IN SEARCH OF TOMORROW

Critical Thinking about the Romanian and International Business Environment

Volume 5

Coordinators: Dr. Ovidiu Oltean, Dr. Alin Băiescu
Transilvania Executive Education

Authors: Ioan-Florin Bucşa, Cristian-Ionel Călbază, Adelina Cotfas, Mihaela-Adela Coroiu, Laura Dragoş-Rădoi, Alexandru-Romulus Harbuzaru, Nicolae Moldovan, Horaţiu-Adrian Pop, Andrei-Adrian Racu, Vasile Rusu, Adrian Sălăjan, Cipriana Stan, and Radu-Ştefan Tărău

UNIVERSITY OF
BUCKINGHAM
PRESS

IN SEARCH OF TOMORROW

Critical Thinking about the Romanian and International Business Environment

Volume 5

Coordinators: Dr. Ovidiu Oltean, Dr. Alin Băiescu
Transilvania Executive Education

Authors: Ioan-Florin Bucşa, Cristian-Ionel Călbază, Adelina Cotfas, Mihaela-Adela Coroiu, Laura Dragoş-Rădoi, Alexandru-Romulus Harbuzaru, Nicolae Moldovan, Horaţiu-Adrian Pop, Andrei-Adrian Racu, Vasile Rusu, Adrian Sălăjan, Cipriana Stan, and Radu-Ştefan Tărău

UNIVERSITY OF BUCKINGHAM PRESS,
AN IMPRINT OF LEGEND TIMES GROUP LTD
51 Gower Street
London WC1E 6HJ
United Kingdom
www.unibuckinghampress.com

First published by University of Buckingham Press in 2025

ISBN: 978-1-918291-88-9

Table of Contents

Introduction

We are proud of our Executive MBA graduates - Class of 2025, together with whom we have succeeded in releasing the fifth volume of *"IN SEARCH OF TOMORROW – Critical thinking about the Romanian and International Business Environment"*. This book continues a tradition started in 2019 when, as in this case, the students enrolled in the Executive MBA organised by Transilvania Executive Education (now, in cooperation with the University of Buckingham), decided to collect and publish their best essays produced during their MBA programme. These contributions reflect both the intellectual discipline and the professional insight that define the EMBA journey. So, the present edition comes as proof of the utility and the appreciations the previous ones have received since their launch.

The Executive MBA programme itself is more than a course of study. It is a platform where professional experience meets academic rigor. Participants enter the programme as accomplished specialists, entrepreneurs, and leaders, and throughout their journey they are challenged to rethink their assumptions, confront complex problems with new tools, and translate theory into action, back in the companies they are coming from. Each essay included in this book is therefore not only an academic deliverable, but also a reflection of the lived experiences of managers who operate in fast-moving, competitive, and, so frequently, uncertain environments. Their writings capture this dynamic interplay between analysis and practice, showing that the EMBA is not about abstract theory but about transformation of self, of organizations, and of communities. The book is not simply an anthology of academic papers. It is, above all, a testimony of applied learning, of how senior professionals use the concepts, theories, and analytical frameworks acquired during their studies to better understand their own organizations and industries. In doing so, they not only fulfil an academic requirement, but also create work of lasting value to their professional communities.

The essays you will read here exemplify the MBA spirit of

learning, unlearning, and relearning: an openness to question established practices, to innovate responsibly, and to adapt to the demands of complex, fast-moving business environments. At the same time, this volume stands as a bridge between academic insight and managerial practice. For EMBA students, it offers models of high-quality essays that combine theory, structure, and critical reflection with practical applicability. For master's and doctoral students in business and economics, it provides access to real-world case studies from Romanian and international contexts, written by managers and entrepreneurs who are not only observers, but active participants in the challenges they describe, with the purpose of moving their enterprises to the next level. And for business practitioners and policymakers, the collection demonstrates how academic learning can be translated into insights for leadership, governance, innovation, and growth.

Publishing such a collection has become a tradition in itself. It affirms the conviction that the work of EMBA students deserves a readership beyond the classroom, and that these essays can inspire others to connect their professional practice with analytical depth. Each volume, including this one, serves as a snapshot of its generation: a portrait of the concerns, priorities, and creativity of a particular cohort of executives who navigated their program in a specific historical and economic moment. The essays gathered here are therefore not only valuable for their immediate insights, but also as markers of how Romania's business community evolves, learns, and positions itself in relation to broader European and global developments.

As in earlier editions, the essays also serve as a mirror of the Romanian and broader European business landscape. They reveal both the challenges and opportunities of industries ranging from IT and advertising to family businesses, financial education, manufacturing, and energy. They also point to recurring themes: the importance of governance and ethical responsibility, the role of innovation and adaptation, and the constant search for balance between people, performance, and long-term sustainability.

The first set of contributions underscores how financial education has become not only a private but a public concern. Adelina Cotfas, in her chapter *Revising Romania's Financial Education Strategy*, offers a critical perspective on Romania's 2030 national strategy, highlighting gaps in inclusivity and behavioural design. She reframes financial education as a matter of *financial well-being and resilience*, particularly for vulnerable groups, while calling for policies adapted to the realities of digital finance. This focus on systemic gaps naturally anticipates the innovation-oriented project of Ioan-Florin Bucşa, whose essay later in the volume develops a youth-focused digital financial education platform, showing how policy and innovation can complement one another in addressing one of Romania's pressing socio-economic challenges. If Cotfas and Bucşa bring our attention to public responsibility and innovation, Adrian Sălăjan reminds us of another key dimension of sustainability: family business governance. His essay, *Ownership Strategy and Governance Solutions: Transgenerational Continuity*, explores the dilemmas of succession and conflict in a family-owned enterprise. By proposing the four-room governance model, he demonstrates how structure and foresight can preserve organizational resilience across generations. In many ways, Sălăjan's insights parallel Cotfas's call for systemic frameworks, since both underline the need for continuity and stability in the face of change.

Yet sustainability is not only a matter of governance but also of leadership culture. This is vividly illustrated in Alexandru Harbuzaru's *From Mad Men to Sad Men: A Self-Reflexive Case Study of a Toxic Triumvirate in a Small Advertising Agency*. His autoethnographic narrative explores the failure of an organization he co-founded, offering a candid reflection on ambition, misaligned visions, and the corrosive effects of personal conflict. Harbuzaru's account resonates with Sălăjan's discussion of governance, for both point to the fragility of organizations when leadership falters—whether through a lack of structure or through a failure of self-awareness. The theme of scrutiny and resilience is carried forward by Andrei Racu, whose essay, *The Company: Information Technology – Software Services*, provides a rigorous financial analysis of one of Romania's leading IT firms. By evaluating performance indicators and acquisitions, Racu situates the company in a sector both dynamic and vulnerable, emphasizing the importance of financial discipline for sustainable growth. His chapter speaks directly to Harbuzaru's reflections: where leadership failures can undo an organization, sound financial strategy can help secure its future. From financial evaluation, the volume moves into entrepreneurial imagination with Cipriana Stan's *Marketing Plan to Launch "Gelateria Dolce Lusso" into the Romanian Marketplace*. Stan proposes the launch of a premium gelato brand in Cluj-Napoca, combining traditional craftsmanship with innovative CSR and digital marketing strategies. Her essay, while entrepreneurial in scope, resonates with Racu's financial analysis, for both show how businesses must navigate competitive environments by aligning creativity with economic rationality.

The question of alignment is also central to Cristian Călbază's contribution, *Applying Operations and Supply Chain Management in a Software Company to Optimise the Bench*. He explores how unallocated human resources can undermine efficiency and proposes Lean and Just-in-Time solutions. Călbază's concern with operational agility transitions smoothly into Horațiu Pop's essay, *Should We or Should We Not Monitor Our Software Development Team Members?*, which addresses the human dimension of efficiency. Where Călbază emphasises optimization, Pop highlights the risks of excessive monitoring, suggesting that trust and engagement are equally critical for organizational performance. Together, these two essays demonstrate that efficiency cannot be separated from human motivation. It is precisely this human and societal dimension that Ioan-Florin Bucșa elaborates in *Empowering the Next Generation: Developing a Financial Education Platform for Youth*. Building on Cotfas's earlier concerns, Bucșa applies the Doblin model of innovation to design a gamified, partnership-driven platform that seeks to improve Romania's poor financial literacy rates among children and young people. His essay closes a thematic arc on financial education while also extending the discussion into digital innovation and systemic transformation.

From national challenges, the volume broadens to global perspectives with Laura Dragoș-Rădoi's *Tesla (TSLA) Financial Analysis*. By analysing Tesla's recent performance, Dragoș-Rădoi shows how a global leader navigates crises such as the pandemic and supply-chain disruptions while pursuing innovation and growth. Her essay complements Racu's Romanian case study: both chapters, taken together, illustrate how financial analysis can illuminate organizational strategies at different scales, from local firms to global giants. The question of leadership during transformation is further developed by Mihaela Coroiu in *Driving Strategic Change: Transformational Leadership in a Manufacturing Context*. Coroiu explores how leaders can guide organizations through resistance and uncertainty, emphasizing the importance of vision and empowerment. Her contribution resonates with Harbuzaru's cautionary tale, but instead of failure, she offers a roadmap for successful change.

This attention to people and organizational culture is echoed by Nicolae Moldovan in *Employee Engagement: A Study in a Corporate Organization*. Moldovan examines how engagement strategies shape performance and retention in large corporations, linking his insights with those of Pop and Călbază. Together, these chapters remind us that at the heart of competitiveness lies not only structure and efficiency but also the capacity to create workplaces that motivate and inspire. Finally, the volume turns toward the broader structural transformations of our time. Radu Tărău, in *Harnessing Energy Transitions: Strategic Pathways in the Electrical Engineering Sector*, situates Romania's energy industry within the European Union's climate agenda. His reflections on sustainability, governance, and infrastructure align with Dragoş-Rădoi's global case, demonstrating how industries from Cluj to California are grappling with the dual imperative of growth and responsibility. In parallel, Vasile Rusu's *Rethinking Organizational Learning in Software Development: Addressing Gen Z's Career Challenges through Soft Systems Methodology* returns us to the world of IT, but through a systemic lens. By analysing generational tensions and remote work practices, Rusu proposes solutions that reinforce team cohesion and mentorship, issues that directly connect back to Pop's and Călbază's essays.

Taken together, these essays illustrate the intellectual breadth and practical orientation of our Executive MBA programme. From financial analysis and marketing strategy to governance reform, leadership reflexivity, innovation, and sustainability, the contributions all share a common thread: they are anchored in the lived experiences of managers and entrepreneurs who are willing to test theory against practice. Each chapter adds a piece to the puzzle of contemporary business challenges: financial education (Cotfas, Bucşa), family governance (Sălăjan), organizational leadership (Harbuzaru, Coroiu, Pop, Moldovan), financial and operational strategy (Racu, Călbază, Dragoş-Rădoi), entrepreneurial innovation (Stan), energy transitions (Tărău), and systemic organizational learning (Rusu). Individually, they reflect personal journeys of inquiry and discovery. Collectively, they demonstrate the capacity of Romania's executives to engage critically with global challenges while grounding their insights in local realities.

This volume therefore continues to serve not only as a compendium of essays, but also as a portrait of a business community in transformation: innovative, reflexive, and increasingly confident on the European and global stage.

In conclusion, we kindly offer you this book: it contains excellent essays, written in compliance with high academic standards, by business practitioners, for you to enrich your theoretical background and to improve your business practice, for the welfare of your community!

Dr. Ovidiu Oltean & Dr. Alin T. Băiescu

OVIDIU OLTEAN, PhD, is the Research Methods Module Leader for the TEE Executive MBA programme. Assistant lecturer in the Political Science Department, College of Political, Administrative and Communication Sciences (FSPAC) at Babeş-Bolyai University, he teaches different subjects related to politics, elections, migration, development, and research methods. He is involved in national and international research projects tackling the topic of migration, where he collaborates with international organisations like the UN and universities from China, France, Germany, the Netherlands, Spain, and South Africa.

ALIN T. BĂIESCU, PhD, is the Economics for Managers and Entrepreneurs Module Leader for the TEE Executive MBA programme. He has over 25 years of experience in the financial insurance sector, in middle and top management positions, within well-known multinational corporations. Dr. Băiescu is also trained and certified in two methodologies for changing behaviours: BCW© – Behaviour Change Wheel (University College London – UK, 2023 – 2024) and the BASIC© framework (iNUDGEyou consulting company – Copenhagen, DK, 2023). Since 2020, he has been a Board Member at TEE, as Alumni Representative and the Programme Director of the "Behavioural Economics in Practice – Executive Training" (2022). In 2022, he founded the Behavioural Economics HUB, a private company focused on training, consultancy, and research in the behavioural economics area.

Editor: Transilvania Executive Education

Authors' Introduction

The authors featured in this volume are **graduated of the TEE Executive MBA – Class of 2025**, who successfully completed the program with **Distinction** in September 2025. The essays presented herein exemplify the intellectual discipline and strategic insight cultivated throughout the EMBA journey. Far exceeding the scope of academic assignments, these contributions offer a nuanced reflection of the professional realities faced by executives operating within dynamic, competitive, and frequently uncertain environments.

Each essay represents a synthesis of analytical rigor and practical experience, underscoring the transformative nature of the EMBA—both at the individual and organizational level. This collection affirms the belief that the work produced by EMBA students merits a broader readership, capable of inspiring others to integrate critical thinking with professional practice.

The authors' profiles and research interests are presented in the following section.

IOAN-FLORIN BUCȘA is a seasoned IT professional with more than 15 years of experience in network management and monitoring background within large enterprise environments. Currently leading a team overseeing network and infrastructure monitoring for a global organization. Ioan is enthusiastic about driving automation, process improvement, and leveraging technology to achieve business objectives. He holds a degree in Telecommunications Engineering from the Technical University of Cluj-Napoca and an Executive MBA from the University of Buckingham.

CRISTIAN-IONEL CĂLBAZĂ is a technology and delivery leader with over 15 years of experience in the software development and IT services industry. He currently serves as Director of Software Engineering at Qubiz, where he leads strategic initiatives across engineering delivery, team development, and innovation. Throughout his career, Cristian has remained committed to people development, agile practices, and continuous improvement. He holds a bachelor's degree in computer science from Babeş-Bolyai University and Executive MBA from the University of Buckingham. He is passionate about blending technical acumen with business vision to drive organizational success.

With a passion for creating meaningful customer experiences, **ADELINA-SÎNZIANA COTFAS** has more than 12 years of experience transforming insights into impactful solutions that enhance customer and employee satisfaction. With a keen interest in behavioural science and a focus on innovation, she is dedicated to delivering value through thoughtfully designed products and services. Drawing on her specialization in methodologies like Design Thinking and Design Sprint, she advocates for a structured yet creative approach to problem-solving. Adelina currently occupies the role of Deputy Director, UX Design and Research at Banca Transilvania. She holds an Executive MBA from the University of Buckingham, with research interests focused on financial education and financial inclusion.

MIHAELA-ADELA COROIU is an accomplished energy executive with over 19 years of leadership experience at EnergoBit, one of Romania's leading energy companies. She has successfully managed business development and commercial strategies across multiple divisions, including Energy Efficiency, Renewable Energy, Total Service, and Industrial Services. With a strong track record in driving sustainable growth, Mihaela oversees complex projects and leads cross-functional teams to deliver innovative energy solutions for clients across Romania and Europe. She also directs EnergoBit's marketing strategy, aligning sustainability objectives with market demands and technological advancements. Holding a PhD in Electrical Engineering and advanced degrees in Environmental Engineering, Sustainable Urbanization, Physics, and Economics, Mihaela combines deep technical expertise with strategic management skills. She graduated from the University of Buckingham EMBA in 2025.

LAURA DRAGOȘ-RĂDOI is a strategic business consultant with close to a decade of experience in operations, HR strategy, and risk management. She has worked with both public institutions and private companies, supporting organizational growth, compliance, and digital transformation across various industries. Her experience spans collaborations with SMEs, startups, and corporate organizations. Laura is the co-founder of a tech startup focused on pet wellbeing and an active stakeholder in several AI projects centered on responsible innovation. She holds an Executive MBA from the University of Buckingham. Her work combines ethical foresight with practical business insight, particularly in the areas of AI and IoT in healthcare. She is especially interested in the ethical implications of singularity theory and quantum computing, and in how emerging technologies can support viable, inclusive, and sustainable business models.

ALEXANDRU ROMULUS HARBUZARU began his professional career in sales - his strongest skill and the foundation of everything he does. Despite running a seven-figure business, he still enjoys sales as much as watching Tarkovsky or Kubrick films or admiring Van Gogh paintings. In 2022, Alexandru joined Hpotech, a Turkish company, becoming one of the company's largest shareholders, exchanging his ability to open markets and drive growth for stock. Their technology is now featured in longevity documentaries and used by NFL, NBA, and Premier League athletes, as well as world-renowned doctors and wellness leaders. His art education taught him to look beyond the obvious, his career taught him to build and lead, and now he is combining the two to shape not just businesses, but entire industries. He started his EMBA studies with the University of Buckingham in 2023.

NICOLAE MOLDOVAN has more than 10 years of experience leading international projects across diverse sectors, including automotive, industrial automation and IT for large organizations like Bosch and Emerson. With a strong background in working within multinational environments, Nicolae has managed cross-functional teams, coordinated global stakeholders, and delivered high-impact solutions on time, within budget, and to the highest quality standards. Possessing extensive hands-on experience with both traditional and agile project management methodologies enables him to seamlessly adapt to a wide range of business needs and technical challenges. His ability to lead with clarity and engage teams effectively has made him a trusted contributor to the success of numerous international projects. He graduated from the University of Buckingham EMBA in 2025.

HORAȚIU-ADRIAN POP is an accomplished manager and software development leader based in Cluj, Romania, with nearly two decades of experience driving technology innovation and operational excellence. Currently serving as Business Group Manager at AROBS Group, he oversees high-performing, multidisciplinary teams across international locations, ensuring the delivery of scalable, AI-enabled software solutions that align with strategic business objectives and consistently exceed client expectations. With a deep-rooted expertise in software development, Horațiu has a proven track record in leading complex projects from conception to successful execution. His hands-on technical background has equipped him with a robust understanding of the software development lifecycle, critical problem-solving skills, and the ability to implement innovative, client-focused solutions. Horaţiu holds an Executive MBA from the University of Buckingham.

ANDREI-ADRIAN RACU is an M&A Manager with strong expertise in business development and cross-border transactions, currently contributing to AROBS Transilvania Software's growth and expansion strategy. With a career spanning over 15 years, Andrei has gained hands-on experience in over 15 countries, delivering complex assignments — from internal audits and financial analysis to operational management — across markets such as the USA, Hong Kong, Germany, South Africa, Chile, India, the Czech Republic, Uruguay, Cyprus, Slovakia, and Lithuania. Known for his analytical approach and problem-solving mindset, Andrei has consistently contributed to the improvement of internal controls, financial processes, and operational efficiency. In 2025, Andrei completed the Executive MBA program offered by Transilvania Executive Education, in partnership with the University of Buckingham (UK).

VASILE RUSU is a Senior Engineering Manager with over 15 years of experience in the IT industry. His career spans various roles including Software Engineer, Team Lead, Tech Lead, Staff Engineer, and Engineering Manager. He has contributed to diverse sectors such as online education, automotive, payments, fintech, and industrial software. Vasile holds a bachelor's degree in economics and informatics from Babeş-Bolyai University and recently completed an Executive MBA through Transilvania Executive Education partnership with the University of Buckingham. Known for his leadership and technical acumen, Vasile brings a strategic perspective on software engineering and team development.

With over 20 years of experience across sectors such as automotive, manufacturing, distribution, FMCG, and IT, **ADRIAN SĂLĂJAN** has built a strong track record in strategic and operational management. He is recognised for driving performance, optimizing processes, and implementing innovative solutions for business growth. Adrian is the CEO of Plasmaserv Metal Connection, a company specializing in advanced welding and cutting technologies for the naval and construction industries. He holds an Executive MBA from the University of Buckingham. His professional interests include business strategy, leadership, and corporate governance.

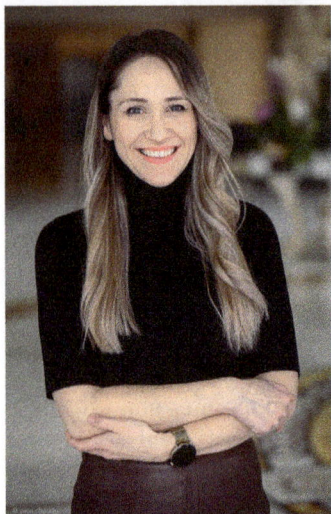

CIPRIANA STAN has over 16 years of experience in marketing, having coordinated numerous projects across digital marketing, internal communications, lead generation, employer branding, and both B2B and B2C marketing. As a senior digital strategist within the Brandocracy team, she brings extensive expertise in developing digital strategies for companies across a wide range of industries, including IT, healthcare, tourism, food, ceramics, education, manufacturing, and SaaS products. Cipriana has marketed software solutions tailored to sectors such as Railway, Telco, Pharma, Airline, and Life Science in European and Asian markets, as well as educational services in the Middle East and Australia. Alongside her strategic marketing work, Cipriana also acts as CMO and manages the family business, Smart RobotX – a robotics and programming school for children, currently expanding through a franchise model. She graduated in 2025 with an Executive MBA from the University of Buckingham (UK).

RADU-ŞTEFAN TĂRĂU is a professional engineer with more than 20 years of experience in the energy industry, licensed by ANRE as a class III electrician. He joined EnergoBit Control Systems team in 2010 as the head of the Energy and Equipment Engineering Department and since 2019 Radu become the Executive Director of the company. Under his leadership, the company has addressed and designed numerous renewable energy systems all over Romania, and in doing so,

Radu have gained in-depth experience and knowledge in a wide range of new technologies: photovoltaic, wind, storage, cogeneration, combined cycle. He holds a bachelor's degree in electronic engineering and Telecommunications, an Executive MBA (EMBA) with Buckingham University. Throughout his career, Radu have developed substantial experience and expertise by being involved in some of the most important energy projects in Romania, coordinating the study and design component.

Ioan-Florin Bucşa

Empowering the Next Generation: Developing a Financial Education Platform for Youth

EMBA Module: Disruptive Innovation: Practices and Processes

Assignment task: Using the Doblin Model: Create an innovation by developing an idea for a new product using the Doblin innovation principles explored in class. This can be one of your own products, a brand-new idea, or an innovation for an existing product or brand on the market. You must apply at least 4 of the Doblin innovation lenses, explaining how and why you have used each lens, and how the lens works in the idea to generate value.

Pitching your idea: You must also consider each of the following concepts and describe them in relation to the idea, as these would be the key considerations in deciding whether the idea is relevant, a large opportunity, and whether it should be progressed.

Executive Summary

This paper aims to advance a conceptual framework for a platform to deliver comprehensive financial literacy to elementary school students. The proposal is for an online platform and a companion mobile application.

In recent years, children have been introduced to digital

products that often have underlying financial components from a very young age. Financial education holds paramount significance for young school children as it equips them with essential life skills necessary for navigating the complexities of personal finance in adulthood. Students develop a profound understanding of financial responsibility and independence by instilling foundational knowledge about budgeting, saving, investing, and managing debt early on. Moreover, such education cultivates prudent decision-making abilities, fostering resilience against financial pitfalls and promoting long-term financial stability. Beyond individual benefits, a financially literate populace contributes to socioeconomic development by bolstering economic growth, reducing poverty rates, and fostering a culture of fiscal accountability. Thus, integrating financial education in the education curriculum, both formal and informal, not only empowers young learners to make informed choices but also lays the groundwork for a prosperous and financially secure society. While the long-term results are difficult to measure, the literature suggests a significant impact on behaviors and attitudes that can have positive second-order effects later in life (Amagir et al., 2018).

Financial literacy is a pressing issue impacting individual economic stability and well-being in general. From a statistical perspective, Romania ranks among the bottom countries globally and in the EU when it comes to financial literacy, with sources estimating the percentage of the population that is financially literate from 8% to 24% (Klapper, Lusardi and van Oudheusden, 2015; Nițoi et al., 2022). In terms of estimating financial literacy knowledge, Romania ranks almost constantly close to the bottom of the sample being analyzed, be it the EU, OECD countries, or a subset of European countries (Reiter and Beckmann, 2018; OECD/INFE, 2020; European Commission, 2023).

The OECD recognises that financial education is critical to individual economic empowerment and financial system stability (OECD, 2015). In 2018, Romanian Ministries, Financial, and Banking authorities signed a collaboration agreement that aimed, among other objectives, to develop a national financial education strategy (European Commission, 2018). Despite this initiative, as evidenced by the preceding data, the National Strategy's effectiveness has been limited.

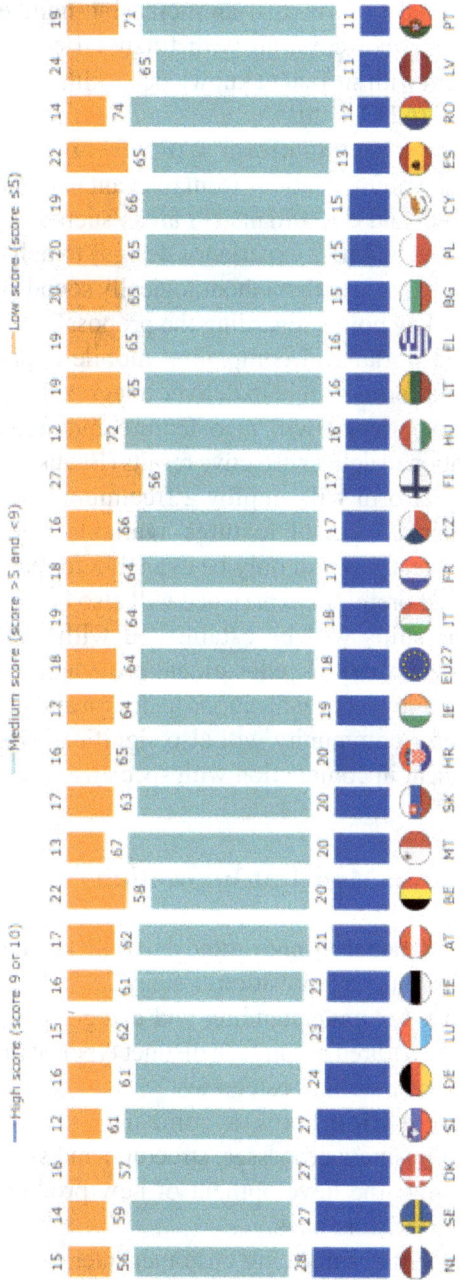

Figure 1 – Overall financial literacy in the EU. Source: (European Commission, 2023)

Case studies show that an increasing number of countries are targeting school children with financial education programs to equip them with sufficient knowledge, skills, and confidence before adulthood (OECD, 2015).

The proposed platform will leverage existing materials, strategic recommendations from relevant national and international authorities, and consultants (in areas such as education, finance, psychology, and user experience design) to deliver comprehensive experience that is both methodologically sound and comprehensive.

A few key points regarding the proposal:

A web portal and companion mobile applications for major mobile platforms will help deliver integrated experience.

The experience will also feature interactive learning using gamification to deliver effective results (Bayuk and Altobello, 2019).

The platform will employ a freemium pricing model, with a comprehensive set of features available free of charge, while advanced features will only be available for paying subscribers. A customised premium experience will also be available.

Partnerships will be established with consultants, national regulatory authorities, educational providers (public and private), and other relevant organizations to design and deliver the curricula.

The user community will also significantly shape the learning environment in conjunction with specialised partners.

The Doblin Model of Innovation

The Doblin model of innovation, developed by Larry Keeley and his team at Doblin, an innovation strategy firm, offers a comprehensive framework for understanding and categorizing innovation. This model is structured around ten distinct types of innovation, grouped into three overarching categories:

Configuration: how a company is organised internally, including business processes, structure, and systems.

Offering: the development of new products or services and improving existing ones.

Experience: enhancing customer interactions and engagement with a company's products or services.

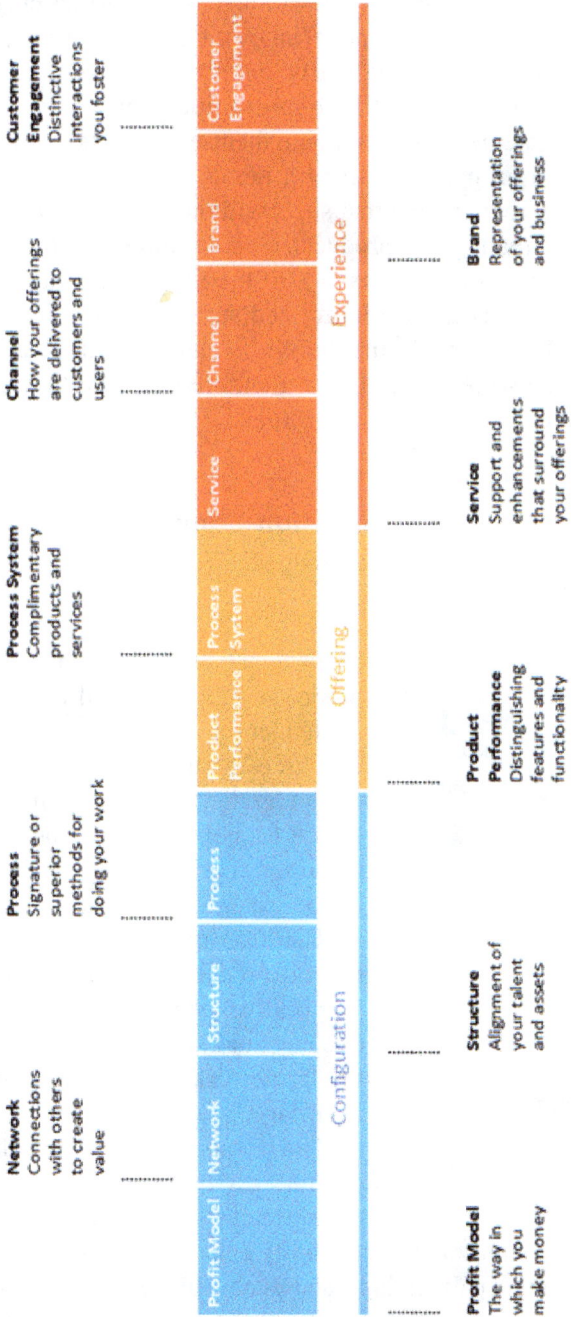

Figure 2 – The Doblin "Ten Types of Innovation" Framework

The ten types of innovation within these categories encompass everything from business model innovation to customer experience innovation. By systematically analyzing these dimensions, organizations can identify opportunities for innovation and develop strategies to differentiate themselves in the market.

The Doblin model's strength lies in its holistic approach to innovation, recognizing that successful innovation often requires more than creating new products. It underscores the importance of considering various aspects of a business and its interactions with customers to drive meaningful and sustainable change (Keeley et al., 2013). As such, the Doblin model is a valuable tool for organizations seeking to foster a culture of innovation and stay ahead in today's dynamic marketplace.

The Ten Types of Innovation Framework in Action

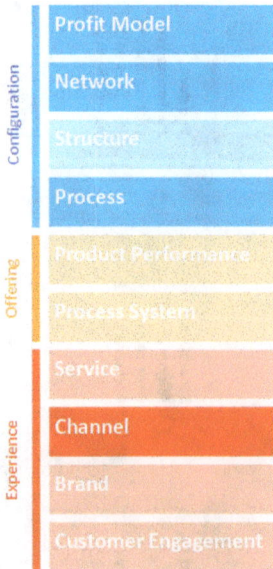

Summary

Using the Doblin model, the innovation proposed will be refined using four of the ten lenses available.

Three of the four lenses selected fall under the 'Configuration' category (Profit Model, Network, and Process), while the fourth belongs to the 'Experience' category (Channel).

The 'Configuration' lenses focus on the core product, while the 'Experience' side is all about the end customer, or as (Keeley et al., 2013) put it, "the left of the framework is backstage; the right is onstage."

The focus will be on achieving profitability by creating multiple revenue streams, incorporating innovative technologies that will significantly enhance the user experience, create strategic partnerships, and establishing diversified channels to the market.

The result will be a robust and differentiated product with a clearly defined value proposition, incorporating risk mitigation strategies from a revenue and distribution perspective.

Profit Model

This lens examines how innovation generates revenue and sustains profitability. The Profit Model lens analyzes various revenue streams, cost structures, pricing strategies, and value propositions associated with the proposed innovation. Identifying innovative ways to monetise the platform while ensuring it delivers value to customers and remains financially viable is paramount.

The current proposal is to utilise a freemium pricing strategy, which will consist of three tiers:

Standard – Users will get access to most of the features, such as learning materials, mobile applications, and interactive experiences, free of charge.

Premium – Users will pay a monthly subscription fee to access more advanced features such as personalised learning experiences, recommendations, or analytics.

Custom – This tier is about delivering a customised learning experience, online or offline, by directly interacting with a professional consultant. Pricing will be established based on the specific requirements and resources allocated.

Additional revenue streams will be generated by publishing sponsored content from relevant partners, referring to additional resources such as books or tickets to events or corporate sponsorships.

Network

The Network lens assesses the ecosystem surrounding innovation, including partnerships, alliances, distribution channels, and interactions with stakeholders. Strategic partners, suppliers, and collaborators are essential for successfully scaling and implementing innovation. Additionally, network effects have to be considered, particularly how they can amplify the value of innovation within the broader ecosystem.

Key partnerships need to be established with the following stakeholders:

Educational providers (both public and private) – Financial education can be included in the curriculum as an optional subject.

Financial authorities – Forming partnerships with government agencies or ministries of education to integrate the platform into national or regional educational initiatives and for strategic guidance.

Financial institutions – Forming partnerships with government agencies or ministries of education to integrate the platform into national or regional educational initiatives to improve youth financial literacy.

Process

The Process lens focuses on optimizing internal processes to enhance efficiency, agility, and innovation capabilities. The processes involved in developing, producing, distributing, and supporting the proposed innovation will be evaluated. Opportunities for streamlining workflows, reducing waste, adopting agile methodologies, and leveraging technology to improve process efficiency will be identified. By optimizing internal processes, innovation can be developed and delivered more effectively, leading to faster time-to-market and better customer experiences.

The proposal shows several innovative features, such as:

Interactive Experiences – Develop interactive simulations and gamified exercises to emulate real-life scenarios and allow learners to practice making financial decisions in a controlled environment.

Data Analytics and Machine Learning for Personalization – Leveraging advanced data analytics techniques to analyze user data and provide personalised recommendations for further learning resources, extracurricular activities, or study opportunities based on each student's interests and aptitudes.

Feedback Loops – Establishing feedback mechanisms to collect input from students, parents, and educators and using this to continuously refine and improve the platform's content, features, and user experience.

Virtual Tutor – Design a virtual tutor using a customised LLM (Large Language Model). The model will be trained using platform materials and other relevant content, allowing students to interact with the course content.

Channel

The Channel lens explores how innovation reaches and interacts with customers. The key focus is identifying distribution, sales, marketing, and customer touchpoints to ensure a seamless and engaging experience. Factors such as convenience, accessibility, and personalization must be considered to deliver a comprehensive product to customers. Diversified channels lead to customer satisfaction, increasing adoption rates, and drive loyalty.

To maximise the success and profitability of the platform, several distribution and promotion channels need to be established:

Mobile App – Creating a mobile app to complement the content and make it accessible to mobile platforms.

Social Media Presence – Leveraging social media platforms to promote the platform's educational content, engage with students and parents, and build a community.

In-Person Events – Organizing in-person events such as workshops, hackathons, or competitions in partnership with schools, community centers, or local businesses to supplement the online learning experience.

Pitching the Idea

Value Proposition

The Problem

Data shows Romania lags behind most EU countries in financial literacy (Reiter and Beckmann, 2018; OECD/INFE, 2020; European Commission, 2023). Although national strategies to address financial education have been proposed, the impact has been limited. Furthermore, financial education is not included in the formal primary or secondary school curriculum. While the long-term results are difficult to assess empirically, research indicates that exposing young students to financial education can positively impact their attitudes and behaviors.

The Solution

The proposed idea is for an online educational platform and a companion mobile application to deliver financial education to primary and secondary school students in Romania. The aim is to equip young students with the knowledge and skills that will enable them to navigate the complexities of personal finance successfully in adulthood. Product differentiation is achieved through leveraging technology, network effects, and diversified market channels.

Product Highlights

Several innovative technologies will be leveraged to deliver superior customer experience:

	Technology	Data Analytics: Analyze progress and provide relevant metrics. LLMs: Design a virtual tutor using a customised LLM trained on platform material. Machine Learning: Deliver a customised learning experience tailored to student skills, requirements, and interests.
	Network Effects	Build key partnerships with: Public and private educational providers Government authorities Financial institutions Consultants (specializing in education, finance, user experience, or psychology)
	Interactive Experience	Users will interact with the content using the virtual tutor, simulations, and exercises. Additionally, user feedback will continuously refine and improve the platform's content, features, and user experience
	Gamification	Simulations and games included in the platform and companion app will help learners apply acquired knowledge and practice making decisions in a controlled environment.

Market Size

According to Statista (2023a), there are 1,607,000 students enrolled in primary and gymnasium education institutions in the school year 2022-2023. Statistical data also shows that in the school year 2021-2022, there were 4,002 primary and secondary schools active in Romania (Statista, 2023b)

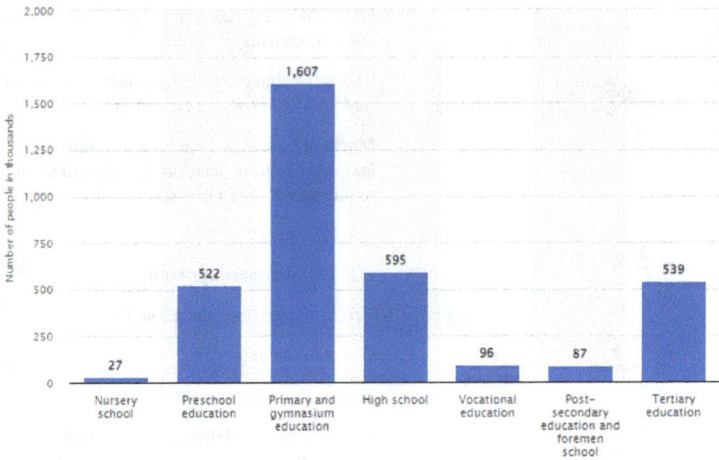

Figure 3 – School population in Romania in the school year 2022-2023. Source: Statista, 2023a

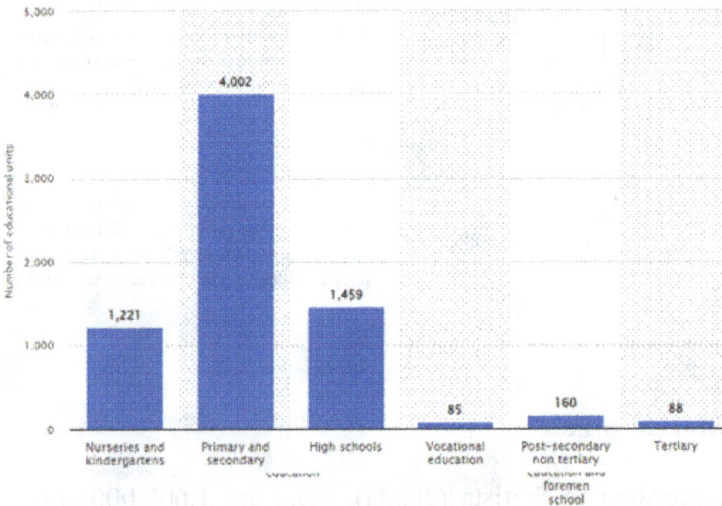

Figure 4 – Educational units in Romania in the school year 2021-2022. Source: (Statista, 2023b)

While data suggest that the Total Addressable Market (TAM) size is about 1,6 million users, due to limitations, in this case represented by the percentage of the population with internet access (89.41% in 2022, according to (Statista, 2023c), the Service Addressable Market (SAM) is closer to 1,4 million users.

Assumptions related to market shares that are split between existing competitors must also be considered. Therefore, estimating a Service Obtainable Market (SOM), which is the more realistic estimate of the serviceable user base, to around 25% of the market (350,000) in the first two years is a more attainable target.

Additional assumptions, such as parents' level of education, family monthly income, or percentage of urban versus rural population, might also influence the estimations.

Competitor Analysis

Preliminary research shows that the financial education market for primary and secondary school students is suitable for disruption due to the small number of platforms identified.

Two distinct types of education providers have been identified:

Educational platforms:

https://www.educatiefinanciaracopii.ro/ – Facilitates events resembling children's theatre plays that feature relatable characters. The platform also contains specialty articles and an online shop.

https://abcdarfinanciar.ro/ – Contains a collection of content that is focused on enabling parents and educators to teach children about specific financial subjects.

https://appe.ro/ – Delivers probably the most comprehensive educational experience among potential competitors. The curriculum includes a manual, student workbooks, software, and games. Most material is available online, and webinars are also organised.

Courses (both online and in person) provided by financial institutions or other parties:

https://www.smarty-kids.ro/educatie-financiara/
https://mbakids.ro/educatie-financiara-mbakids-cursuri-copii
https://www.bcr.ro/ro/csr/proiecte/educatie-financiara-pentru-toate-varstele

Go-to-Market Strategies

By leveraging multiple channels such as mobile apps, web platforms, and partnerships with educational institutions, the platform can cater to diverse learning preferences and access points. Ultimately, diversified distribution channels amplify the platform's impact, fostering greater adoption, engagement, and effectiveness in delivering financial literacy education to students.

Online Platform

The main point of presence will feature educational content, specialty blog posts, interactive games, and a virtual tutor.

Mobile Compan-ion App

The mobile app will complement the platform and extend the learning experience to mobile platforms. The app will be available for iOS and Android.

In-Person Events/ Courses

Organizing offline events such as workshops, hackathons, or competitions in partnership with schools, community centers, or local businesses to supplement online learning experience.

Social Media Presence

Presence on social media platforms will increase awareness, foster an online community, and facilitate the delivery of customised complementary content (short videos, event notifications, or sponsored content).

Revenue Streams

The primary source of recurring revenue will be represented by subscriptions. The platform will feature a freemium pricing strategy with three distinct tiers:

Standard — Users will get access to standard features, such as learning materials, mobile applications, and interactive experiences, free of charge.

Premium — For a monthly subscription fee, users receive access to advanced features such as personalised learning experiences, recommendations, analytics, or a virtual tutor.

Custom — The aim is to deliver a customised learning experience, online or offline, by directly interacting with a professional consultant or via a tailored experience. Pricing will be established based on the specific requirements and resources allocated.

Additional revenue streams would maximise the profitability and increase the robustness of the platform:

Sponsored Content — Sponsored content from our partners will be published as blog posts while being adequately marked as such.

Merchandise Referrals — Blog posts will also refer to merchandise such as books or other educational materials, event tickets, or other relevant products.

Corporate Sponsorships — Partners with corporations are interested in promoting financial literacy among youth. Corporate partners could sponsor the platform, provide free access to schools or offer scholarships to students who excel in financial education.

Risk Mitigation

Several risk categories have been identified, and mitigation strategies will need to be devised for each.

Financial Sustainability – Challenges related to revenue generation, funding, or resource allocation may affect the platform's financial sustainability. The multiple revenue streams previously identified will help mitigate this type of risk.

Market Competition – Intense competition from other financial education platforms, educational institutions, or traditional learning methods could impact the platform's market share and user adoption. Mitigation will be achieved by implementing the proposed set of features that will significantly differentiate the product from the competition's offerings. Key partnerships will also be crucial in providing a unique learning experience.

Distribution – Relying on a particular channel or a less optimal set of channels can negatively impact the product. Implementing the proposed mix of go-to-market strategies will significantly increase the platform's robustness regarding market reach.

Intellectual Property Infringement – This risk occurs when the original content created by the platform is unlawfully copied, reproduced, or distributed without proper authorization or attribution. Mitigation strategies could include watermarking content, copyright protection, or digital rights management. The unique set of features and network effect additionally increase resilience.

User Engagement and Retention – Low user engagement or high churn rates could undermine the platform's long-term success and impact. Mitigation involves continuously improving the platform's user experience by designing feedback loops, ensuring content relevance and accuracy, leveraging data analytics to understand user behavior and preferences, and implementing targeted marketing and retention strategies.

Final Considerations

The development of a financial education platform for school kids offers significant potential to address critical needs in financial literacy education, especially considering Romania's overall level of financial literacy. The innovative approach to addressing unmet needs, maximizing consumer benefits, and continuously adapting the content ensures the platform's relevance, scalability, and sustainability in a rapidly evolving educational landscape.

By continuously adapting and establishing strategic partnerships, the education platform can realise its vision of equipping school kids with the knowledge and tools to navigate the complexities of the modern financial world confidently. This will not only compound individual economic stability, but it will also create benefits on a societal level.

References

Amagir, A., Groot, W., Maassen van den Brink, H., Wilschut, A., 2018. A review of financial-literacy education programs for children and adolescents. Citizenship, Social and Economics Education. https://doi.org/10.1177/2047173417719555

Bayuk, J., Altobello, S.A., 2019. Can gamification improve financial behavior? The moderating role of app expertise. International Journal of Bank Marketing 37. https://doi.org/10.1108/IJBM-04-2018-0086

European Commission, 2023. Monitoring the level of financial literacy in the EU [WWW Document]. URL https://europa.eu/eurobarometer/surveys/detail/2953 (accessed 3.4.24).

European Commission, 2018. Romania: a Working Agreement signed for the National Financial Education Strategy's development [WWW Document]. Romanian Eurydice Unit. URL https://eurydice.eacea.ec.europa.eu/news/romania-working-agreement-signed-national-financial-education-strategys-development (accessed 3.2.24).

Keeley, L., Walters, H., Pikkel, R., Quinn, B., 2013. Ten types of innovation: the discipline of building breakthroughs, Ten types of innovation: the discipline of building breakthroughs. John Wiley & Sons.

Klapper, L., Lusardi, A., van Oudheusden, P., 2015. Financial literacy around the world, Standard and Poor.

Niţoi, M., Clichici, D., Zeldea, C., Pochea, M., Ciocîrlan, C., 2022. Financial well-being and financial literacy in Romania: A survey dataset. Data Brief 43. https://doi.org/10.1016/j.dib.2022.108413

OECD. (2015). *NATIONAL STRATEGIES FOR FINANCIAL EDUCATION.* https://www.oecd.org/daf/fin/financial-education/National-Strategies-Financial-Education-Policy-Handbook.pdf (accessed 3.4.24).

OECD/INFE, 2020. OECD/INFE 2020 International Survey of Adult Financial Literacy, OECD/INFE 2020 International Survey of Adult Financial Literacy.

Reiter, S., Beckmann, E., 2018. How financially literate is CESEE? Insights from the OeNB Euro Survey, Oesterreichische Nationalbank Focus on European Economic Integration.

Statista, 2023a. School population in Romania in the school year 2022/2023, by level of education [WWW Document]. URL https://www.statista.com/statistics/1200381/romania-school-population-by-education-level/ (accessed 3.4.24).

Statista, 2023b. Number of educational units in Romania in the academic year 2021/2022, by type [WWW Document]. URL https://www.statista.com/statistics/1235337/romania-educational-units-by-type/ (accessed 3.4.24).

Statista, 2023c. Share of households with internet access in Romania from 2009 to 2022 [WWW Document]. URL https://www.statista.com/statistics/377760/household-internet-access-in-romania/ (accessed 3.4.24).

Cristian-Ionel Călbază

Applying O&SCM in a Software Company to Optimise the Bench

EMBA Module: Operations and Supply Chain Management

Assignment task: Drawing upon either your own organisation (or previously worked for) or an organisation with which you are familiar, identify an area of activity and suggest how the current management of operations could be improved. It is important that you explain the area of activity and its purposes clearly by providing adequate information and contextual information of the chosen organisation. For the area of activity identified, define, and critically evaluate suitable operational objectives or performance outcomes, and suggest how the current management of the operations could be improved. It is important that you seek, where possible, to apply the various models, concepts, tools, and techniques considered during the course.

Executive Summary

Evaluates the resource management practices of ABC Company and identifies inefficiencies in the current approach to allocating developers to projects.

Examines the application of Operations and Supply Chain Management (O&SCM) principles, including Lean Management, Just-in-Time (JIT), Value Stream Mapping (VSM), and

Operations Research (OR), to optimise resource allocation and reduce bench time.

Recommends strategic improvements in resource planning using the SCOR model, engaging developers in internal projects, automating HR functions, and conducting continuous training.

Proposes a cost-benefit analysis to determine the feasibility of implementing internal software solutions versus purchasing them and integrating Lean with digital transformation initiatives.

Highlights the importance of aligning resource management initiatives with the company's strategic goals to achieve competitive advantage and sustained growth in the IT industry.

Introduction

Context

In the fast-paced and competitive world of IT, managing human resources effectively is crucial for maintaining operational efficiency and competitiveness. The concept of "bench management" refers to the practice of having a pool of employees, particularly software developers, who are not currently assigned to any billable (active and revenue-generating projects) projects. While maintaining a bench allows flexibility and quick response to new project demands, it also presents challenges related to cost management and resource optimization.

Purpose

This research aims to investigate and propose improvements in bench management within a specific Romanian IT software solutions company (ABC), where the author holds a delivery manager role. The primary focus is on identifying strategies to optimise bench management, thereby reducing operational waste and improving overall efficiency. This study will utilise relevant models and frameworks from Operations and Supply Chain Management (O&SCM) to provide actionable insights tailored to the organization's needs.

Background of the Organization

The organization in focus, based in Cluj-Napoca, is a software solutions company known for providing a wide range of IT services to global clients. The company has a substantial number of employees and has experienced fluctuating demand for its services, leading to periods where developers are on the bench. Recent economic challenges and market fluctuations have heightened the need for an effective bench management strategy to ensure operational efficiency and cost-effectiveness.

Relevance of the Study

The relevance of this study is underscored by recent trends in the Romanian IT industry, particularly in Cluj-Napoca, where several companies have faced significant layoffs due to economic pressures and market shifts (Razvan, 2024) (Reştea, 2023) (Roberts, 2024) (Şupeală, 2024) (www.actualdecluj.ro, n.d.). By examining bench management practices and proposing improvements within the selected organization, this research aims to provide a framework that can help mitigate similar challenges.

With the IT industry in Cluj-Napoca undergoing significant changes, including layoffs and restructuring, understanding and improving bench management practices is more critical than ever. The findings of this study will not only provide insights into optimizing operations within the company but also contribute to broader discussions on how IT companies can navigate economic uncertainties while maintaining a flexible and efficient workforce.

Literature Review

Introduction to Operations and Supply Chain Management

O&SCM involves the strategic coordination of business functions within a company to improve the long-term performance of the individual enterprises and the supply chain as a whole. It is a crucial aspect of any organization, for optimizing processes, managing resources efficiently, and delivering value to customers. O&SCM

integrates multiple activities such as production planning, inventory management, procurement, logistics, and distribution (Chopra & Meindl, 2016; Slack, Brandon-Jones, & Johnston, 2016). In the context of IT, these principles help manage the lifecycle of software development projects, from planning and sourcing to execution and delivery. The SCOR (Supply Chain Operations Reference) model is one framework that can be adapted for this purpose. Developed by the Supply Chain Council, it provides a standardised approach to evaluate and improve supply chain performance. This model encompasses five main processes:

Plan: Involves forecasting demand for software projects, planning resource allocation, and scheduling project timelines.

Source: Refers to procuring the necessary resources, including hiring and assigning developers.

Make: Involves the actual development of software.

Delivery: Ensures timely completion and deployment of projects.

Return: Deals with post-delivery support and potential project revisions.

Figure 1 – the SCOR model (Arif, 2022)

Applying O&SCM principles offers several advantages, including streamlining operations and reducing costs through efficient resource management, enhancing customer satisfaction by improving delivery times and quality, and providing a framework for continuous improvement. However, implementing these principles can be complex and resource-intensive, requiring continuous monitoring and adjustment to remain effective. For ABC, the

SCOR model may help map out the entire development process, identifying bottlenecks and inefficiencies. By benchmarking against best practices, IT companies can optimise their workflows, reduce waste, and ensure that resources, especially developers in this case, are allocated effectively.

Lean Management and Waste Reduction

Lean Management is a systematic approach to identifying and eliminating waste through continuous improvement. It aims to enhance efficiency and value by focusing on activities that add value to the end customer and eliminating those that do not (Womack & Jones, 1996).

Moreover, the Lean methodology identifies seven types of waste (Muda): defects, overproduction, waiting, non-utilised talent, transportation, inventory, motion, and extra-processing (Liker, 2004). In the IT sector, these wastes can translate into idle time for developers (bench time), unnecessary documentation, redundant processes, and delays in task assignments. Consequently, Lean Management could increase efficiency by eliminating non-value-added activities, enhance product quality while reducing costs, and engage employees in the improvement process, thereby boosting morale and productivity. However, it requires a cultural shift towards continuous improvement, which can be met with resistance. The initial implementation can be resource-intensive, and success depends on sustained commitment and involvement at all levels.

Lean principles can be applied to ABC by focusing on reducing bench time for developers. This involves streamlining processes to ensure that developers are always engaged in value-adding activities. The 5S methodology can organise and standardise the workplace to enhance productivity, but for ABC more relevant would be implementing continuous improvement (Kaizen) initiatives to help identify inefficiencies in the assignment of tasks to developers.

Value Stream Mapping in Software Development

Value Stream Mapping (VSM) is a Lean tool used to visualise and analyze the flow of information and materials through a process. In software development, VSM helps identify bottlenecks, inefficiencies, and waste, providing a basis for process improvements (Rother and Shook, 2003).

VSM involves creating a visual representation of the entire software development process, from initial requirements gathering to final delivery and this visualization helps in identifying areas where developers are idling or waiting for tasks, thus pinpointing inefficiencies (Martin and Osterling, 2013).

Advantages:
- Provides a comprehensive view of the process, highlighting non-value-added activities.
- Forms the foundation for process optimization by identifying bottlenecks.
- Enhances communication and collaboration by making the process transparent.

Disadvantages:
- Can be time-consuming to create and interpret the maps.
- Requires expertise to analyze and implement changes effectively.
- Initial disruptions may occur when implementing changes based on VSM findings.

Just-in-Time

Just-in-Time (JIT) is a production strategy that aims to reduce in-process inventory and associated costs by producing goods in response to demand rather than in anticipation of it. In the IT industry, JIT principles can be adapted to manage resources efficiently, ensuring that developers are assigned to projects as they are needed.

JIT helps in reducing the time developers spend on the bench by aligning their availability with project requirements. The Kanban system, associated with JIT, uses visual signals to control the flow of work, ensuring that tasks are pulled from one stage to the next only when they are needed. By visualizing the workflow, IT managers can ensure that developers are allocated to projects just in time, reducing idle periods and enhancing productivity.

Applying the JIT strategy offers several advantages, including reducing inventory costs by minimizing excess resources, improving efficiency by ensuring that resources are available as needed, and increasing flexibility to respond to changing project demands. However, it can provide high dependence on accurate demand forecasting, risks of shortages if resources are not available when needed, and require seamless coordination between departments (Schonberger, 1982).

Operations Research in Resource Optimization

Operations Research (OR) applies mathematical and analytical methods to aid decision-making and optimise resource allocation. Techniques such as linear programming, queuing theory, and simulation can help IT organizations allocate resources efficiently and reduce bench time.

OR involves developing models that optimise the allocation of developers to projects, considering various constraints such as skills, availability, and project deadlines. For example, linear programming can determine the best combination of developers for different projects to minimise idle time and maximise productivity. According to Hillier and Lieberman (2014), OR provides optimal solutions, enhancing strategic planning and resource allocation, while improving decision-making through quantitative analysis and scenario planning. It allows for the simulation of different scenarios to predict outcomes and plan accordingly. However, OR requires specialised knowledge and tools for effective implementation, can be data-intensive, necessitating accurate and comprehensive data, and the implementation and maintenance of OR models can be complex.

Findings and Improvements on ABC Organization

Resource Planning Using the SCOR Model

To begin, the author will address the first process of the SCOR model – Plan. One of the key findings when evaluating how ABC Company manages its resource planning is the overly simplistic approach currently in use. Typically, when a new project is initiated, a team is assembled by randomly selecting developers from a list of available personnel. This method presents several disadvantages, including missed opportunities for initiating other potential projects due to the premature allocation of key resources to ongoing projects where they may not be critically needed.

A more strategic approach to resource planning is essential. The current practice of arbitrarily assigning developers can lead to inefficiencies and suboptimal use of talent, particularly when key personnel are assigned to projects that do not fully leverage their skills. This practice can also result in a shortage of essential resources for future projects, thereby limiting the company's capacity to undertake new initiatives.

To enhance resource planning, the following recommendations are proposed for the group of delivery managers at ABC Company:

Forecasting Future Projects: It is crucial to conduct a thorough analysis of potential upcoming projects. This involves anticipating the types of projects that may commence in the near future, their scope, and their requirements. By forecasting future projects, managers can better align current resource allocations with anticipated needs.

Project Size and Complexity Assessment: Delivery managers should evaluate the size and complexity of each potential project. This assessment will help in understanding the resource demands and ensuring that projects are staffed with the appropriate number and level of developers.

Identifying Key and Suitable Profiles: It is essential to identify developers who possess the key skills and profiles best suited for specific projects. This requires a detailed understanding of each developer's strengths, experience, and areas of expertise.

Reallocation of Resources: Managers should regularly review current projects to identify developers who may be better suited for other initiatives. This may involve reallocating developers from projects where their skills are underutilised to those where they can make a more significant impact.

<u>Periodic Alignment of Delivery Managers</u>: Regular meetings and alignment sessions among delivery managers are necessary to discuss and coordinate resource planning. These sessions should focus on aligning resource allocation strategies, sharing insights on project demands, and ensuring that all managers have a consistent understanding of priorities.

<u>Integration into Resource Allocation Software</u>: All the above strategies should be integrated into the company's existing resource allocation software. This will provide a centralised and systematic approach to resource planning, enabling better visibility and control over resource distribution.

Lean Management and Waste Reduction

The principles of Lean Management are fundamentally aimed at waste reduction and process optimization, which are crucial for enhancing operational efficiency in any organization, including ABC Company. In this section, we explore how ABC Company can implement Lean principles to streamline its operations and reduce waste:

<u>Internal Projects</u>: One effective way to utilise idle resources (bench time) is to allocate them to internal projects that add value to the company. For instance, resources can be allocated to the enhancement of the existing Resource Allocation system, automating HR functions, and engaging in R&D for innovative solutions. Volianska-Savchuk & Hlushko (2023) emphasise the importance of digitalization for optimizing business processes, making them simpler, more economical, and of higher quality. Automating HR functions can significantly improve efficiency and reduce costs, aligning with the digital transformation trends discussed by Volianska-Savchuk & Hlushko (2023).

<u>Training and Development</u>: Implementing a Kaizen approach, which focuses on continuous improvement, can help identify the training needs of employees. Conducting thorough internal analyses and interviews with leadership can uncover areas where employees need skill enhancement or exposure to new technologies demanded

by the market. Although ABC Company has initiated some training programs, it is recommended to develop a comprehensive mid- to long-term training plan aligned with the company's strategic goals. This will ensure that the workforce remains competitive and adaptable to market changes.

Cost-Benefit Analysis

Implementing internal projects and training programs requires an analysis of the associated costs versus the benefits. Investing in internal software solutions or purchasing them from the market should be evaluated based on factors such as cost, implementation time, scalability, and potential return on investment. Volianska-Savchuk & Hlushko (2023) highlight that digitalization and automation can lead to significant efficiency gains and cost reductions, making them worthwhile investments for ABC Company.

More agile and responsive organization

The digital transformation of business processes is essential for optimizing operations and maintaining competitiveness. As Volianska-Savchuk & Hlushko (2023) suggest, digitalization involves not only the use of digital technologies but also a fundamental change in organizational design, management models, and incentive systems. For ABC Company, integrating Lean principles with digital transformation initiatives can create a more agile and responsive organization.

Strategic Alignment and Competitive Advantage

It is crucial that Lean initiatives are aligned with the overall strategic goals of ABC Company. Developing a strategic plan for mid- to long-term initiatives that focus on continuous improvement and innovation can provide a competitive advantage. This plan should include specific milestones and performance metrics to ensure that the initiatives are on track and delivering the expected benefits.

Skill Matrix for Optimal Resource Allocation

To further optimise resource allocation at ABC Company, implementing a Skill Matrix for all employees is highly recommended. A Skill Matrix is a visual tool that maps the skills of employees against the needs of the organization. It displays the proficiency levels of various skills across the workforce, enabling managers to make informed decisions about resource allocation.

In the context of ABC Company, integrating a Skill Matrix into the internal resource allocation software can streamline the decision-making process for delivery managers. By having a comprehensive overview of the skills and proficiency levels of each employee, managers can more easily allocate the right people to the right projects, thereby enhancing efficiency and project outcomes.

Implementation Steps

Skill Identification: Begin by identifying the key skills required for various roles within the organization. This can include technical skills, soft skills, and domain-specific knowledge.

Skill Assessment: Assess the current skill levels of all employees through self-assessments, peer reviews, and performance evaluations. This should be an ongoing process to keep the Skill Matrix up to date.

Skill Mapping: Create the Skill Matrix by mapping the assessed skills against the required skills for each project or role. Use a scale (e.g., novice, competent, proficient, expert) to rate the proficiency levels.

Integration with Software: Integrate the Skill Matrix into the existing resource allocation software. Ensure the software allows for easy updates and access by all relevant stakeholders.

Training and Development: Use the Skill Matrix to identify skill gaps and plan targeted training programs. Encourage continuous learning and skill development to keep the workforce adaptable and competitive.

<u>Regular Updates and Reviews</u>: Regularly update the Skill Matrix to reflect new skills acquired by employees and changes in project requirements. Conduct periodic reviews to ensure its accuracy and relevance.

Advantages

Implementing a Skill Matrix at ABC Company offers several advantages. It enhances decision-making by providing a clear and detailed overview of employee skills, which facilitates better project assignments. This improved efficiency ensures that the right skills are deployed for the right tasks, reducing mismatches and inefficiencies. Additionally, the Skill Matrix helps identify skill gaps and informs targeted training programs, fostering continuous employee development. Increased flexibility is another key benefit, as it enables quick and informed adjustments to resource allocation based on changing project needs.

By integrating it into the internal resource allocation software, delivery managers can quickly identify the best-fit employees for new projects and ensure that key skills are not over-allocated to non-critical projects. This integration facilitates the reallocation of resources to maximise efficiency and project success. Additionally, it allows managers to plan and implement targeted training programs to address skill gaps, thereby keeping the workforce competitive and adaptable to market changes

Conclusions

Integrating these O&SCM principles – Lean Management, JIT, VSM, and OR – can provide a robust framework for optimizing bench management in IT. Lean Management and JIT focus on reducing waste and ensuring timely resource allocation, which directly addresses the issue of developers spending excessive time on the bench. VSM provides a visual tool for identifying inefficiencies and streamlining processes, while OR offers advanced analytical techniques for optimizing resource allocation.

By combining these approaches, IT organizations can create a more efficient and responsive resource management system.

For instance, VSM can identify bottlenecks in the current bench management process, Lean principles can guide the elimination of waste, JIT can ensure developers are assigned to projects as needed, and OR can optimise the allocation of resources.

However, the successful implementation of these principles requires a comprehensive understanding of the existing processes, a cultural shift towards continuous improvement, and a commitment to sustained effort. Additionally, the integration of these models must be tailored to the specific needs and context of the organization, considering factors such as project variability, developer skills, and market dynamics.

In conclusion, applying O&SCM principles to bench management in IT not only enhances operational efficiency but also contributes to a more engaged and productive workforce. By reducing idle time and optimizing resource utilization, IT organizations can better navigate economic uncertainties and maintain a competitive edge in the dynamic tech industry.

References

Arif (2022). *Supply Chain Operations Reference Model (SCOR) | AIMS UK.* [online] AIMS. Available at: https://aims.education/study-online/supply-chain-operations-reference-model-scor/ (Accessed: 10 May. 2023)

Chopra, S. and Meindl, P. (2016). *Supply chain management : strategy, planning, and operation. 6th ed.* Boston, Mass.: Pearson.

Hillier, F.S. and Lieberman, G.J. (2014). *Introduction to Operations Research. McGraw-Hill Europe.*

Liker, J.K. (2004). *The Toyota Way.* McGraw Hill Professional.

Martin, K. and Osterling, M. (2013). *Value stream mapping : how to visualise work and align leadership for organizational transformation.* New York Mcgraw Hill Professional.

Razvan, R. (2024). *Concedieri masive la două firme mari de IT din cluj-Napoca.* [online] Ziar Gazeta de Cluj. Available at: https://gazetadecluj.ro/concedieri-masive-la-doua-firme-mari-de-it-din-cluj-napoca/ (Accessed 20 May. 2024).

Reștea, K. (2023). *Lovitură pe piața IT și în România, după valul masiv de concedieri ale giganților Tech la nivel global: Compania Telenav își închide sediul din Cluj/ 172 de angajați sunt afectați/ Activitatea se mută în locațiile din SUA și China.* [online] Economedia.ro. Available at: https://economedia.ro/lovitura-pe-piata-it-si-in-romania-dupa-valul-masiv-de-concedieri-ale-gigantilor-tech-la-nivel-global-compania-telenav-isi-inchide-sediul-din-cluj-172-de-angajati-sunt-afectati-activitatea-se-muta.html (Accessed 20 May. 2024].

Roberts, A. (2024). *Another One: Gameloft to Close Cluj-Napoca Studio, 136 Employees to Be Laid Off.* [online] Cluj XYZ. Available at: https://clujxyz. com/news/business/another-one-gameloft-to-close-cluj-napoca-studio-136-employees-to-be-laid-off/ (Accessed 20 May. 2024).

Rother, M. and Shook, J. (2003). *Learning to see : value stream mapping to create value and eliminate muda. – Version 1.2.* Brookline, Mass.: The Learning Enterprise Institute.

Schonberger, R. (1982). *Japanese manufacturing techniques : nine hidden lessons in simplicity.* New York: Free Press.

Slack, N., Brandon-Jones, A. and Johnston, R. (2016). *Operations management. 8th ed.* Harlow, England: Pearson.

Șupeală, D. (2024). *Concedieri în masă la Gameloft – 200 de oameni dați afară la Cluj.* [online] DoruSupeala.ro. Available at: https://dorusupeala.ro/concedieri-in-masa-la-gameloft-200-de-oameni-dati-afara-la-cluj/ (Accessed 20 May. 2024).

Volianska-Savchuk, L. and Olena KOSHONKO (2023). *DEVELOPMENT TRENDS IN THE USE OF DIGITAL TECHNOLOGIES IN PERSONNEL MANAGEMENT*, (68), pp.112–120. [online] Available at: doi:https://doi.org/10.24025/2306-4420.68.2023.284582. (Accessed: 21 May. 2023)

Womack, J.P. and Jones, D.T. (1996). *Lean Thinking : Banish Waste and Create Wealth in Your Corporation.* London: Simon & Schuster, Limited.

www.actualdecluj.ro. (n.d.). *NTT Data, a treia cea mai mare companie de IT din Cluj, renunță la oameni din echipă. Mai mulți angajați se plâng de concedieri mascate/ Compania: „Fluxul de personal la nivelul NTT DATA este pozitiv".* [online] Available at: https://actualdecluj.ro/ntt-data-a-treia-cea-mai-mare-companie-de-it-din-cluj-renunta-la-oameni-din-echipa-mai-multi-angajati-se-plang-ca-li-se-propune-sa-plece-amiabil-compania-fluxul-de-personal-la-nivelu/ (Accessed 20 May. 2024).

Adelina-Sinziana Cotfas

Revising Romania's Financial Education Strategy

EMBA Module: Governance and Business Ethics

Assessment task: *The assignment is a 3000-word report that will consist of students' own organisations' approaches to corporate governance, with recommendations for improvements. Alternatively, you can choose other business organisations or make a policy proposal.*

Executive Summary

In 2024, Romania introduced its National Financial Education Strategy 2030, designed to establish a framework for enhancing the financial well-being of its citizens. However, the Strategy presents several problematic aspects that undermine its intended purpose.

Firstly, the Strategy suffers from ambiguous governance, lacking clear ownership and accountability, featuring poorly defined objectives, unmeasurable targets, and unclear funding sources. Secondly, it targets three broad groups—children, adults, and businesses—while overlooking vulnerable subpopulations such as low-income individuals, women, the Roma community and those living in rural areas. Thirdly, it places disproportionate emphasis on objective knowledge, neglecting financial attitudes and behaviours, contrary to OECD guidance. It also fails to address critical prerequisites like improving digital literacy, which is essential in an increasingly digital financial landscape. Finally, the Strategy misses the opportunity to foster meaningful institutional collaboration, both across public bodies and with the private sector.

In this context, Romania should rethink and relaunch its Financial Education Strategy as a Financial Well-Being and Resilience Strategy—one that prioritises stronger governance, effective institutional collaboration, and targeted actions for all vulnerable population groups.

Furthermore, both public institutions and private companies should support individuals in making better financial decisions by embedding behavioural science principles and ethical nudges across the Romanian financial ecosystem.

Introduction

As of 2023, Romania recorded the lowest financial literacy score in the European Union, with only 13% of its population demonstrating high overall literacy—compared to the EU average of 18% (European Union, 2023). This result is unsurprising, given the overall performance of Romania's education system[1] and the well-documented link between financial literacy, GDP per capita and education levels (Demertzis, M. et. al., 2024).

Low financial literacy affects numerous aspects of Romania's society and economy, from limited financial inclusion to unhealthy financial behaviours.

As of 2021, 42% of Romanians remained unbanked, positioning Romania as the **12th most unbanked country globally** (Ventura, L., 2021). The primary reasons include a lack of trust in financial institutions, low levels of financial literacy (Romanian National Bank, 2019), and a general reluctance among Romanians to have

---

[1]. The entire Romanian educational system is underperforming, with 42% of Romanian students being functionally illiterate, as stated by Romania Insider: https://www.romania-insider.com/romanian-students-functional-literacy-skills-report-2023. Romania's education has the lowest financing level in the EU and the country has a very low participation of adults in learning programmes, as pointed out by the World Bank: https://documents1.worldbank.org/curated/en/763281530905054127/pdf/128056-SCD-PUBLIC-P160439-RomaniaSCDBackgroundNoteEducation.pdf.

their financial transactions monitored by authorities (Romanian Banks Association, 2022).

The low level of financial inclusion leads to an **underdeveloped financial sector**, characterised by shallow credit intermediation and one of the least developed capital markets in the EU (World Bank, 2023). In terms of **savings and investments**, only 18% of Romanians have deposits, 3% own stocks and only 1% own bonds—while 53% of the population reports never having saved or invested money (Nițoi, M. et. al, 2022).

When it comes to **personal finance management**, many Romanians display unhealthy behaviours—such as compulsive shopping or a lack of clear financial objectives (OECD, 2020)— which can eventually lead to over-indebtedness, either through non-bank financial institutions which practise huge interest rates[2] or through the Buy Now, Pay Later options, which are becoming increasingly popular (Demertzis, M. et. al., 2024).

Financial literacy also plays a key role in **retirement preparedness** (Fernandes, D. Lynch, J.G. and Netemeyer, R. G., 2014). When asked about their pension plans, 39% of Romanians declared they intend to continue working after the official retirement age (OECD, 2020).

In this context, the World Bank has identified closing the financial inclusion gap as one of Romania's key priorities (World Bank, 2023). Enhancing financial literacy and behaviour is considered essential for fostering healthy financial habits and supporting economic growth.

However, without a thorough revision of the current Strategy, Romania is unlikely to meet these objectives. This paper will first present the existing Strategy, followed by a critical analysis based on best practices and relevant theoretical frameworks. The aim is to propose concrete improvements that can shift the Strategy's focus from *financial education* towards financial *well-being and resilience.*

---

2. The Non-bank financial institutions' assets has doubled in Romania since 2014, according to The Financial Supervisory Authority: https://www.asfromania.ro/uploads/articole/attachments/61c22508d748d656752824.PDF. Only in 2024, the Parliament regulated the interest rates practised by NBFIs, by setting a 16% cap: https://www.profit.ro/povesti-cu-profit/financiar/banci/parlamentul-a-adoptat-plafonarea-dobanzilor-la-creditele-acordate-de-ifn-noi-limitari-la-recuperarea-de-creante-21536406.

Key elements of Romania's current Financial Education Strategy

The new National Financial Education Strategy for 2024-2030 (Education Ministry, 2024) begins by outlining the rationale for its development and recognises the need for a coordinated effort among various institutions and authorities.

The financial education *value proposition* is also articulated: the Strategy aims to *enhance the medium- and long-term well-being of financial product consumers by improving financial knowledge, resilience, and awareness of financial and fiscal rights and obligations.*

The Strategy proceeds by presenting data to contextualise the European and Romanian landscape, highlighting the country's socio-economic conditions and the current level of financial knowledge among Romanians. It includes a detailed overview of Romania's financial system, with a particular focus on the banking sector.

Additionally, the document outlines the existing formal education offerings in financial topics at the eighth, tenth, eleventh, and twelfth grade levels – namely, Social and Financial Education, Entrepreneurial Education, Economics, and Applied Economics, respectively.

The Strategy focuses on three target groups, children and young people, adults, and companies, all with proposed initiatives, such as:

- **Children and young people**: integrating financial education into the formal curriculum, organising events and awareness campaigns, introducing economics courses in universities, promoting healthy financial behaviours through mass media, providing dedicated online training for teachers and launching awareness campaigns targeted at parents.
- **Adults**: promoting financial education and consumer rights via mass media and facilitating financial literacy workshops in the workplace.
- **Companies**: encouraging business owners to participate in financial literacy programmes.

The document also proposes general and specific objectives for all target groups, as well as corresponding indicators, as illustrated in Figure 1.

Target group	General objectives	Specific objectives	Examples of indicators
Children and young people under 25	Enhancing financial education by developing the financial skills that children and young people need to become informed consumers of financial products and services;	1. Enhancing the financial knowledge of pupils and students. 2. Elevating the financial knowledge of educators. 3. Integrating a financial education component into parental education programs.	Schools involved Participants Activities Classes and events Workshops Digital services offered Press releases Online attendees
Adults	Improving the knowledge and skills that the adult population needs to plan their finances better, save money, and become informed consumers of financial products and services;	1. Increasing adult consumers' financial knowledge to ensure proper usage of financial products and services for their personal benefit, and to understand their rights and obligations. 2. Cultivating financial behaviours and attitudes in adults to enhance individual economic well-being.	Surveys TV and radio programmes Social media Campaigns
Companies	Enhancing companies' access to information with the purpose of improving their financial discipline.	1. Developing financial and fiscal skills and behaviours to enhance economic outcomes. 2. The continuous education of companies' representatives regarding the financial market.	Classes Participants Beneficiaries

Figure 1. *Target groups, general and specific objectives and indicators (Author's own, adapted from Education Ministry, 2024)*

The Strategy is signed by the Ministry of Education, the Ministry of Finances, Romania's National Bank, the Financial Supervisory Authority, Romania's Banking Association, and the National Consumer Protection Agency. Representatives from these institutions form the Financial and Economic Education Committee.

Regarding funding, the proposed activities will be subject to annual budgets, which must be approved by the relevant authorities. Additional resources may be sourced from the European Union or from private sector partners affiliated with the signatory institutions.

As an Annex, the Strategy includes a more detailed action plan for the three target groups. Examples of activities include:

- **For children and young people:** organising workshops and classes during international events such as Financial Education Week, partnering with universities to offer optional financial education courses, collaborating with publishers to produce educational materials, working with video game developers to create educational games, developing an online platform with resources for teachers, conducting Zoom-based training sessions for educators and organising workshops for both teachers and parents.

- **For adults:** engaging influencers to promote financial education and consumer rights on social media and providing workplace education through various workshops offered by employers.
- **For businesses:** conducting online seminars on fiscal responsibility, offering courses and workshops on financial products and services.

Problems with the current Strategy

In its current form, Romania's Financial Education Strategy faces several shortcomings that may hinder its ability to achieve its stated objectives:

3.1. Ambiguous governance

The Strategy is endorsed by six major Romanian institutions and, although it mentions the creation of the Financial and Economic Education Committee, the person or group of specialists accountable for both the direction and the implementation of the Strategy remain unclear, as a continuation of the *regulatory uncertainty* surrounding the topic over the last 30 years[3].

Progress monitoring and impact evaluation are particularly challenging under the current Strategy[4], as neither the objectives nor the indicators outlined in Figure 1 are measurable, time-bound or linked to specific targets. The accompanying action plan is equally vague: all activities are assigned the same broad timeframe (2024 to 2030), indicators are presented not as quantitative metrics, but as examples of actions or target audiences, and budgeting remains unclear and non-specific across all initiatives.

In summary, the absence of clearly assigned responsibilities,

---

3. Considering that Romania has had nearly 30 Ministers of Education over the past 30 years, (https://www.zf.ro/eveniment/world-vision-romania-faptul-ca-am-avut-30-de-ministri-ai-educatiei-19425200), the educational landscape has been characterised by a lack of accountability and a tendency towards short-term focus.

4. Although the European Commission's report cited by Bruegel (https://www.bruegel.org/policy-brief/state-financial-knowledge-european-union) in 2023 clearly states the need for better and more systematic monitoring of the financial literacy progress.

defined timelines, specific budget allocations, and a structured process for review and adjustment significantly undermines the Strategy's potential to achieve meaningful outcomes.

3.2. Broad targeting resulting in generic measures

The Strategy adopts a one-size-fits-all approach, overlooking the significant disparities in financial literacy across different segments of the population.

For instance, there are notable gender differences: only 4% of women correctly answered advanced financial literacy questions, compared to 8% of men (Nițoi, M. et. al, 2022). Similar gaps exist across income levels, with fewer than 1% of minimum wage earners answering all three core financial literacy questions correctly (Nițoi, M. et. al, 2022).

Despite Romania's rapidly ageing and declining population (World Bank, 2018), older adults are not addressed as a distinct target group. Globally, the longevity economy is gaining significance, with projections estimating 2.1 billion people over the age of 60 by 2050 (World Economic Forum, 2024).

Additionally, 70% of Romania's poor live in rural areas, where disparities in transportation, access to public services, and resilience to natural disasters further marginalise communities (World Bank, 2023). The Roma population—Romania's second-largest minority group, estimated at 1.85 million people (European Commission, 2022)—faces distinct challenges, including low literacy, lack of documentation, and limited access to healthcare and financial services.

In summary, the Strategy fails to propose targeted interventions or *differentiated communication strategies* for Romania's most vulnerable groups, significantly limiting its potential impact.

3.3. Overemphasising *objective knowledge* and neglecting the behavioural dimension

As financial products become increasingly diverse and complex, individuals with low financial literacy are at greater risk of selecting inappropriate products or misusing them (OECD, 2017). In this context, customer expertise—defined as the ability to perform product-related tasks (Alba and Hutchinson, 1987, cited in Fernandes, D. Lynch, J.G. and Netemeyer, R. G., 2014)—is critical. Yet, financial literacy continues to be predominantly measured as objective knowledge of concepts such as compound interest or product features.

While Romania's Strategy declares the goal of enhancing citizens' financial well-being, its actions focus primarily on delivering financial education that builds objective knowledge, particularly through formal school curricula and optional classes. However, meta-analyses indicate that such approaches often result in weak correlations between financial literacy and actual financial **behaviour**[5] (Fernandes, D. Lynch, J.G. and Netemeyer, R. G., 2014).

Without integrating behavioural components, the Strategy is likely to produce only minimal impact or yield benefits over an extended timeframe, once today's students reach adulthood and begin managing their finances independently.

3.4. Neglecting the role of digital skills in financial literacy

Given the increasing digitalisation of financial services, attention must be given to how digital skills interact with financial products and services (Demertzis, M. et. al., 2024).

Despite good digital connectivity, Romania continues to lag behind the EU in terms of digital adoption[6]. As of 2023, only 28% of Romanians possessed basic digital skills, compared to the EU average of 55% (Eurostat, 2024). Moreover, internet usage in Romania is largely focused on communication and entertainment rather than education or online banking (World Bank, 2023).

In this context, the Strategy misses the opportunity to lay the groundwork for *institutional complementarity* and address digital skills as prerequisites for enhancing financial literacy.

---

5. Finland's Financial Literacy Strategy has the following objectives: preventing people from getting into difficulties with their own finances and supporting people to make advantageous choices in the financial markets (https://publications.bof.fi/bitstream/handle/10024/43727/Talousosaamisen-strategia-EN.pdf?sequence=1&isAllowed=y).

6. 18% of Romanians aged 16-74 have never used the internet, versus the EU average of 9%, according to the World Bank's Systematic Country Diagnostic (https://documents1.worldbank.org/curated/en/099134003102323181/pdf/BOSIB0480d508207e0805908b215a1d78b8.pdf).

3.5. Lack of engagement with *institutional investors*

While the Strategy references partnerships with the Romanian Banking Association and the National Bank of Romania, it does not include any collaboration with key institutional investors such as commercial banks, pension funds, or insurance companies, despite their significant regulatory influence and capacity to support joint educational initiatives.

By overlooking these actors, the Strategy misses a critical opportunity to foster public trust in financial institutions, an especially urgent issue given the high percentage of Romania's unbanked population[7].

Towards a Financial Well-Being and Resilience Strategy for Romania. Recommendations

In its current form, the Strategy is unlikely to deliver on its stated value proposition. Two key interventions are essential, drawing on the four benchmark strategies analysed[8] and the national context outlined in the Introduction. First, the structural shortcomings identified throughout this analysis must be addressed. Second, principles of *behavioural economics* should be integrated through coordinated efforts between the public and private sectors, with the aim of *ethically nudging* individuals toward sound financial decisions (Thaler, R. H. and Sunstein, C. R., 2009).

---

7. Romania's National Bank stated, in its 2019 Financial Stability Report, that the low level of financial inclusion in Romania is due, in part, to the lack of trust in financial institutions (https://www.bnr.ro/PublicationDocuments.aspx?icid=19966).

8. Any measure meant to improve the current Strategy with the end goal of increasing Romania's financial literacy level must consider the country's characteristics in terms of individual responsibility, private sector involvement and institutional collaboration. To this purpose, the strategies of countries placed on different points on the Varieties of Capitalism spectrum (Hall, P. and Soskice, D., 2001) were analysed, both Liberal Market Economies and Coordinated Market Economies. An extended analysis on the financial literacy strategies of Canada, Finland, Estonia and Slovenia can be found in **Appendix 1**. Liberal in terms of social cohesion and coordinated in terms of labour market and business regulation, Romania is considered a mix of the two ideal types (Lane, D. and Myant, M., 2007), more specifically an investment-led Dependent Market Economy (Ban, C., 2019).

1. Set the right foundation with better governance and strong partnerships

To ensure accountability from the onset (Keping, Y., 2017), a Coordinator should be appointed to establish the necessary governance structures, convene all relevant stakeholders, and ultimately lead the revision of the Strategy.

The coordinator's priority should be to establish a Research Subcommittee, whose mandate is outlined in Figure 2.

Research subcommittee capabilities	Research subcommittee responsibilities
Qualitative research	Performing a Macro study at national level to:
Quantitative research	• understand Romanians' current level of financial literacy in more details, on all
Sociology	three pillars: knowledge, attitude and behaviours;
Culture and anthropology	• repeat the study with the needed
Behavioural design	frequency to assess the efficiency of the actions performed.
	Identifying all target groups that the new Strategy must focus on
	Designing experiments meant to test different approaches before rolling them out nationally;
	Promoting a data-oriented approach in the Committee.

Figure 2. *The capabilities and responsibilities of the Research Subcommittee (Author's own)*

Establishing partnerships with both public entities and private organisations is essential for leveraging business-specific capabilities (Porter, M. et al., 2011). Each partner should have clearly defined responsibilities and, where relevant, focus on specific target groups. Based on the preceding analysis, the following partners could be incorporated into the revised Strategy, with additional stakeholders to be identified through the initial macro-level study:

Type	Institution	
Public entities	• Ministry of Finance • Ministry of Education • Romania's National Bank • Romania's Banking Association • National Consumer Protection Agency • Financial Supervisory Authority • Romania's Digitisation Authority	• Insurance Supervisory Authority • Private Pensions Supervisory Authority • Romania's Roma Agency • National Gender Equality Agency • National Anti-Poverty Commission • The Bucharest Stock Exchange
Commercial banks	Top five banks by market share: • Banca Transilvania • Banca Comerciala Romana • CEC Bank • BRD • ING Bank	
Insurance companies	Top five insurance companies: • Groupama • Allianz-Tiriac • Omniasig • Asirom • Generali	
Pension providers	Pillar II • Allianz-Tiriac • BCR • BRD • Metropolitan Life • NN	Pillar III • AEGON • BCR Plus • BRD • NN Activ & Optim • BT Pensions • Raiffeisen
NGOs		

Figure 3. Initial list of potential partners for rewriting the Strategy (Author's own)

Representatives from each partner should form the new Committee for Financial Well-Being and Resilience. A *two-tier board structure* should be adopted for the Committee (Bryne, D., n.d.), comprising a *management board* responsible for drafting, piloting, and implementing the Strategy and a *supervisory board* tasked with safeguarding the interests of all stakeholders and ensuring transparency and accountability throughout the process.

To align the Strategy with measurable outcomes, the *Objectives and Key Results (OKR) framework* can be applied (Niven, P. R. and Lamorte, B.). Objectives should be anchored in the overarching goal of enhancing financial well-being and resilience, with a focus on reducing debt and irresponsible financial behaviour, while increasing pension preparedness and overall savings (Kaiser, T., & Menkhoff, L., 2017).

2. Place the Strategy in the context of other related systemic issues

As previously discussed, functional literacy and digital skills are critical enablers for the success of any financial well-being strategy. The Digital Decade 2030 policy explicitly identifies low financial literacy as a barrier to advancing digital competencies in Romania (The Research, Innovation and Digitisation Ministry and Romania's Digitisation Authority, 2022). These initiatives must be strategically aligned—for instance, by sharing the Research Subcommittee to ensure that both strategies are grounded in the same evidence base, and by establishing joint objectives where appropriate.

To address functional illiteracy, a standalone policy should be developed. This policy must assess the socio-economic background of functionally illiterate populations and propose tailored interventions.

3. Target the right groups with tailored approaches

Children remain a key demographic, as appropriately highlighted in the current Strategy. However, section 3.2 presents some of the vulnerable subgroups left unaddressed, such as women, seniors, low-income Romanians, people living in rural areas or the Roma community.

Problematic target groups are more difficult to educate in general (Kaiser, T., & Menkhoff, L., 2017) and should therefore be targeted through tailored programmes designed to meet their specific needs. Potential measures include:

- *Timing* the interventions properly and taking advantage of *teachable moments* might prove more effective for these groups, such as important life events: the birth of a child or turning around age (Milkman, K. et. al., 2011);
- The concept of *just-in-time financial education —linking learning to specific financial decisions—* could also prove useful for harder-to-reach groups, especially if coupled with *teaching soft skills*, like propensity to plan, confidence and proactivity (Fernandes, D. Lynch, J.G. and Netemeyer, R. G., 2014);

A good practice example in targeting different groups comes from Cyprus, where a *spillover effect* was proven: parents living with children who took financial education classes also improved their own financial literacy—an effect that is even more pronounced among parents with lower initial financial literacy levels (Kallenos, T., Milidonis, A. and Zenios, S., 2023), similar to Romania.

One of the new Committee's initial priorities should be to identify all relevant target groups through evidence-based research. Tailored interventions should then be designed for each group, with their effectiveness tested on representative samples to ensure relevance, impact, and scalability. Such interventions include:

- Identifying the most effective communication channel for each sub-group.
- Testing and adapting different messages.
- Working closely with public entities (such as the Roma Agency) to design targeted learning programmes.
- Designing *customer journey maps* for each sub-group's interaction with the financial system and identifying key pain points to be addressed.
- Collaborating with companies in the financial sector to improve the overall financial products environment by simplifying the choice architecture (Linke, R., 2017).
- Providing debt counselling (Republic of Estonia Ministry of Finance, 2021).

4. Nudge people into financial well-being and resilience

Governments around the world are increasingly leveraging behavioural science to advance policy objectives. Decision nudges have been successfully used to increase retirement savings, college enrolment, and influenza vaccination—generating a high impact per dollar spent (Benartzi, S. et. al., 2017). For example, a 2001 study found that automatically enrolling people in a 401(k) increased participation rates from 49% to 86% (Madrian and Shea, 2001, cited in Committee, Nobel Prize, 2017).

Behavioural science offers a range of principles that can be applied to improve financial well-being, including:

Behavioural principle	Intervention idea	Actors involved
Loss aversion *"losses loom larger than gains"* *(Kahneman & Tversky, 1979)*	Ads comparing the monetary loss of a bank loan (net interest) VS loans from other types of loan providers.	Romania National Bank
Anchoring *"Initial exposure to a number serves as a reference point and influences subsequent judgments" (Kahneman & Tversky, 1979)*	Set a default contribution rate for retirement plans (e.g., 5% of salary) that people must opt out of rather than opt into.	Ministry of Finance Retirement plans providers
The paradox of choice *"The fact that some choice is good doesn't necessarily mean that more choice is better."* *(Joseph, S., 2015)*	Limit the number of choices when it comes to financial products	Commercial banks Insurance companies Pension providers
Social norms *Changing behavior by emphasising the statistical reality. [...] If you want to nudge people into socially desirable behavior, do not, by any means, let them know that their current actions are better than the social norm. (Thaler, R. H. and Sunstein, C. R., 2009, p. 67-68).*	Present people with statistics about the saving rates / retirement plans contribution of their peers (if the numbers respect the principle presented to the left).	National Bank Ministry of Finance Retirement plans providers Commercial banks

Figure 4. Ideas for using behavioural principles to nudge Romanians into a better financial behaviour (Author's own, adapted from Kahneman D., Tversky A., 1979; Joseph, S., 2015; Thaler, R. H. and Sunstein, C. R., 2009, p. 67-68)

> *"A nudge is any aspect of the choice architecture that alters people's behavior in a predictable way without forbidding any options or significantly changing their economic incentives. To count as a mere nudge, the intervention must be easy and cheap to avoid. Nudges are not mandates. Putting the fruit at eye level counts as a nudge. Banning junk food does not".*
>
> *Thaler, R. H. and Sunstein, C. R., 2009, p. 6*

Nudges have faced criticism, when perceived as a form of libertarian paternalism that disempowers or infantilises people (Banerjee, S. and John, P., 2022), so ensuring that people retain the ability to make informed judgments for themselves is therefore paramount.

Nudging should always align with the main objective. For example, while default enrolment in retirement plans increases participation rates, it was proven to result in lower overall contributions compared to voluntary enrolment (Thaler, R. H. and Sunstein, C. R., 2021).

In conclusion, when appropriately applied alongside traditional methods, nudge interventions can deliver significant benefits (Committee, Nobel Prize, 2017). It is therefore recommended that all Strategy partners test and integrate behavioural science-based nudges to develop improved protocols, products and services—ultimately facilitating adherence to desirable financial behaviours (Linke, R., 2017).

Conclusion

Romania has the lowest financial literacy rate in the European Union and ranks as the 12th most unbanked country globally—challenges that significantly impact its social and economic landscape.

The current Financial Education Strategy falls short due to ambiguous governance, limited attention to vulnerable populations, vague objectives, a narrow focus on objective knowledge over behavioural change, a lack of partnerships with institutional investors, and insufficient focus on digital skills. Collectively, these shortcomings hinder the Strategy's ability to meaningfully address the country's financial literacy gap.

To overcome these challenges, a new approach is required—one that ensures clear accountability, fosters institutional collaboration to improve low digital literacy, delivers targeted interventions for vulnerable groups, and leverages behavioural science to support better financial decision-making and long-term resilience.

References

Ban, C. (2019), 'Dependent development at a crossroads? Romanian capitalism and its contradictions', *West European Politics*, pp. 1-28.

Banerjee, S. and John, P. C. (2022), *Nudge and Nudging in Public Policy*, Encyclopedia of Public Policy.

Bank of Finland (2020), *Proposal for a national strategy to promote financial literacy in Finland.* Available at: https://publications.bof.fi/bitstream/handle/10024/43727/Talousosaamisen-strategia-EN.pdf?sequence=1&isAllowed=y (Accessed: 8 July 2024).

Bank of Finland Museum (n.d.), *Financial Literacy Centre.* Available at: https://www.rahamuseo.fi/en/museum/financial-literacy-centre/ (Accessed: 12 July 2024).

BBVA (2023), 'Why does China top the ranking in financial literacy?', *BBVA Education* [online]. Available at: https://www.bbva.com/en/sustainability/china-top-ranking-financial-literacy/ (Accessed: 12 July 2024).

Benartzi, S., Beshears, J., Milkman, K. L., Sunstein, C. R., Thaler, R. H., Shankar, M., Tucker-Ray, W., Congdon W. J. and Galing, S. (2017), 'Should Governments Invest More in Nudging?', *Association for Psychological Science*, 28(8), pp. 1041-1055.

Bryne, D. (n.d.), 'What is a two-tiered board structure?', *The Corporate Governance Institute* [online]. Available at: https://www.thecorporategovernanceinstitute.com/insights/lexicon/what-is-a-two-tiered-board-structure/ (Accessed: 4 July 2024).

Calin, G. (2023), 'The Parliament has adopted a cap on NBF loans', *Profit.ro* [online]. Available at: https://www.profit.ro/povesti-cu-profit/financiar/banci/parlamentul-a-adoptat-plafonarea-dobanzilor-la-creditele-acordate-de-ifn-noi-limitari-la-recuperarea-de-creante-21536406 (Accessed: 9 July 2024).

Cornea, R. (2020), 'World Vision Romania: The fact that we had 30 Education ministers in the last 30 years is one of the causes of our systemic issues', *Ziarul Financiar* [online]. Available at: https://www.zf.ro/eveniment/world-vision-romania-faptul-ca-am-avut-30-de-ministri-ai-educatiei-19425200 (Accessed: 12 July 2024).

Demertzis, M., Moffat, L. L., Lusardi, A., Lopez, J. M., (2023), 'State of Financial Knowledge in the European Union', *Bruegel* [online]. Available at: https://www.bruegel.org/policy-brief/state-financial-knowledge-european-union (Accessed: 12 July 2024).

Dumitrescu, R. (2023), 'Romanian students' functional literacy skills report 2023', *Romania Insider* [online]. Available at: https://www.romania-insider.com/romanian-students-functional-literacy-skills-report-2023 (Accessed: 29 June 2024).

European Commission (2020), *A new Vision for Europe's capital markets*. Available at: https://finance.ec.europa.eu/system/files/2020-06/200610-cmu-high-level-forum-final-report_en.pdf (Accessed: 12 July 2024)

European Commission (2022), *Strategy of the Romanian Government on Inclusion of Romanian Citizens Belonging to the Roma Minority for the period 2022 to 2027*. Available at: https://commission.europa.eu/document/download/d6eacde7-c02e-4ec5-88e8-e35727b1032a_en?filename=1_1romania_national_roma_strategic_framework_2022_2027.pdf (Accessed: 2 July 2024).

European Union (2023), *Monitoring the level of financial literacy in the EU*. Available at: https://europa.eu/eurobarometer/surveys/detail/2953 (Accessed: 11 July 2024).

Eurostat (2024), *Digital skills in 2023: impact of education and age*. Available at: https://ec.europa.eu/eurostat/web/products-eurostat-news/w/ddn-20240222-1 (Accessed: 12 July 2024).

Fernandes, D., Lynch, J. G., and Netemeyer, R. G. (2014), 'Financial Literacy, Financial Education, and Downstream Financial Behaviors', *Management Science*, 60(8), pp. 1861-1883.

Financial Consumer Agency of Canada (2021), *National Financial Literacy Strategy 2021-2026*. Available at: https://www.canada.ca/content/dam/fcac-acfc/documents/programs/financial-literacy/financial-literacy-strategy-2021-2026.pdf (Accessed: 27 June 2024).

Government of Canada (2023), *Implementing the National Strategy for Financial Literacy – Count me in, Canada: Progress report 2015-2019*. Available at: https://www.canada.ca/en/financial-consumer-agency/programs/financial-literacy/progress-report-financial-literacy.html (Accessed: 2 July 2024).

Government of Slovenia (2021), *National Financial Education Programme*, Available at: https://www.gov.si/assets/ministrstva/MF/Financni-sistem/DOKUMENTI/Financno-izobrazevanje/NPFI_EN.pdf (Accessed: 6 July 2024).

Hall, P. and Soskice, D. (2001), *Varieties of Capitalism*, New York: Oxford University Press.

Joseph, S. (2015), *Positive Psychology in Practice: Promoting Human Flourishing in Work, Health, Education, and Everyday Life*, New Jersey: John Wiley & Sons, Inc.

Kahneman, D. and Tversky, A. (1979), 'Prospect theory: An analysis of decision under risk', *Econometrica*, 47, pp. 263–291.

Kaiser, T. and Menkhoff, L. (2017), 'Does Financial Education Impact Financial Literacy and Financial Behavior, and If So, When?', *The World Bank Economic Review*, 31(3).

Kallenos, T., Milidonis, A. and Zenios, S., 2023, 'The Ripple Effect of Financial Education', *Bruegel* [online]. Available at: https://www.bruegel.org/analysis/ripple-effect-financial-education (Accessed: 17 July 2024).

Keping, Y. (2018), 'Governance and Good Governance: A New Framework for Political Analysis', *Fudan Journal of the Humanities and Social Sciences*, 11, pp. 1-8.

Linke, R. (2023), 'Nonprofit Uses Behavioral Science to Nudge People Towards Making Good Choices', *MIT Sloan* [online]. Available at: https://mitsloan.mit.edu/ideas-made-to-matter/nonprofit-uses-behavioral-science-to-nudge-people-towards-making-good-choices (Accessed: 5 July 2024).

Milkman, K. L., Beshears, J., Choi, J. J., Laibson, D., and Madrian, B. C. (2011), 'Using implementation intentions prompts to enhance influenza vaccination rates', *Proceedings of the National Academy of Sciences*, 108(26), pp. 10415–10420.

Ministry of Justice Finland (2023), *Promoting financial literacy and the national financial literacy strategy*. Available at: https://oikeusministerio.fi/en/

promoting-financial-literacy#:~:text=The%20financial%20literacy%20 function%20at,on%20the%20financial%20literacy%20strategy. (Accessed: 2 July 2024).

Niţoi, M., Clichici, D., Zeldea, C., Pochea, M. M., Ciocîrlan, C. (2022), 'Bunăstarea financiară şi alfabetizarea financiară în România', *Institutul de Economie Mondială Working Paper 2022*.

Nobel Prize Committee (2017) ,'Richard H. Thaler: Integrating Economics with Psychology', *Nobel Prize in Economics documents* [online]. Available at: https://ideas.repec.org/p/ris/nobelp/2017_001.html (Accessed 3 July 2024).

OECD (2017), *Behavioural Insights and Public Policy*. Available at: https://www. oecd.org/en/publications/2017/03/behavioural-insights-and-public-policy_ g1g7590e.html (Accessed: 12 July 2024).

OECD (2020), *Financial Literacy of Adults in South East Europe*. Available at: https://www.oecd-ilibrary.org/finance-and-investment/financial-literacy-of- adults-in-south-east-europe_c639aa3c-en (Accessed: 2 July 2024).

Republic of Estonia Ministry of Finance (2021), *Money Smart Estonia. Strategy for developing the financial wisdom of the inhabitants of Estonia for 2021- 2030*. Available at: https://www.fin.ee/en/media/10094/download (Accessed: 1 July 2024).

Romania's Government (2024), *National Financial Education Strategy 2024-2030*. Available at: https://www.edu.ro/sites/default/files/_fi%C8%99iere/Strategii/ SNEF_2024_2030.pdf (Accessed: 20 June 2024).

Romanian Banks Association (2022), *Half of Romanians make payments using Internet/Mobile Banking*. Available at: https://www.arb.ro/wp-content/ uploads/CP-incluziune.pdf (Accessed: 28 June 2024).

Romanian National Bank (2019), *Financial Stability Report for December 2019*, Year IV, 8(18). Available at: https://www.bnr.ro/PublicationDocuments. aspx?icid=19966 (Accessed: 12 July 2024).

Thaler, R. H. and Sunstein, C. R. (2009; 2021), *Nudge*, New York: Penguin.

The Financial Supervisory Authority (2021), *Report on the stability of non-bank financial markets*. Available at: https://www.asfromania.ro/uploads/articole/ attachments/61c22508d748d656752824.PDF (Accessed: 7 July 2024).

Ventura, L. (2021), 'World's Most Unbanked Countries', *Global Finance Magazine* [online]. Available at: https://gfmag.com/data/worlds-most- unbanked-countries (Accessed: 2 July 2024).

World Bank (2018), *Romania: Systematic Country Diagnostic. Background Note on Education*. Available at: https://documents1.worldbank.org/curated/ en/763281530905054127/pdf/128056-SCD-PUBLIC-P160439-RomaniaSCD BackgroundNoteEducation.pdf (Accessed: 2 July 2024).

World Bank (2023), *Systematic Country Diagnostic Update Romania*. Available at: https://documents1.worldbank.org/curated/en/099134003102323181/pdf/BOSIB0480d508207e0805908b215a1d78b8.pdf (Accessed 8 July 2024).

World Economic Forum (2024), *Longevity Economy Principles*. Available at: https://www3.weforum.org/docs/WEF_Longevity_Economy_Principles_2024.pdf (Accessed: 5 July 2024).

Appendix 1. Comparative analysis of financial literacy strategies

Four financial literacy programmes from around the world were analysed. The comparative analysis included countries with great results in terms of financial literacy (Canada, Finland, Estonia) and one country that shares similarities with Romania but scores well in financial literacy, Slovenia (both formerly communist countries, now democracies and part of the EU).

Table 1. *A comparative view of four Financial Literacy strategies*

Component	Canada	Finland	Estonia	Slovenia
Main takeaways. Elements that can travel in the Romanian context	Evidence-based research and Collaboration are the two main pillars for the entire strategy. The concept of just-in-time knowledge. The main objective is financial resilience, defined as the ability to persevere and adapt through challenging times and negative life events (FCAC, 2021). It includes a guide for all stakeholders, for translating each objective into specific actions in their area (How can stakeholder X advance this priority) (FCAC, 2021). It includes actions grounded in behavioural research. A Research Sub-Committee was established together with the previous Strategy to provide evidence-based advice to the main Committee (FCAC, 2015)	It has a two-tier governance structure: one entity wrote it and other deals with the implementation. It includes media literacy and digital literacy. Two types of target groups: based on demographics and based on life moments. Measurable objectives and targets.	All three strategic priorities are broken down into clear objectives and indicators, although the targets (increasing/decreasing) could have been more specific. It explores the relationships with other strategies, such as social security, research and development, innovation and entrepreneurship, and the fields of youth and education. Partnering with a major bank.	Adding advisory as an important component of the programme. Proposing pilot programmes which will be evaluated before full rollout.

Component	Canada	Finland	Estonia	Slovenia
Governance and institutional cooperation	Owner: The Financial Consumer Agency of Canada (FCAC) Four main stakeholder groups: - Community groups: NGOs, consumer advocacy organisations etc. - Financial services: banks, fintech's, financial advisors, credit bureaus, insolvency trustees etc. - Governors and regulators: FCAC, federal/territorial/municipal government, indigenous governments etc. - Others: research, academia, financial influencers. (FCAC, 2021)	Owners: Bank of Finland and the Ministry of Justice A project group from Bank of Finland was responsible for writing the strategy proposal. (Bank of Finland, 2021) The steering instrument was the Financial Literacy function in the Ministry of Justice, in charge of coordinating the work of all private and public entities collaborating on this matter (Ministry of Justice, n.d.)	A strong collaboration with Nordea Bank is emphasised, with thousands of students being taught by bankers both on basic financial skills and financial crime (Nordea, 2024)	Written by an Inter-ministerial Working Group. Each of the nine sub-programmes has a specific institution as owner. A strong collaboration with the Consumers Protection Agency is emphasised. (Ministry of Finance, 2010)
Objectives	The strategy has the following strategic priorities: A. Reduce barriers: 1. Communicate in ways people understand. 2. Build for different needs. 3. Increase digital access and literacy. B. Catalyse action: 4. Improve access to quality and affordable financial help. 5. Simplify financial decisions with behavioural design. 6. Enhance consumer protection measures. Supporting measures to improve: - Skills needed to navigate the financial marketplace - Capacity: just-in-time knowledge. - Behaviour: managing expenses, debt, savings. (FCAC, 2021)	"Finns will have the world's best financial literacy by 2030" (Bank of Finland, 2021). The strategy's mission is to make people understand the importance of finance and help them act in an ethical and sustainable manner. The objectives: - To prevent people from getting into difficulties with their finances. - To support people to make advantageous financial choices. (Bank of Finland, 2021)	The strategy is "Money smart Estonia" (Ministry of Finance, 2021). The objectives follow the same OECD-recommended structure: knowledge, attitude and behaviours: 1.People will plan their finances better and make better decisions. 2.People will understand financial products better. 3.Financial services will be offered more responsibly.	The strategy breaks financial capability into five components: 1. Making ends meet: keeping up with financial commitments, having a positive payment account balance. 2. Keeping track of finances: checking the cash inflow and outflow, budgets for unpredicted expenses. 3. Planning ahead: having enough provisions for unexpected income drops, having retirement provisions. 4. Choosing financial products and services: seeking advice from appropriate advisers, comparing products etc. 5.Staying informed on financial matters. The programme has four main pillars: - Prevention. - Universality. - Guidelines and consultancy. - Selection of potential education providers. (Ministry of Finance, 2010).

Component	Canada	Finland	Estonia	Slovenia
Target groups	Each strategic priority mentions the types of publics it addresses, for example: - Women. - Indigenous Peoples. - Racialised Canadians - Older Canadians. - Newcomers to Canada. - Linguistic minorities. - People with disabilities or cognitive challenges. - People with limited digital access and/or digital skills, including seniors, recent immigrants etc. - Children and youth. - Low-income Canadians. - Unbanked Canadians. (FCAC, 2021)	Three demographics addressed: - Children - Adults - Retirement age Three categories based on the most favourable moments for embracing financial literacy: - Predictable life changes (starting a family). - Unexpected risks (illness). - Financially vulnerable groups. Special sub-categories: - Women - Low-income citizens - Lowly educated citizens	A single target group is mentioned specifically besides the general addressability, namely women.	Children Young persons Adults Special target groups (young people outside the education system, low-education groups, unemployed people, those in debt, socially disadvantaged persons and financially excluded groups), Educators (Ministry of Finance, 2010)
Targets / expected outcomes	Example of expected outcome for Strategic priority 1 (Communicate in ways people understand): Fewer Canadians experience negative outcomes due to the lack of understanding of the characteristics, risks or benefits of financial products, or from an inability to determine which product best fits their needs. (FCAC, 2021)	The three dimensions suggested by OECD—knowledge, attitude and behaviours—are applied, with measurable indicators defined for each, for example: At least 80% of individuals can correctly define inflation (knowledge) At least half of them make a monthly budget for their finances (behaviour) At most half get pleasure from spending money at once (attitudes).	Three targets are set: Financial wisdom is accessible to everyone. - Example of indicator: % of educational institutions that added entrepreneurship to their curriculum. As is: 55%. Target: growing. Financial wisdom is used practically, in daily decisions - Example of indicator: Number of people having joined III pillar. As is: 167,200. Target: growing. The environment encourages financial wisdom. - Example of indicator: volume of investment fraud. As is: €5.6 million. Target: declining. (Republic of Estonia Ministry of Finance, 2021).	Sub-programmes are designed for each target group, with designated owners, different budgets and targets. Most initiatives are proposed pilots which will be evaluated before full rollout. Expected outcomes are mostly based on the target audiences' exposure to the provided content: number of websites hits, number of brochures printed, media coverage. Ministry of Finance, 2010)

Component	Canada	Finland	Estonia	Slovenia
Examples of initiatives	Initiatives for Strategic priority 1: For FCAC: - Develop targeted education outreach programmes. - Ensure all communication is understood. For Financial Services: - Pilot alternative communication styles. - Work with experts to create a plain language. For regulators: - Use a variety of channels to convey messages. - Test all communication before rolling out. For community groups: - Advocate on behalf of their clients. - Share communication best practices with the other institutions. Initiatives for Strategic priority 5: For FCAC: - Adapt best practices of behavioural design to finances. - Implement behavioural-based experiments. For Financial Services: - Implement user testing and apply behavioural design approaches to make sure consumers are not overwhelmed by all the choices. - Apply ethical nudges to increase the chances of people making healthy financial decisions. - Simplify decision making. For regulators: - Design programs that include a "default" state to ethically aid consumers in the decision-making process. For community groups: - Just-in-time, simplified communication. - Using games and incentives grounded in behavioural research. (FCAC, 2021)	A Financial Literacy Centre was established at the Bank of Finland Museum, which organises different events and tours. (Bank of Finland Museum, n.d.) No specific list of actions is presented in the Strategy, but a corresponding 5-year action plan was being prepared at the time of this analysis.	No clear examples of initiatives are provided.	At least one sub-programme for each target group, for example "Education scheme for Elderly People". No specific actions are designed within the programmes, which will be the prerogative of each programme owner. Ministry of Finance, 2010)

Mihaela–Adela Coroiu

Systemic Management Insights Based on the Viable System Model for an Energy Services Company

EMBA Module: Systemic Management: Seeing the Bigger Picture

Assignment task: This assignment is a 3000-word report on a full application of a chosen systemic methodology in the students' business. It will be a 'consulting' type of report, with a briefing to the Board of Directors, providing the results of the systemic analysis undertaken, and the recommendations for improvements resulting from it.

1. Introduction

This paper presents a case study analysing the organizational structure of ENERGIA S.A. – a Romanian company operating in the energy services sector, identifying current managerial challenges and exploring potential solutions.

Today, many companies focus on optimizing individual processes within their internal functions to reduce costs. However, this approach does not necessarily ensure overall process optimization. Contemporary management faces difficulties in both internal and external relationships due to pressure for rapid decision-making and a lack of coordination, adaptability, and flexibility. Organizations often overlook their holistic nature and their potential to interact and build cooperative ecosystems. A systemic approach is essential for organizations to navigate their internal and external environments effectively (Gallego-García and García-García, 2019).

This paper explores the application of the Viable System Model (VSM) as a tool for visualizing and analysing a complex organization active in Romania's energy sector. Based on key principles such as viability, recursion, and autonomy, VSM emphasises the importance of a system's ability to respond to internal and external disruptions to remain viable.

2. Brief presentation of the company analysed

The case study refers to a Romanian company founded more than two decades ago, referred to in this paper as ENERGIA S.A. Over this period, the company has evolved into a major player on the local energy market, focusing on domestic development. With nationwide offices and its own production facilities, the company has become a significant actor in the energy sector.

A key moment in its evolution occurred between 2008 and 2013, when the company played an important role in the construction of new renewable energy plants in Romania during the first wave of green energy investments. During this period, the company experienced significant business growth, reaching its peak turnover in 2012.

At the same time, Romania and Europe experienced a surge in clean energy investments. The company, organised as a group with national coverage, distinguished itself as a general contractor for large-scale wind and photovoltaic park projects.

Currently, the company provides complex energy services structured into four main divisions, as presented in Figure 1.

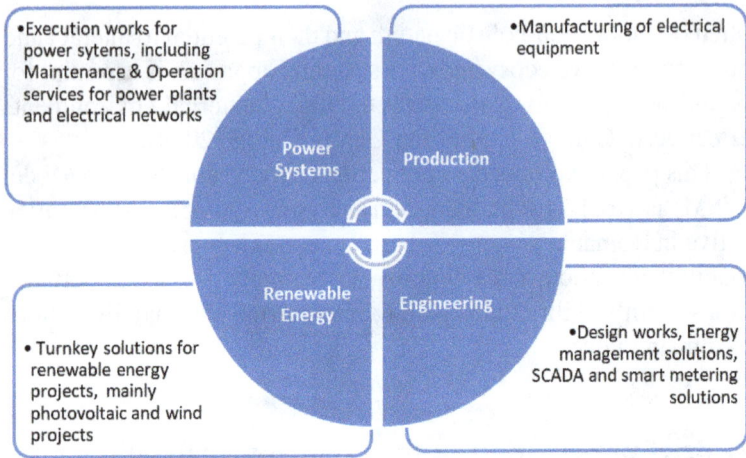

Power Systems
•Execution works for power sytems, including Maintenance & Operation services for power plants and electrical networks

Production
•Manufacturing of electrical equipment

Renewable Energy
• Turnkey solutions for renewable energy projects, mainly photovoltaic and wind projects

Engineering
•Design works, Energy management solutions, SCADA and smart metering solutions

Figure 1. Main business divisions and core activities of the energy services company

The board of directors is including the founding partners, and the company is managed by a General Manager (GM), who oversees all support services through seven departments: Legal, Marketing, Finance, IT, Human Resources, HSEQ, and Development. Reporting to the GM is a Deputy General Manager responsible for production structures, including the Procurement Department, Products Sales Department, and the two factories. Apart from the production-related profit centre managed by the Deputy GM, the remaining profit centres — six regional branches and four core departments (Lighting, Green Energy, Electrical Engineering, and Power Systems) — are directly coordinated by the GM.

Currently, most of its managers have been with the company for 10-15 years, and numerous new engineers are being hired to support upcoming projects.

In the current landscape, the energy market is undergoing a second wave of development to support decarbonization, and ENERGIA, a well-established company in the local market, is encountering significant competition from major international energy firms. While maintaining a strong presence, ENERGIA has reached a business maturity and pinnacle in its current portfolio development. To sustain its current business level and profitability, the company must comprehend emerging industry trends and challenges, necessitating a successful reinvention of its portfolio and service delivery methods. Failure to identify innovative market approaches may confine its activities to subcontracting for major players in the future.

Customer expectations are evolving, with a growing emphasis on ensuring business sustainability. Simply offering a competitive price for satisfactory quality is no longer enough. Customers now seek additional features such as zero emissions, minimised environmental impact, services throughout the product lifecycle, social involvement, and support for vulnerable groups. These aspects align with the trending concept of energy sustainability, requiring the company to be prepared to offer enhanced solutions while preserving performance and profitability.

The business growth potential is significant in the next 10 years, raising questions about the company's preparedness to meet new challenges and remain among the major players in the industry. If the market allows for fantastic development, how can the company organise itself to enhance its performance? What are the key internal issues, and how can they be addressed to be able to capture new businesses? ... To find answers to these questions, an analysis of the management system is required.

3. Self-transformation methodology overview

The chosen methodology refers to the Viable System Model (VSM) and Espinosa's Methodology for self-transformation (Espinosa and Walker, 2017). The VSM is a widely utilised methodological tool globally (Espinosa, 2015), developed by Beer in 1994 as a theory of organizational viability grounded in cybernetics and neurophysiology. It presents a cybernetic model of organizations conceived as viable systems. Beer proposes that the human nervous system establishes survival rules through processes of regulation, learning, adaptation, and evolution.

The methodology selection is based on the reviews showing that:

- VSM offers significant advantages by providing holistic organizational management support (Stich & Blum, 2015).
- Recognised for its dynamism and flexibility, VSM assists management in formulating strategic policies, decision-making regarding the environment, partners, and internal arrangements.

- Its capacity for recursive optimization ensures the organization's sustainability and that of its related environment.
- It offers a conceptual system for organizational structure development; has not been rejected to date. (Vahidi et al, 2019)
- Numerous instances highlight VSM's superior response in all Key Performance Indicators (KPIs), addressing efficiency, effectiveness, and service aspects.
- For complex companies, VSM serves as a key to success, enabling preventive actions and strengthening coordination and oversight. (Arista Hakiki, 2023)

Espinosa (2023) highlights Beer's assertion that VSM possesses necessary conditions for organizational viability: an operational component addressing the variety of specific external niches (recursive), meta-systemic roles managing operational variety, and the organization addressing the variety of the external system.

As Espinosa (2023) emphasises, Beer defined a viable system as one capable of independent existence, specifying necessary and sufficient conditions for the viability of any living organism. Beer's theory of viability and effective organization aimed to uncover fundamental patterns in organizational systems, challenging traditional management approaches. The VSM, a recursive model and meta-language inspired by the human brain's physiological aspects, serves as a guide for systemic intervention and managing organizational complexity (see Figure 2).

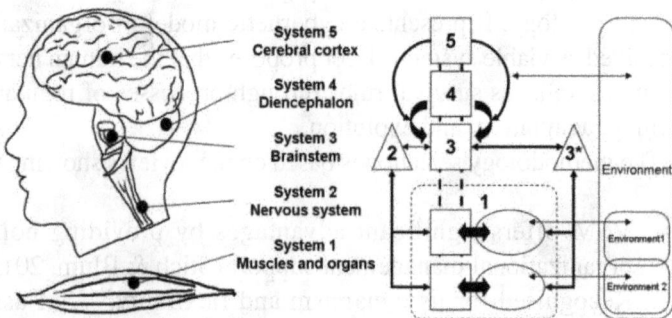

Figure 2. The Viable System Model Structure (Stich and Blum, 2015)

As presented in Figure 3, the VSM comprises five subsystems connected by relation channels, establishing links among subsystems and with the external environment, as follows (Sadi et al, 2016):

- System 1 (S1): The operational unit that produces outcomes (goods or services). It iteratively interacts with the environment, sharing information and knowledge with other subsystems.
- System 2 (S2): The regulatory centre for S1 units, providing rules and guidelines for smooth operations and minimizing oscillations between S1 units.
- System 3 (S3): The overseeing entity engaged in resource negotiations with S1 units, carrying out strategic directives, and fostering collaboration in operations rather than relying solely on autocratic methods.
- System 3*(S3*): The audit-oriented unit that facilitates audits and offers supplementary information regarding the status of operational units.
- System 4 (S4): The strategic unit, focusing on strategic planning by continuously monitoring the potential future environment to anticipate changes. It collaborates with S3 in discussing the need for action.
- System 5 (S5): The policy and normative management, defining the mission, goals, objectives, values, and culture of the organization. S5 also resolves disagreements between S3 and S4.

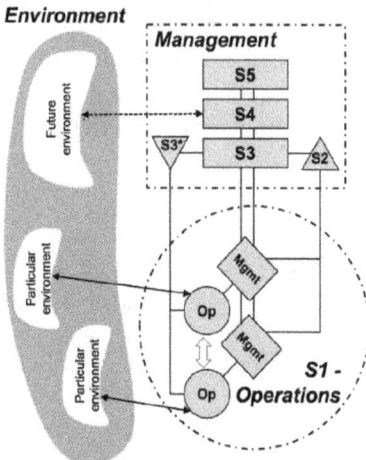

Figure 3. The Viable System Model Structure (Sadi et al, 2016)

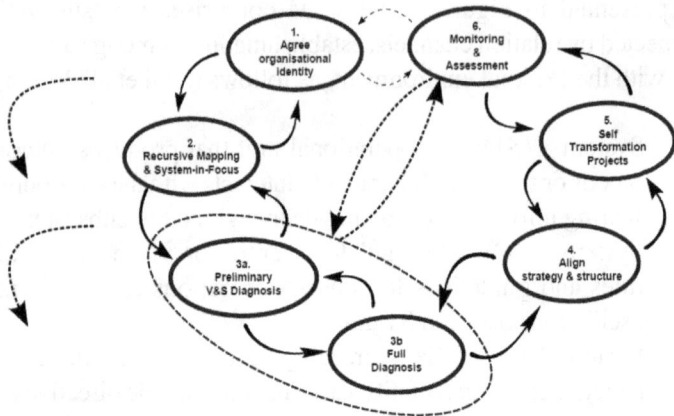

(Illustration by Jon Walker[2])

Figure 4. Self-transformation Methodology (STM) stages according to Espinosa, 2023

Espinosa's (2023) Self-Transformation Methodology (STM) helps organizations observe their current interaction patterns and identify issues. As shown in Fig. 4, the methodology involves three phases for organization diagnosis:

1. Define the system in focus clarify organizational identity and map levels of recursiveness.
2. Identify and map the 5 VSM systems: Operational Units (S1), Harmonization (S2), Self-Regulation and Synergies (S3), Monitoring (S3*), Adaptation and external communication (S4), Identity and Closure (S5).
3. Assess the balance in interactions between the different systems.

In the subsequent sections of this paper, the author will aim to align ENERGIA's current organizational structure with the VSM, addressing diagnostic issues, proposing implementation solutions, and suggesting a monitoring system.

4. Defining the system in focus

4.1 Statement of Organizational Identity

To formulate an effective organizational statement, Espinosa (2023) suggests using a 'TASCOI analysis' (Harwood, 2020), because this tool helps identify key organizational actors (Actors, Suppliers, Customers, Owners, and Interveners) and connect them to define the organizational identity during the main transformation process (T).

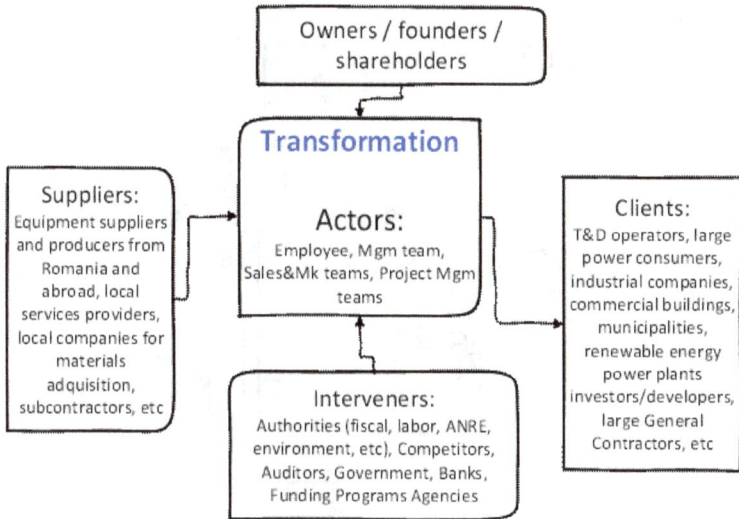

Figure 5. ENERGIA – TASCOI Analysis (Harwood, 2020)

Identity statements for ENERGIA:

"ENERGIA is a high-performing energy company, among leaders of the Romanian market, offering turnkey solution for a wide range of energy projects, being a reliable and long-term partner for its clients, suppliers and collaborators, providing energy sustainable tailored solutions through highly qualified staff that are well-informed in recent technological innovations."

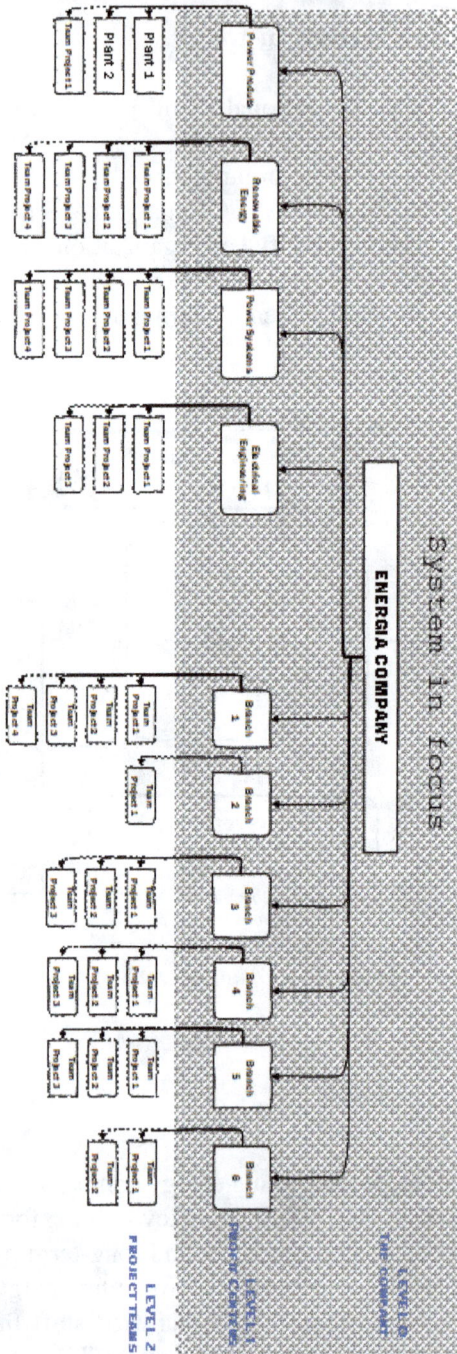

Figure 6. ENERGIA – Recursive Levels and System in focus for VSM

4.2 Recursive analysis

In a recursive organizational structure, each system component can have multiple embedded sub-components, each with the potential for independent viability as a standalone system. (Espinosa, 2023)

As presented in the Fig. 6. (**Annex 2**), for ENERGIA level 0 is considered to be represented by the company itself, level 1 comprises profit centres encompassing both business lines and territorial branches, and recursive level 2 is defined by project teams within each profit centre. The company's support services cater to all profit centres, but specific profit centres hold dedicated positions for roles assumed by the meta-system, ensuring proper integration with the company's overall meta-system.

The system in focus selected for VSM application consist in level 0 and level 1.

5. Applying Viable System Model

5.1 Mapping the Viable System of the System in Focus

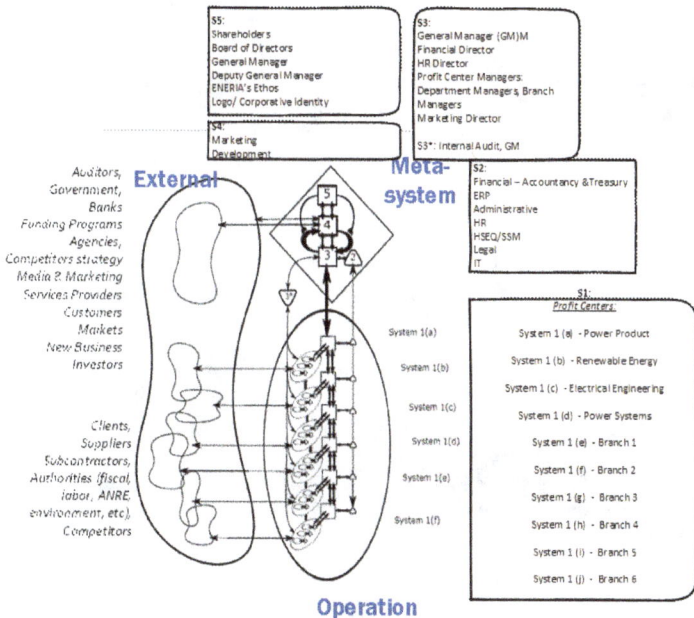

Figure 7. ENERGIA – VSM mapping for system in focus

Graphical representation of VSM mapping in presented in Figure 6 and detailed in **Annex 3**, next to the graphic representation **in Annex 4.**

5.2 Diagnosis (detailed in Annex 5)

Actual issues and problems the management team faces are linked to the communication problem inside company, resources allocation and share between profit centres, commercial activity integration and coordination, development strategy, sharing expertise and knowledge.

The VSM diagnosis reveals several issues and possibilities to improve activity in ENERGIA presented in **Annex 5**. The briefing of the diagnosis issues are presented as the big picture in Figure 8.

No.	Related to System	Issue/Problem description
D1	S1	Profit centers lack collaboration and experience exchange
D2	S2	Poor communication
D3	S2	Lack of performant ICT
D4	S3	Lack of experience sharing
D5	S3	Inefficient resource negotiation
D6	S3	Lack of well-defined operational Key Performance Indicators
D7	S3	Staff assessment criteria may lack clarity, objectivity, or alignment with organizational goals, leading to challenges in identifying and encouraging high-performing individuals.
D8	S3	The absence of an Improvement & Development Plan
D9	S3*	The lack of Client Care tools and compliance operational-level responsibilities
D10	S3*	Delays and inefficiencies in addressing complains
D11	S4	Lack of structured guidance and support for employees' professional
D12	S4	Missing activity for technological innovations and development
D13	S4	Lacks a structured approach to sustainability actions
D14	S4	The absence of a systemic approach in project management
D15	S5	The absence of individual Action Plans and Investment Plans for each profit center poses challenges in coordinating and aligning development efforts with the company's overarching goals.
D16	S5	Missing a clear and disseminated company's long-term strategy, the short-term profitability being the main concern.

Figure 8. ENERGIA – Diagnosis big picture

6. Supporting self-transformation plan

Table 1 – Proposed self-transformation projects based on the solutions to the diagnosis issues

No.	Improvements needed	Proposed Projects	Monitoring and assessment – KPIs
S1	Synergizing Profit Centres (PC): Fostering collaboration through project performance exchange	Monthly internal workshops for project performance exchange	- no. of internal workshops. - no. of profitable projects performed based on shared experience and resources.
S2	Cultivating a culture of clear communication: transforming team dynamics for project success	Introducing "Alignment meetings" – involve team members presenting project/task details, encouraging feedback exchange.	- No of meetings. - Profitability increases for project performed based on incentive from alignment meetings
S3	Implement ICT app (ERP) with CRM & Project Planning tool and centralised procurement	Implementation of ERP	- ERP app
S4	Experience sharing	"How It's Made" – video tool to record challenging operations or project activities as lessons for colleagues and to conduct a documented analysis of closed projects and development of a Virtual library	- Virtual library - No. of trainings records - No. of visualizations by internal staff
S5	Transparent and supportive resource allocation to sustain overall effectiveness and performance.	Planning tool – associated with ERP and CRM	- % decrease overload for PC - Procedures and methodology for sharing resources - Transfer prices policy
S6	Precision in performance: enhance accuracy in performance assessments, promote alignment with organizational goals, and provide a foundation for fair and effective reward structures	Establishing clear operational KPIs	- New operational KPIs
S7	Encourage high performers	Review staff assessment methodology and implement carrier development plan	- staff assessment methodology - carrier development plan for staff
S8	Charting a Course for Growth: continuous improvement and development mechanism	Introducing an Improvement & Development Plan	- Improvement & Development Plan - Idea Box & Folder on server - No. of idea registered - No of improvements implemented

Table 1 (continued)

No.	Improvements needed	Proposed Projects	Monitoring and assessment – KPIs
S9	Elevating Client Experience: Implementing Client Care Tools and Operational Responsibilities	Implement Client Care mechanism: Client feedback form distributed after each project closure; Implement CRM tool for registration of Client and supplier feedback	- Client feedback forms. - CRM feedback registrations
S10	Investing in Success: Establishing a Structured Professional Development Program	Implement a coaching program	- No. of coaches - No. of employees assisted - No. of employees who advanced in their careers following the coaching program
S11	Driving Innovation Excellence: Promoting Technology and Involving Senior Experts in Development Planning	Empowering Development Department with the support of senior experts, creating a development committee as a matrix team formed by senior experts and set a monthly committee meeting to address development and innovation issues	- Team of senior experts for development role. - Monthly committee meetings - No. of development and innovation projects initiated
S12	Recognizing the importance of environmental and social responsibility, our organization is embarking on a transformative journey. Elevating Responsibility: Implementing a Structured Sustainability Approach and Annual Reporting	Implement ESG	- ESG yearly report - ESG projects implemented
S13	Transforming Project Dynamics: Implementing a Systemic Approach to Project Management	Systemic Approach to Project Management Training Program	- No. of trainings - No. of attendees
S14	Driving Coordinated Growth: Introducing Individual Action and Investment Plans for Profit Centres	Implement and monitor yearly Action Plan and Investment Plan for each profit Centre	- Action plans - Investment plans - % implementation results
S15	Define and communicate the company's long-term strategy	Company's strategy toward sustainability	- The strategy - Dissemination events

7. Conclusion and critical reflection

In my opinion, to prepare ENERGIA for sustainability amid the European energy market's transition to decarbonization, it is essential to set ambitious company targets for the next five to ten years. Although this transformation brings new opportunities, the company's long-term strategy remains unclear, and its sustainability objectives have not yet been defined. Therefore, System 5 (S5) / shareholders must decide whether to expand operations and pursue growth or to focus on short-term profitability by running a low-risk business model.

The author raises the question of how the Viable System Model (VSM) could be applied to ENERGIA to identify and address internal weaknesses, particularly those contributing to declining performance in high-potential profit centres. However, the longstanding tenure of some key managers may hinder a comprehensive analysis of the system and restructuring of the organizational framework in line with VSM principles, as it may prevent them from honestly acknowledging the actual roles they fulfil within the company.

From my observations, there are several cases where experienced managers—each with over ten years in the company—are appointed to roles that conflict with their preferences or the tasks they carry out. This may result from their diverse backgrounds and previous experience in areas where they were more competent than in their current positions. This situation raises questions about whether appointments are made based on individual strengths and whether these individuals are truly suited for the roles they occupy. It also points to the need for a well-designed performance management system tailored to ENERGIA's needs.

The author hopes that applying the VSM will shed light on this issue, leading to a realignment of roles within the company, supporting strategic development initiatives, and enhancing performance.

Mapping ENERGIA's organizational structure would also highlight the need to revisit the meta-system and improve the balance—particularly among Systems 3, 4, and 5—to support adaptation and achieve alignment between "inside and now" and "outside and then."

Furthermore, VSM offers a clearer explanation of the importance of creating the right conditions for System 1 (profit centres) to enhance their self-governance. Viability depends on maintaining balanced relationships between the organization and its market, which leads to greater resilience and adaptability. Therefore, profit centres must ensure this balance with their external environment, without relying exclusively on the meta-system.

*Appendixes are available upon requested in order to better understand the financial analysis done by the author.

References

Gallego-García, S. and García-García, M. (2019). Design and Simulation of an Integrated Model for Organisational Sustainability Applying the Viable System Model and System Dynamics. HAL (Le Centre pour la Communication Scientifique Directe), pp.555–563. Doi: HTTPs://doi.org/10.1007/978-3-030-29996-5_64. In-text citation: (Gallego-García and García-García, 2019)

Espinosa, A. (2015). Governance for sustainability: learning from VSM practice. Kybernetes, 44(6–7), 955–969. https://doi.org/10.1108/K-02-2015-0043

Angela Espinosa, Jon Walker, (2017). A Complexity Approach to Sustainability: Theory and Application. (Espinosa and Walker, 2017)

Espinosa, A. (2023). Sustainable Self-Governance in Businesses and Society. Taylor & Francis. In-text citation: (Espinosa, 2023)

Arista Hakiki (2023). Viable System Model (VSM): A Holistic Approach to Organizational Sustainability. International Journal of Management Studies and Social Science Research, 05(03), pp.161–170. Doi: HTTPs://doi.org/10.56293/ijmsssr.2022.4625. In-text citation: (Arista Hakiki, 2023)

Stich, V. and Blum, M. (2015). A Cybernetic Reference Model for Production Systems Using the Viable System Model. IFIP Advances in Information and Communication Technology, pp.169–176. Doi: HTTPs://doi.org/10.1007/978-3-319-22756-6_21. In-text citation: (Stich and Blum, 2015)

Vahidi, A., Aliahmadi, A. and Teimoury, E. (2019). Researches status and trends of management cybernetics and viable system model. Kybernetes, 48(5), pp.1011–1044. Doi: HTTPs://doi.org/10.1108/k-11-2017-0433. In-text citation: (Vahidi, Aliahmadi and Teimoury, 2019)

Tarek Sadi, Julian Wilberg, Iris D. Tommelein, Udo Lindemann, (2016), Supporting the Design of Competitive Organizations by a Domain-Specific Application Framework for the Viable System Model, 18th INTERNATIONAL DEPENDENCY AND STRUCTURE MODELING CONFERENCE, DSM 2016

Harwood, S. (2020). Introducing the VIPLAN Methodology (with VSM) for Handling Messy Situations – Nine Lessons. Systemic Practice and Action Research. Doi: HTTPs://doi.org/10.1007/s11213-020-09545-6. In-text citation: (Harwood, 2020)

Hildbrand, S. and Bodhanya, S. (2015). Guidance on applying the viable system model. Kybernetes, 44(2), pp.186–201. Doi: HTTPs://doi. org/10.1108/k-01-2014-0017. In-text citation: (Hildbrand and Bodhanya, 2015)

Ramírez-Gutiérrez, A.G., Cardoso-Castro, P.P. and Tejeida-Padilla, R. (2020). A Methodological Proposal for the Complementarity of the SSM and the VSM for the Analysis of Viability in Organizations. Systemic Practice and Action Research. Doi: HTTPs://doi.org/10.1007/s11213-020-09536-7. In-text citation: (Ramírez-Gutiérrez, Cardoso-Castro and Tejeida-Padilla, 2020)

Laura Dragoş-Rădoi

Tesla (TSLA) Financial Analysis

EMBA Module: Finance and Accounting for Business

Assignment task: Assess the financial performance of a listed company of your choice. Produce a written research report basing your analysis on the company's most recent financial reports (for the past 3 years) using the financial ratios discussed during the module.

BUSINESS OVERVIEW

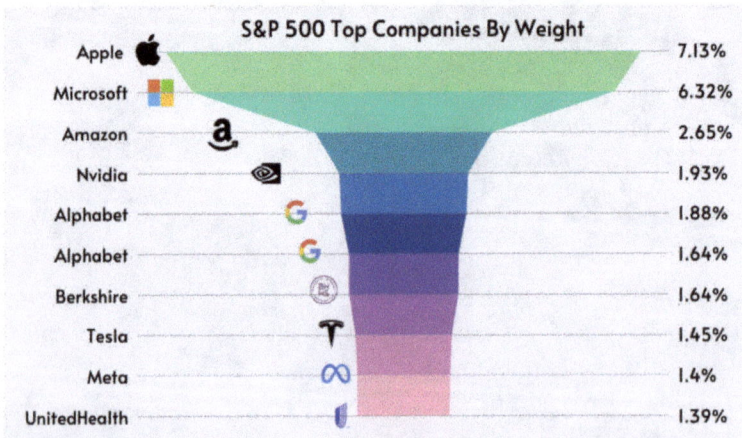

Exhibit 1: SP 500 Index
Source: finasko.com

Description

Established in 2003 and headquartered in Palo Alto, California, Tesla has been publicly listed since 2010 on the Nasdaq Stock Market and since 2020 enters the S&P 500 Index, currently holding the 8th position (Exhibit 1). Tesla operates as a vertically integrated sustainable energy enterprise with the additional goal of driving the global transition to electric mobility through the production of electric vehicles. The firm vends solar panels and solar roofs to facilitate energy generation, along with batteries designed for stationary storage and superchargers across residential, commercial, and utility settings. Tesla maintains a diverse range of vehicles in its lineup, encompassing both upscale and medium-sized sedans, as well as crossover SUVs.

Exhibit 2: Tesla, Inc. Common Stock (TSLA)
Source: Nasdaq

The company is also strategising the introduction of more economical sedans, compact SUVs, a lightweight truck, a semi-truck, and a sports car. In the year 2022, their worldwide deliveries totalled slightly over 1.3 million vehicles. Remarkably, despite the pandemic, the company's revenue has not only remained unaffected but has risen from 2019 levels. With a net profit sustained for the sixth consecutive year and a Revenue Growth (YoY) of 70,67%, Tesla secured its position as the global electric car market leader in 2020, marked also on green as NAS YTD (Exhibit 2).

Tesla managed to disrupt the market introducing its AI assistant Optimus and has over 127 800 employees.

Ownership structure and governance

Leadership ———————— Board of Directors ————

Elon Musk	Andrew Baglino	Elon Musk	Robyn M. Denholm	Ira Ehrenpreis	Joe Gebbia
Tom Zhu	Vaibhav Taneja	James Murdoch	Kimbal Musk	JB Straubel	Kathleen Wilson-Thompson

Exhibit 3: Tesla Leadership
Source: Tesla.com

Exhibit 4: Tesla Board of Director
Source: Tesla.com

Committee Composition

Audit	Disclosure Controls	Compensation	Nominating and Governance
Robyn M. Denholm Chairperson Finance expert Independent director	**Robyn M. Denholm** Chairperson Finance expert Independent director	**Ira Ehrenpreis** Chairperson Independent director	**Ira Ehrenpreis** Chairperson Independent director
Joe Gebbia Independent director Member	**James Murdoch** Independent director Member	**Robyn M. Denholm** Finance expert Independent director Member	**Robyn M. Denholm** Finance expert Independent director Member
James Murdoch Independent director Member	**Kathleen Wilson-Thompson** Independent director Member	**Kathleen Wilson-Thompson** Independent director Member	**James Murdoch** Independent director Member
			Kathleen Wilson-Thompson Independent director Member

Exhibit 5: Tesla Committee
Source: Tesla.com

Tesla started trading on the NASDAQ Global Select Market under the symbol TSLA on June 29, 2010, with an initial public offer of 1.12$ per share and went to two Stock Splits (2020 and 2022), with a current value of 254 $ per share (Nasdaq, 2023). Tesla currently has 8686 holders (most of them are 'street names', whose shares are held by third parties, conforming to Tesla's 10k annual report, 2022) but also major and top institutional holders listed in Appendix 1. Tesla does not anticipate paying cash dividends on the common stock. At the forefront of individual shareholders stands CEO Elon Musk, designated by Tesla as the "Technoking," possessing 412.6 million shares, equivalent to 13.04% of the company's stock. This positions his ownership value in the company at $84.89 billion. Additional Tesla executives hold ownership stakes below 1% (Capital, 2023).Elon Musk has been Tesla's CEO since 2008 and the company's Leadership, Board of Directors and Committee Composition are presented in Exhibit 3,4 and 5.

Key People Tesla Inc.

Board of Directors

Name/Title	Current Board Membership
Robyn M. Denholm Chairman	Tesla, Inc.
Elon Reeve Musk Chief Executive Officer & Director	Tesla, Inc., X Corp. (United States), X Holdings Corp., Musk Foundation, Space Exploration Technologies Corp., OpenAir, Inc.
Kimbal Musk Director	Medium, Inc. (Colorado), The Access Media Network & Technology Co., Inc, The Kitchen Community, Space Exploration Technologies Corp., Anschutz Health & Wellness Center, Square Roots Urban Growers, Inc., Tesla, Inc., Keith Glen Media Corp.

Executives

Robyn Denholm Board Chair	Elon Reeve Musk Chief Executive Officer & Director
Vaibhav Taneja Chief Financial & Accounting Officer	

Exhibit 6: Tesla Key People
Source: WJS Markets

The Board follows Corporate Governance Guidelines (Tesla digital assets, 2021) helping the management pursue Tesla's objectives for the benefit of their stockholders. A majority of directors need to be independent due to Nasdaq requirements, have substantial investments within Tesla and are subject to performance review. Also, the directors are re-elected every 3 years and must have a Lead Independent Director working alongside the CEO. Exhibit 6 displays Key people and current board membership.

INDUSTRY OVERVIEW AND COMPETITIVE POSITIONING

Market & Industry Dynamics

Tesla is operating in one of the largest automotive markets around the globe. The US represents the second-largest market for vehicle sales and production. With great R&D capabilities, the total foreign investments reached $143.4 billion in 2019, generating a total of 4.8 million jobs (Trade Gov.)

The pandemic has severely affected the automotive industry, producing shortages in the supply chain of semiconductors, but also a decrease in light vehicle sales (Exhibit 7 and 8). The US Automotive Market retained a worth of $15.9 million in 2021, and it is projected to expand to $37.8 million by 2029, exhibiting a compound annual growth rate (CAGR) of 13.17%. (MMR, 2022, Appendix 2).

Light Vehicle Sales
2015 – 2025F (millions)

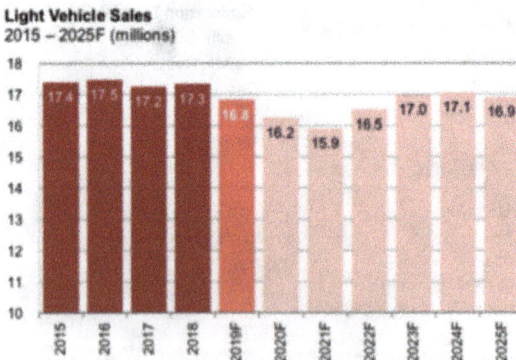

Exhibit 7: Light Vehicle Sales Drop
Source: Automotive Logistics

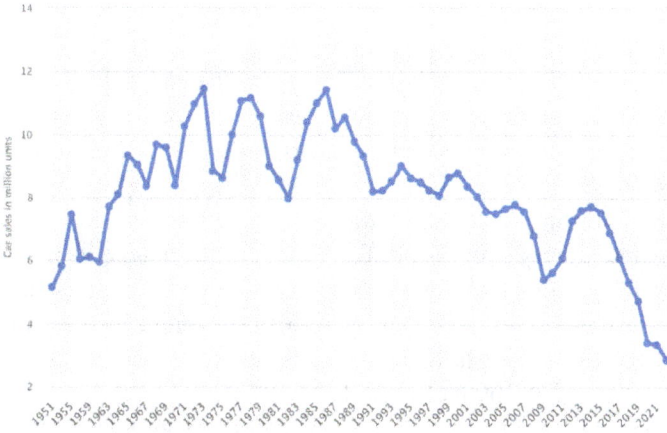

Exhibit 8: US Car Sales in the US from 1951 to 2022
Source: Statistica

Tesla: Innovation Over Advertising?

Expenditure on advertising/research and development per car sold in 2020

■ Ad spend per car sold   ■ R&D spend per car sold

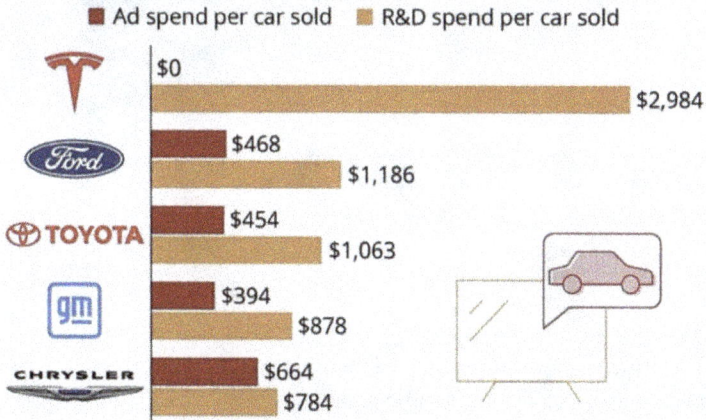

	Ad spend per car sold	R&D spend per car sold
Tesla	$0	$2,984
Ford	$468	$1,186
Toyota	$454	$1,063
GM	$394	$878
Chrysler	$664	$784

Source: SEC filings via Visual Capitalist

Exhibit 9: Tesla Comparison

'Optimus' time for Tesla

Tesla runs its business by offering end-to-end high premium services related to fully electric vehicles, solar energy generation system and storage (service & product diversification after acquiring SolarCity, 2016).

Despite the pandemic challenges related to logistics, supply chain and factory shutdowns, Tesla managed to extend its business by building 2 Gigafactories in Shanghai and Grundheide, reaching a number of 7 manufacturing facilities (Appendix 3). Remaining a market leader, Tesla highlights attainments, encompassing the production of 1,369,611 vehicles (with 1,313,851 successfully delivered), as well as the deployment of 6.5 gigawatt-hours of energy storage products and 348 megawatts of solar systems. The company also reported a $27.64 billion revenue increase and a $4.48 billion cash increase in its 10K annual report.

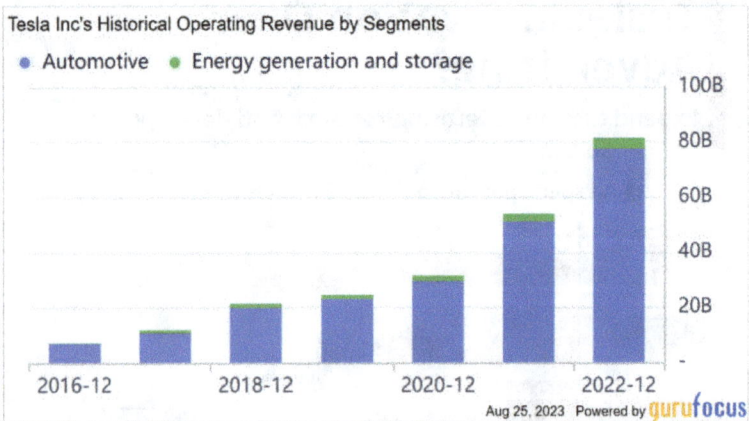

Exhibit 10

Also the CEO announces Optimus, as a triumph of AI over unsafe job tasks. Tesla has partnerships with SpaceX, Neuralink, The Boring Company (high-tech innovating companies under Elon's umbrella), but without any capital implications. The company prefers to innovate, rather than advertise (Exhibit 9) and still be well positioned in the global market (Exhibit 10, 11, 12, 13, 14).

Tesla (TSLA) Financial Analysis

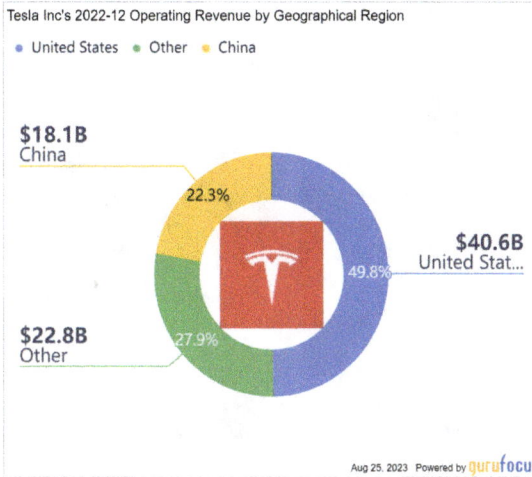

Tesla Inc's 2022-12 Operating Revenue by Geographical Region

● United States ● Other ● China

$18.1B
China

22.3%

$40.6B
United Stat...

49.8%

$22.8B
Other

27.9%

Aug 25, 2023 Powered by gurufocus

Exhibit 11

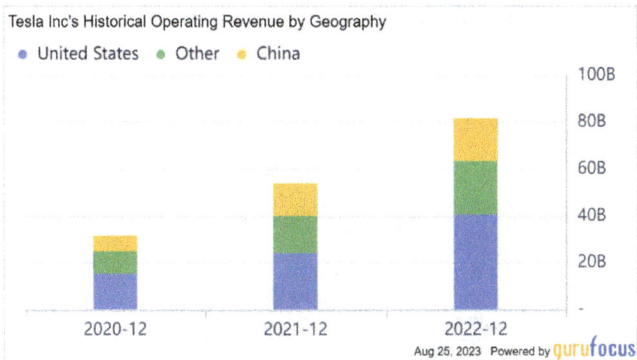

Tesla Inc's Historical Operating Revenue by Geography

● United States ● Other ● China

100B
80B
60B
40B
20B

2020-12   2021-12   2022-12

Aug 25, 2023 Powered by gurufocus

Exhibit 12

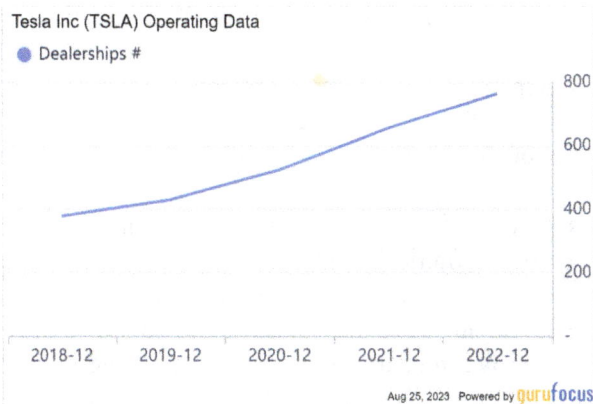

Tesla Inc (TSLA) Operating Data

● Dealerships #

800
600
400
200

2018-12   2019-12   2020-12   2021-12   2022-12

Aug 25, 2023 Powered by gurufocus

Exhibit 13

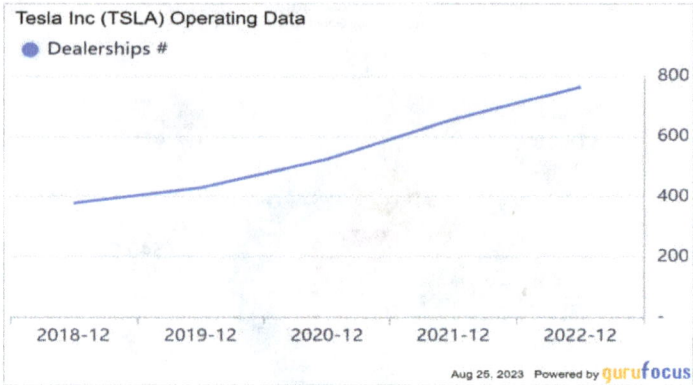

Tesla Inc (TSLA) Operating Data
● Dealerships #

Aug 25, 2023 Powered by gurufocus

Exhibit 14

FINANCIAL ANALYSIS

Computation, Description & Annotation

*	Source: Tesla, Inc. Annual reports,10-k forms (Tesla, 2023)
**	Source: Ford Annual reports, 10-K forms (Ford, 2023)
***	Source: Industry Ratios for Manufacturing: Transportation Equipment (Ready Ratios, 2023)

Exhibit 15: Source of Financial Data and Industry Ratios

The following ratios are calculated based on the financial data captured in Appendix 4, referring to Tesla's Consolidated Balance Sheets, Statement of Operations, Comprehensive Income and Cash Flows (years: 2020, 2021, 2022) in comparison to the financial statements of Ford (one of Tesla's direct competitors) and the industry ratios.

The sources of financial data are provided in Exhibit 15. The source of ratios definition is provided by *Investopedia (2022)*. This analysis uses financial data from the Pandemic and the Ukrainian war timeframe, adjusting for their impact on values, especially in the automotive industry, by factoring in averages in our ratio calculations.

Activity Ratios

Total Asset Turnover	Receivables Turnover	Inventory Turnover	Working Capital Turnover
$\text{Total asset turnover} = \dfrac{\text{Revenue}}{\text{Average total assets}}$	$\text{Receivables turnover} = \dfrac{\text{Revenue}}{\text{Average receivables}}$	$\text{Inventory turnover} = \dfrac{\text{Cost of goods sold}}{\text{Average inventory}}$	$\text{Working capital turnover} = \dfrac{\text{Revenue}}{\text{Average working capital}}$
Shows how many total assets are needed in order to generate revenues. Ideal case: Lower assets with higher sales.	Measures the difficulty of a company to collect its payments from its clients. Measures how many times receivables are converted to cash in a certain period of time. Ideal case: An efficient company has a higher accounts receivable turnover ratio while an inefficient company has a lower ratio.	Measures how efficiently a company uses its inventory. Ideal case: Inventory should not be hold too long on a yearly basis (low inventory may be a sign of weak sales or excess inventory, while a higher ratio signals strong sales but may also indicate inadequate inventory stocking.	Measures the effectiveness of a business at generating sales for every dollar of working capital put to use (to support sales and growth). Ideal case: Higher is better => that a company is able to generate a larger amount of sales.

Ratios	Tesla*			Ford**			Industry***		
	2022	2021	2020	2022	2021	2020	2022	2021	2020
Activity Ratios									
Asset turnover	1.13	0.94	0.73	0.62	0.52	0.48	0.77	0.82	0.79
Receivables turnover	33.49	28.34	19.65	-60.47	14.70	19.90	7.26	6.75	6.4
Inventory turnover	6.52	8.16	6.51	12	1	12	4.93	5.61	5.06
Working capital turnover	5.73	7.28	2.53	8.07	7.46	6.50	N/A	N/A	N/A

Asset turnover ratio

While Tesla is showing an upward trend, with a slight variance compared to the industry, we can observe a significant growth of this ratio in 2022. This is also connected with the opening of the Giga-Brandenburg factory. A higher asset turnover ratio shows a company's improved capacity to generate revenue utilizing its assets. Conversely, a lower ratio implies that the company is not efficiently employing its assets to produce income.

On the other hand, Ford is continuously unable to meet the industry ratios, showing that the company is underutilizing his assets. Exhibit 16 displays Tesla's assets over the past 5 years.

Receivables turnover

Tesla Inc., assets: selected items

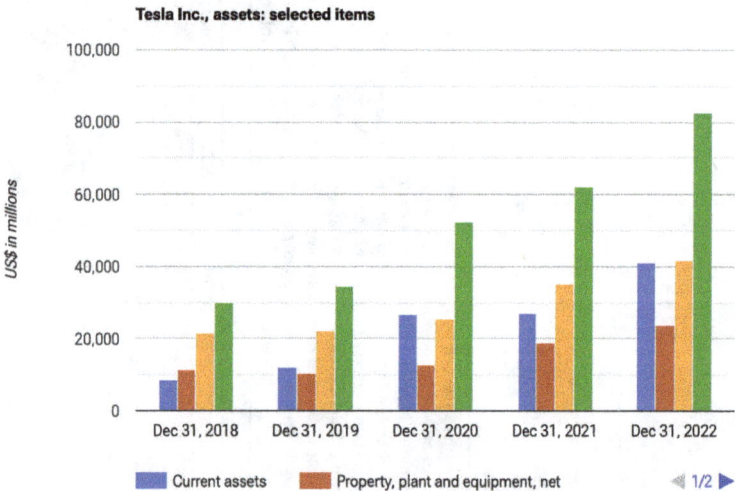

Exhibit 16: Graphic containing Tesla's Assets
Source: Stock Analysis on Net

Tesla is showing an outstanding accounts receivable strategy, with a constant evolution of this ratio, compared to the industry averages. Ford showed a descending trend, very difficult for 2022, when the ratio became negative, meaning ineffective collection procedures, insufficient credit strategies, or customers lacking financial viability or creditworthiness.

Inventory turnover

Tesla Inc., short-term (operating) activity, turnover ratios

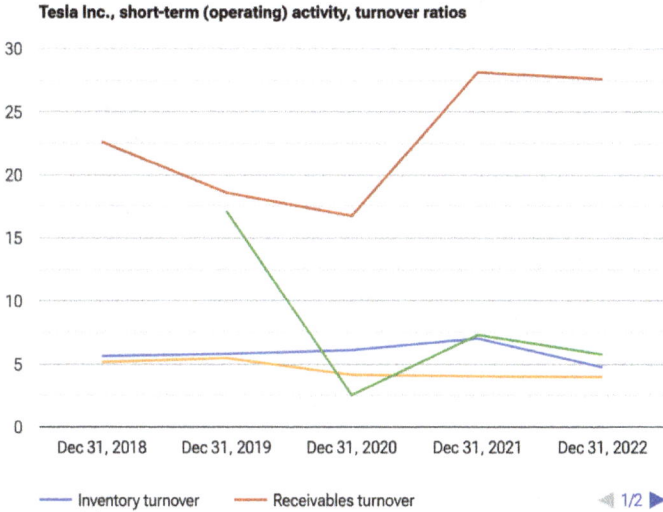

— Inventory turnover   — Receivables turnover   ◄ 1/2 ►

Exhibit 17: Graphic containing Tesla's short-term activity, turnover ratios
Source: Stock Analysis on Net

While Tesla and Ford registered a fluctuation on this ratio, the industry displays fluctuation over the years and a decrease from 2021 to 2022. Historically, Ford is facing instability when it comes to inventory stocking. Tesla managed to hold more inventories within 2021, as declared in the 10-k report, the company faced shortage after the Ukrainian war started and semiconductor crisis still exists in the market, sales have dropped. Also, the company added in its report the impact of the Covid-19 spikes related to new virus variants. A sales strategy was put in place for 2023.

Working capital turnover

For this ratio the industry has no data to provide. While Ford managed to increase this ratio in the past 3 years and secure a better position than Tesla, Tesla faced volatility. 2021 was a better year than 2022, when the company registered a decrease. Analysing Tesla's investments in Brandenburg Gigafactory and research and development, the number of sales have suffered. The company forecasted new contracts and sales for its products and services. Exhibit 17 and 18 shows Tesla's activity ratios.

Tesla Inc., long-term (investment) activity ratios

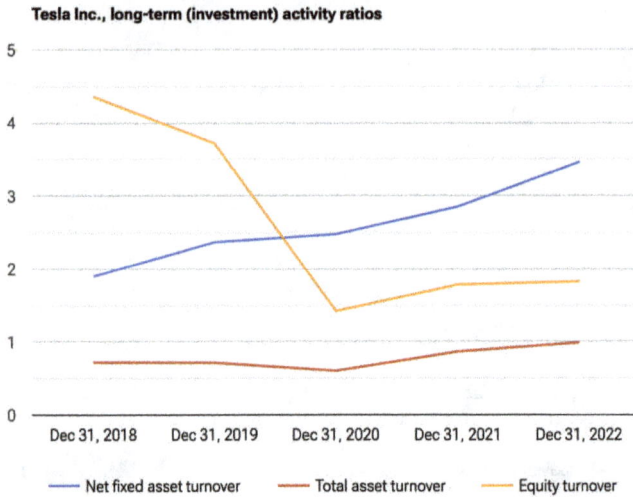

— Net fixed asset turnover   — Total asset turnover   — Equity turnover

Exhibit 18: Graphic containing Tesla's long-term activity ratios
Source: Stock Analysis on Net

Current ratio

Tesla Inc., current assets: selected items

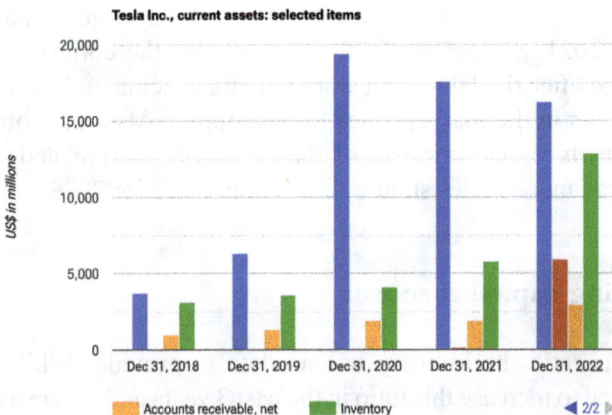

■ Accounts receivable, net   ■ Inventory   ◄ 2/2 ►

Exhibit 19: Graphic containing Tesla's current assets
Source: Stock Analysis on Net

Liquidity Ratios

Current Ratio

$$Current\ ratio = \frac{Current\ assets}{Current\ liabilities}$$

Measures the ability to pay short-term obligations or those due within one year. It tells how to maximise the current assets to satisfy the current debt and other payables. Ideal case: To be in line or slightly higher with the industry average.

Quick Ratio

$$Quick\ ratio = \frac{Cash + Short\text{-}term\ marketable\ investments + Receivables}{Current\ liabilities}$$

Also known as acid test* ratio, this measures the capacity to pay the current liabilities without needing to sell the inventory or obtain additional financing (ability to meet the short-term obligations with most liquid assets).

Ideal case: Higher ratio => better liquidity & financial health.
*An "acid test" is a slang term for describing a quick test designed to produce instant results.

Ratios	Tesla*			Ford**			Industry***		
	2022	2021	2020	2022	2021	2020	2022	2021	2020
Liquidity Ratios									
Current ratio	1.53	1.38	1.88	1.20	1.20	1.20	1.87	1.97	1.88
Quick ratio	0.94	1.00	1.49	0.33	0.62	0.64	0.89	0.95	1.05

While Tesla's showing a slight decrease in 2021 compared to 2020, the current ratio of 2022 is improving, although for the past 2 years the data registered is under the industry ratio. This reflected a difficulty in covering the short-term debt, mostly generated by the geopolitics factors (the starting of the war in 2021, but also Covid that impacted Shanghai in 2022, Tesla being forced to suspend its activity for a significant period). The ratio can be improved through increased sales. Ford's ratio remains constant, but lower when compared to the industry. Both companies are liquid, taking into consideration that the ratio is higher than 1.

Quick ratio

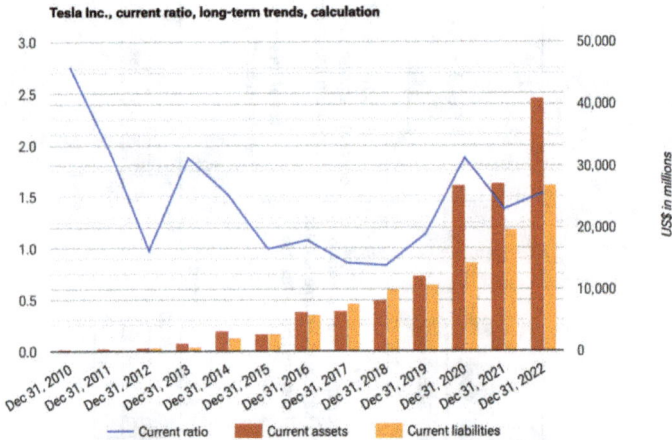

Tesla Inc., current ratio, long-term trends, calculation

Exhibit 20: Graphic containing Tesla's current ratios
Source: Stock Analysis on Net

Tesla is showing better liquidity than Ford, managing to exceed the industry average, being higher. Ford is facing difficulties related to payments. Exhibits 19 and 20 are graphic representations of Tesla's current assets and current ratios.

Solvency Ratios

Debt-to-Assets Ratio

$$\text{Debt-to-assets ratio} = \frac{\text{Total debt}}{\text{Total assets}}$$

Defines how much debt a company owns compared to its assets and shows the degree to which a company has used debt to finance its assets. Can reflect how financially stable a company is. The higher the ratio, the higher the degree of leverage (DoL) and, consequently, the higher the risk of investing in that company. Ideal case: tend to 0, never higher than 1.

Debt-to-Equity Ratio

$$\text{Debt-to-equity ratio} = \frac{\text{Total debt}}{\text{Shareholders' equity}}$$

Helps understanding a company's economic health and if an investment is worthwhile or not. It is considered to be a gearing ratio that compares the owner's equity or capital to debt, or funds borrowed by the company. Ideal case: it should not be above a level of 2.0 and to decrease over a period of time.

Interest Coverage Ratio

$$\text{Interest coverage ratio} = \frac{\text{EBIT}}{\text{Interest payments}}$$

Measures a company's ability to handle its outstanding debt. A higher value means that a company is more poised to pay its debts while the opposite is true for lower ratios. Creditors can decide whether they will lend to the company. A lower ratio may be unattractive to investors because it may mean the company is not poised for growth. Ideal case: To be at least at 2 or 3.

Ratios	Tesla*		Ford**			Industry***		
	2022	2021	2020	2021	2022	2022	2021	2020
Solvency Ratios								
Debt to assets	0.45	0.50	0.56	0.54	0.54	0.6	0.54	0.59
Debt to equity	0.82	1.03	1.31	2.84	3.22	0.94	0.78	0.95
Interest Coverage	71.50	17.58	2.67	4.02	-0.34	1.77	3.08	-0.23

Debt to assets

While Tesla is on a descending wave, tending to 0, mapping a better position than the industry average; Ford has recorded a decrease in 2021 (after being higher than the benchmark industry ratio in 2020), and remaining constant in 2022. Both companies are managing their debt well.

Debt to equity

Tesla's values are close to the industry average (slightly higher between 2020 and 2021), showing a good debt dealing strategy, while Ford has the worst values.

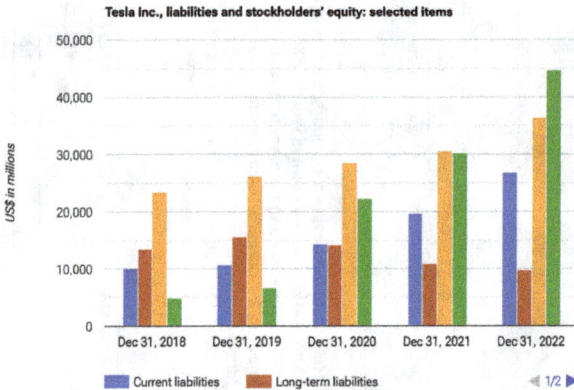

Tesla Inc., liabilities and stockholders' equity: selected items

Current liabilities   Long-term liabilities   1/2

Exhibit 21: Graphic containing Tesla's liabilities and stockholders' equity
Source: Stock Analysis on Net

Interest coverage

Compared to the industry and Ford, Tesla has outstanding values. Exhibit 21 is a visual representation of Tesla's liabilities and stockholders' equity.

Profitability Ratios

Net Profit Margin

$$\text{Net profit margin} = \frac{\text{Net profit}}{\text{Revenue}}$$

Measures how much net income or profit is generated as a percentage of revenue. Ideal case is this ratio to increase and to be as high as possible.

Operating Profit Margin

$$\text{Operating profit margin} = \frac{\text{Operating profit}}{\text{Revenue}}$$

Represents how efficiently a company is able to generate profit through its core operations. It measures how much profit a company makes on a dollar of sales after paying for variable costs of production, such as wages and raw materials, but before paying interest or tax. Ideal case: Higher margins.

Return on Equity

$$\text{Return on equity} = \frac{\text{Net income}}{\text{Average total equity}}$$

Is the measure of a company's net income divided by its shareholders' equity. Ideal case: The higher the ROE, the better a company is at converting its equity financing into profits.

Return on Assets

$$\text{ROA} = \frac{\text{Net income}}{\text{Average total assets}}$$

Indicates how profitable a company is in relation to its total assets. Can determine how efficiently a company uses its assets to generate a profit. Ideal case: Growth over a period of time.

Ratios	Tesla*			Ford**			Industry***		
	2022	2021	2020	2022	2021	2020	2022	2021	2020
Profitability Ratios									
Net profit margin	15.45%	10.49%	2.73%	-1.25%	13.16%	-1.01%	0.50%	3.20%	1.10%
Operating profit margin	16.76%	12.12%	6.32%	3.97%	3.32%	-3.47%	2.20%	3.70%	0.90%
Return on Equity (ROE)	33.61%	21.54%	5.98%	-4.69%	45.09%	-3.98%	-2.50%	5%	-3.60%
Return on Assets (ROA)	17.43%	9.88%	1.99%	-0.84%	6.83%	-0.49%	0.60%	2.60%	-0.70%

Tesla Inc., net profit margin, long-term trends, calculation

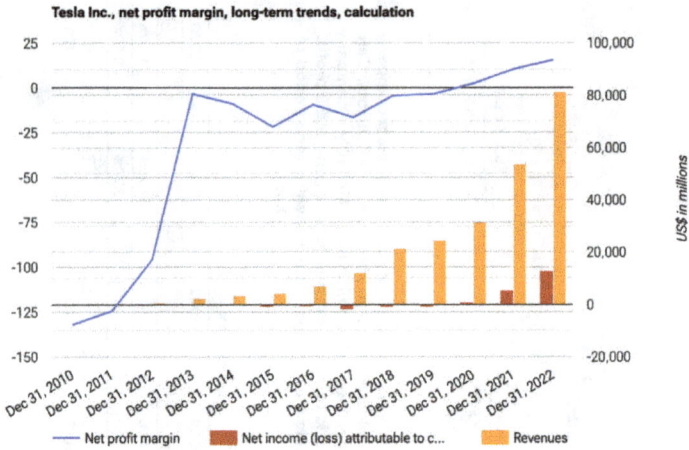

Exhibit 22: Graphic containing Tesla's net profit margin
Source: Stock Analysis on Net

Net profit margin

Except 2021 when Ford excelled over Tesla and the industry, Tesla shows clear footage of high efficiency when it comes to generating profit, with an upward trend.

Operating profit margin

While Ford faced difficulties during 2020 and 2021, Tesla recorded outstanding values (particularly in 2021-2022), keeping an upward direction.

Return on equity

Ford led through 2021, but its volatility and negative trends created instability. The same happened with the industry, while Tesla grew rapidly, becoming an investor's star from a rentability point of view.

Return on assets

Compared to the industry rates, Ford managed to obtain good results for 2021 (slightly better than 2020), but Tesla again sets high standards when coming to its profitability in relation to its assets.

In Exhibit 22, 23 and 24 we can observe Tesla's profit margin, net vs comprehensive income and ROA during the years.

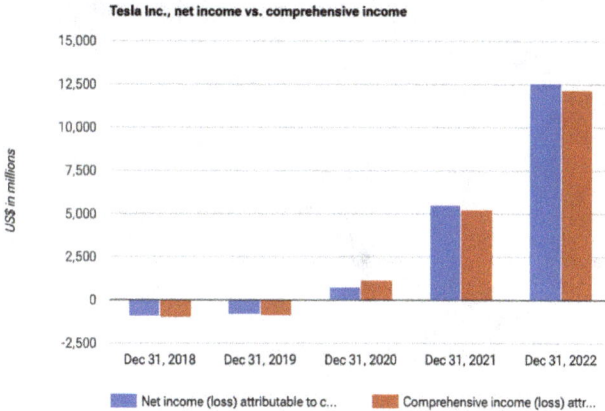

Exhibit 23: Graphic containing Tesla's net vs comprehensive income
Source: Stock Analysis on Net

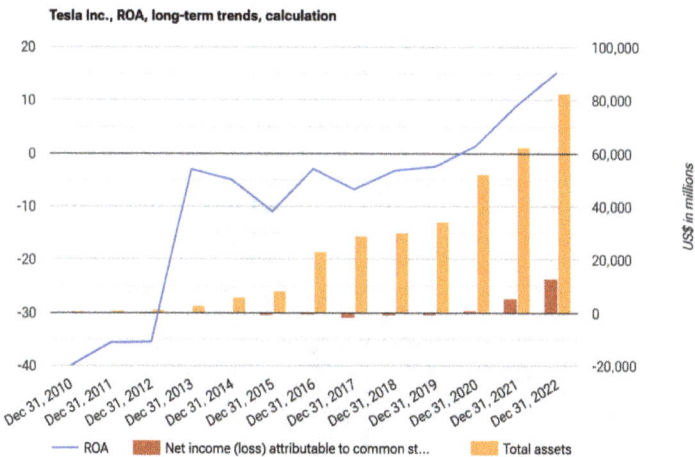

Exhibit 24: Graphic containing Tesla's Return of Assets ratio
Source: Stock Analysis on Net

Valuation Ratios

Price-to-Earnings Ratio

$$P/E = \frac{\text{Price per share}}{\text{Earnings per share}}$$

Relates a company's share price to its earnings per share.

A high P/E ratio could mean that a company's stock is overvalued, or that investors are expecting high growth rates in the future. This is used by investors and analysts to determine the relative value of a company's shares in an apples-to-apples comparison to others in the same sector.

Ideal case: to grow in time.

Dividend Payout Ratio

$$\text{Dividend payout ratio} = \frac{\text{Common share dividends}}{\text{Net income attributable to common shares}}$$

The sum of declared dividends issued by a company for every ordinary outstanding share. This is an important metric for investors because the amount a firm pays out in dividends directly translates to income for the shareholder.

A growing DPS over time can also be a sign that a company's management believes that its earnings growth can be sustained.

Ratios	Tesla*			Ford**			Industry***		
Valuation Ratios	2022	2021	2020	2022	2021	2020	2022	2021	2020
P/E	34.03	216.11	1120.10	-21.82	4.16	-24.31	N/A	N/A	N/A
Dividend payout	0.00	0.00	0.00	0.00	0.00	0.00	0.09	0.29	0.24

Price to earnings

While the industry is not providing data, Ford shows negative values (excepting 2021). Tesla kept the bar high, even if it has recorded a decrease of this ratio, this is explained through the 2 stock splits. First, in August 2020, on a five-for-one basis (explaining the huge gap) and the second one in August 2022 on three-for-one basis.

Dividend Payout

Tesla Inc., consolidated income statement: selected items

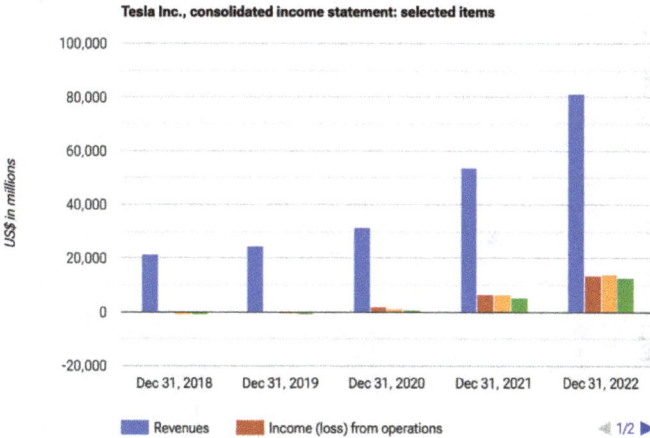

Exhibit 25: Graphic containing Tesla's consolidated income statement
Source: Stock Analysis on Net

Tesla doesn't pay and does not intend to pay dividends in the nearest future, while Ford has insignificant values related to common share dividends and negative values for the net income attributable to common shares that its value tends to 0.

The industry has no applicable data related to this ratio. Exhibits 25 and 26 conclude by showing the visual representation of Tesla's consolidated income statement and the Financial Position and performance history for the past 7 years.

Financial Position and Performance History

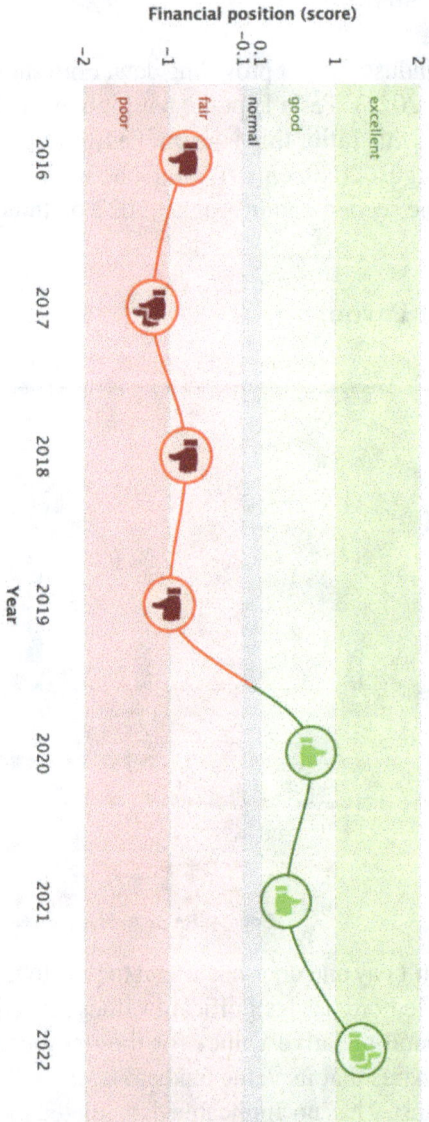

Exhibit 26: Graphic containing Tesla's Financial Position and Performance History
Source: Stock Analysis on Net

Appendixes 5 and 6 are displaying key financial data from financial statements in the form of charts, but also visual images related to market ranks (provided by Guru Focus). For a full breakdown of the calculations, please refer to Appendix 8.

INVESTMENTS RISKS

As a public company, Tesla must disclose business and stock-related risks in its Annual Report's "Risk Factors" section. The top three risk categories—Growth, Operations (>50% of risks), Regulations, and Ownership. This analysis will highlight a subset of these risks (Appendix 7). Exhibits 27 and 28 shows Tesla's operational Risk profile and pillars.

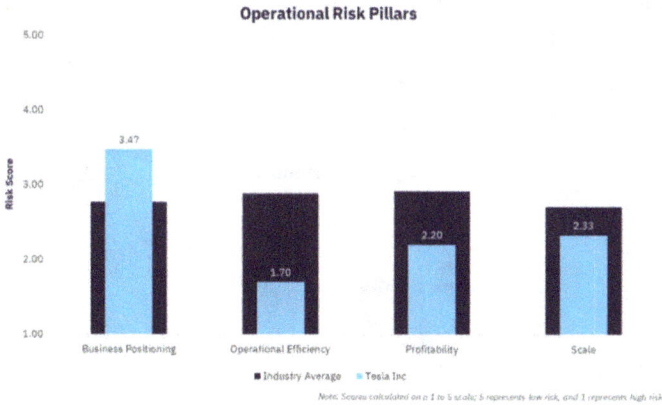

Exhibit 27: Graphic containing Tesla's Operational Risk Pillars
Source: GlobalData

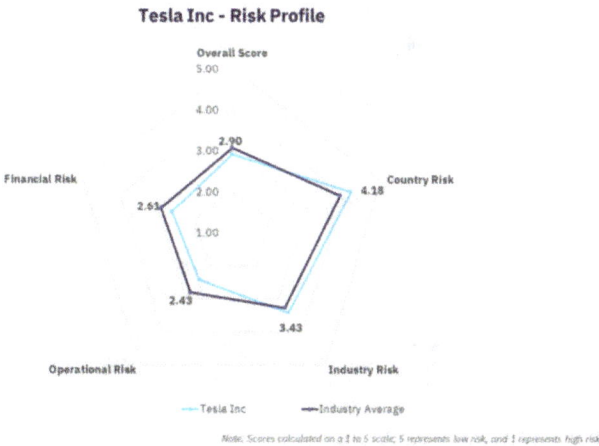

Exhibit 28: Graphic containing Tesla's Risk Profile
Source: GlobalData

ENVIRONMENTAL, SOCIAL AND GOVERNANCE

Even if Tesla was excluded in 2022 from the S&P 500 ESG Index due to several car crashes and employee conflicts involving racism (Bloomberg and Reuters, relates), Sustainalytics and MSCI are rating the company with a medium risk, displaying also a rating history for it, but also the key issues compared to other peers (Exhibit 29, 30, 31, 32).

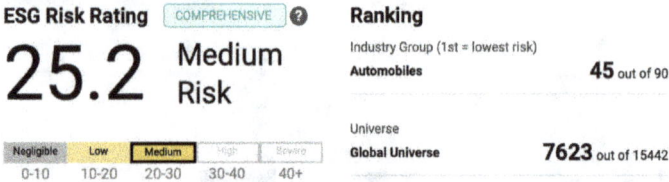

Exhibit 29: Tesla ESG Rating
Source: Morningstar, Sustainalytics

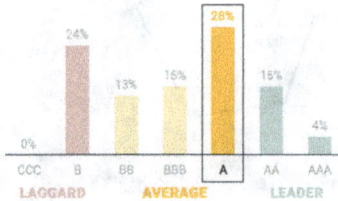

Exhibit 30: Tesla ESG Rating
Source: MSCI

Tesla's rating remains unchanged since May, 2021.

ESG Rating history

MSCI ESG Rating history data over the last five years or since records began.

Exhibit 31: Tesla ESG Rating history
Source: MSCI

Key Issues distribution in relation to industry peers

We focus on the key issues material to the **automobiles industry**. Here is how **Tesla** compares to industry peers. For more details, visit the ESG investing page.

Exhibit 32: Tesla ESG Key Issues
Source: MSCI

Environmental	Social	Governance
Tesla is one of the most innovative company at the moment, continuously investing in better-greener world. Besides the Fully Electric vehicles, Tesla has started to develop more sustainable methods related to energy regeneration and usage, by offering complete services related to solar energy generation and storage. For Tesla, Environment come first and the company have not fail in complying to any of the Environmental Regulations across al of its production sites. Even if the product carbon footprint is ranked average, this is not related to the electric vehicles per se, rather with the production. Tesla is still not managing in decreasing the Implied temperature rise, being misaligned with the global climate goal (Exhibit 33), but remains a leader as respects the opportunities in clean tech. Related to MSCI's SDG (Sustainable Development Goal) - (Exhibit 34) - Tesla was rated as aligned in regards to Responsible Consumption, Production and Climate Action.	Tesla does not need any marketing to sell its products, yet the company has noted at the moment, continuously investing in problems related to customers and product safety and quality related to autonomus driving capacity. Some controversy was also recorded related to some racism scandals among employees. All the above were solved and Tesla is continuously trying to strive all of these challenges. The company has collaborations with several institutions in which commitments are made in order to create jobs and to sustain local economy. Tesla encourages every employee to be part of their mission in transitioning to a cleaner world and have introduced stocks in their benefit plans, that are offered exclusively to its employees. Optimus robot came in the market as an AI revelation, but it's main duty is to protect Tesla's employees of harmful situations, doing the most difficult tasks around production areas.	MSCI is mapping Tesla as average when it comes to corporate governance and behaviour. Despite some press scandals that are sometimes involving Tesla's CEO Elion, the company promotes an ethical leadership, followed by best practice guidelines. The primary role of the board is to supervise ESG matters, while various separate committees have the responsibility of overseeing compensation, audits, and the governance structure. Tesla is also a clean company when it comes to MSCI's ESG Business Involvement Screening (Exhibit 35) and it's not in partnership with controversial industries such as Tobacco, Alcohol, Gambling or Banned Controversial Weapons.

Exhibit 36 is helping us understand the significant controversies using a scale indicator.

MSCI IMPLIED
TEMPERATURE RISE

2.1°C

MISALIGNED

An Implied Temperature Rise of between 2°C and 3.2°C indicates that TESLA, INC. is misaligned with global climate goals and is in line with a business-as-usual scenario.

2°C Trajectory   ❓

Absolute emissions [Megatons CO2e]

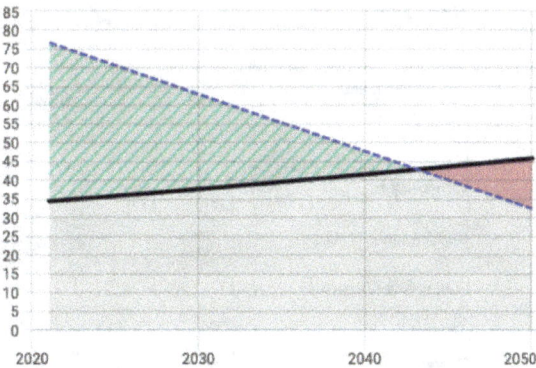

- — Annual Projected Carbon Emissions
- ▪▪▪ MSCI 2°C Trajectory (Annual Budget)
- ▪ Absolute Carbon Budget Overshoot
- ▨ Absolute Carbon Budget Undershoot

**Exhibit 33: Tesla: MSCI
Implied Temperature Rise**
Source: MSCI

Goals	Strongly Aligned	Aligned
1: No Poverty		
2: No Hunger		
3: Good Health and Well-Being		
4: Quality Education		
5: Gender Equality		
6: Clean Water and Sanitation		
7: Affordable and Clean Energy		
8: Decent Work and Economic Growth		
9: Industry, Innovation and Infrastructure		
10: Reduced Inequalities		
11: Sustainable Cities and Communities		
12: Responsible Consumption and Production	●	
13: Climate Action	●	
14: Life under Water		
15: Life on Land		
16: Peace, Justice and Strong Institutions		
17: Partnerships for the Goals		

Exhibit 34: Tesla: MSCI SDG
Source: MSCI

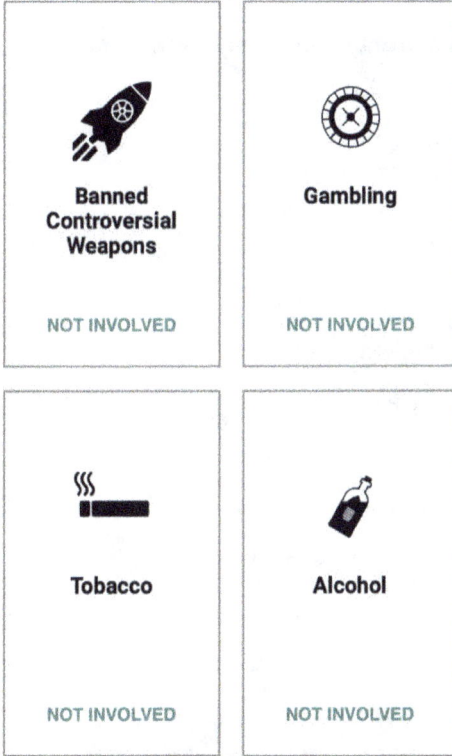

Banned Controversial Weapons

NOT INVOLVED

Gambling

NOT INVOLVED

Tobacco

NOT INVOLVED

Alcohol

NOT INVOLVED

**Exhibit 35: Tesla: MSCI
ESG Business Involvement Screening**
Source: MSCI

Significant Controversies by Indicator

Environment	G
Social	O
Customers	O
Marketing & Advertising	Y
Privacy & Data Security	Y
Product Safety & Quality	O
Human Rights & Community	Y
Impact on Local Communities	Y
Labor Rights & Supply Chain	Y
Collective Bargaining & Union	Y
Discrimination & Workforce Diversity	Y
Labor Management Relations	Y
Governance	Y
Bribery & Fraud	Y
Governance Structures	Y

Performance Flag

R **Red**: Indicates that a company is involved in one or more very severe controversies.

O **Orange**: Indicates that a company has been involved in one or more recent severe structural controversies that are ongoing.

Y **Yellow**: Indicates that the company is involved in severe-to-moderate level controversies.

G **Green**: Indicates that the company is not involved in any major controversies. However, this could indicate that the company is involved in minor or moderate controversies.

Exhibit 36: Tesla: MSCI ESG Controversies
Source: MSCI

CONCLUSIONS

Based on Tesla's financial data from the past 3 years (up to 2023), the company has rejoined the S&P 500 ESG index and is undergoing rapid growth. Analyzing key stock selection ratios, including working capital, quick ratio, EPS, P/E, debt-to-equity, and ROE, Tesla shows an upward trend. In 2022, Tesla secured a substantial contract with Hertz Global Holdings, projecting higher revenues (Seeking Alpha, 2022).

BCG MATRIX TESLA

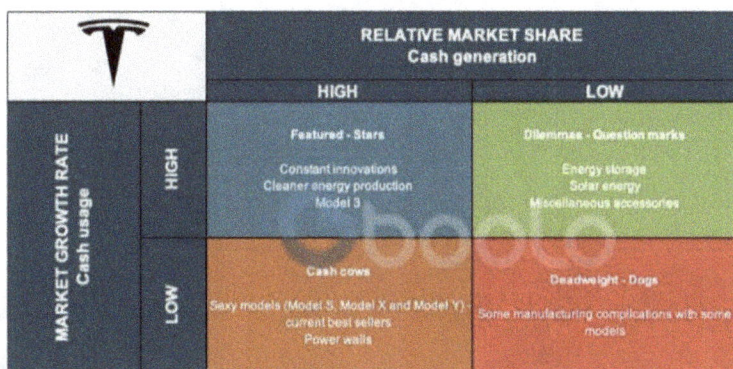

Credit Photo : Oboolo

Exhibit 37: Tesla: BCG Matrix
Source: Oboolo

Exhibit 37 (The BCG Matrix) displays Tesla's few product vulnerabilities, with decreasing dilemmas due to ongoing research and development enhancements. Guru Focus suggests Tesla's value could be notably underestimated (Exhibit 38). This resource offers valuable insights into Tesla's performance, including DuPont Analysis on ROE, a score linked to long-term stock performance, and Stock Price data (Exhibit 39, 40, 41, 42).

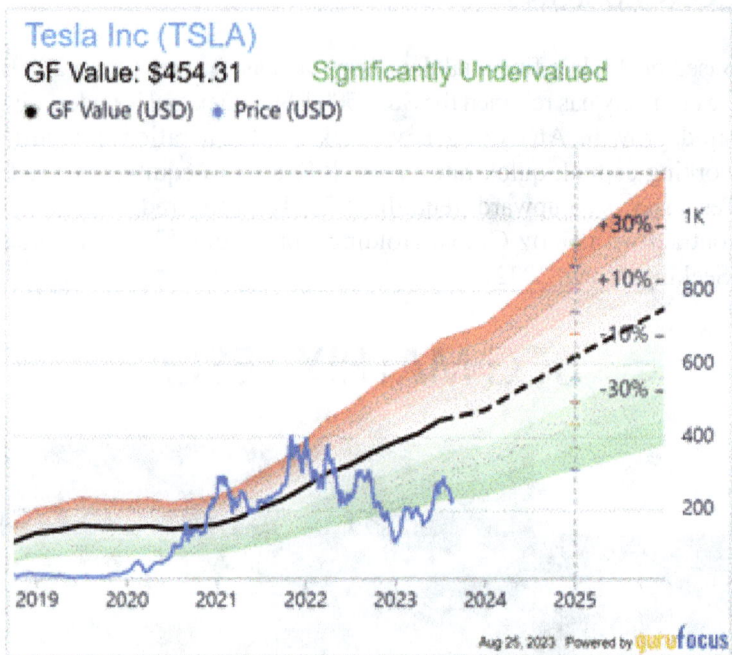

Exhibit 38: Tesla Guru Focus Value
Source: Guru Focus

With two stock splits from 2020-2022 and a current value of $254 per share, Tesla might see another split next year based on its technical analysis (Exhibit 43). Despite its tech volatility and risks, Tesla is a strong investment option, suitable for both short and long-term strategies, helping to counteract FOMO associated with these investments.

The prediction suggests Tesla will reach the $400 mark again, with Exhibit 44 chart implying a potential quick resurgence, resembling an Elliott pattern where retracements bolster momentum rather than stall it (Nasdaq, 2023). The question is not 'can Tesla regain its heights?', it's actually 'When?'

Decomposition of Tesla Inc (TSLA)'s Return on Equity (ROE) ?

5-Step DuPont Analysis as of 2023-06-29 (Quarterly)

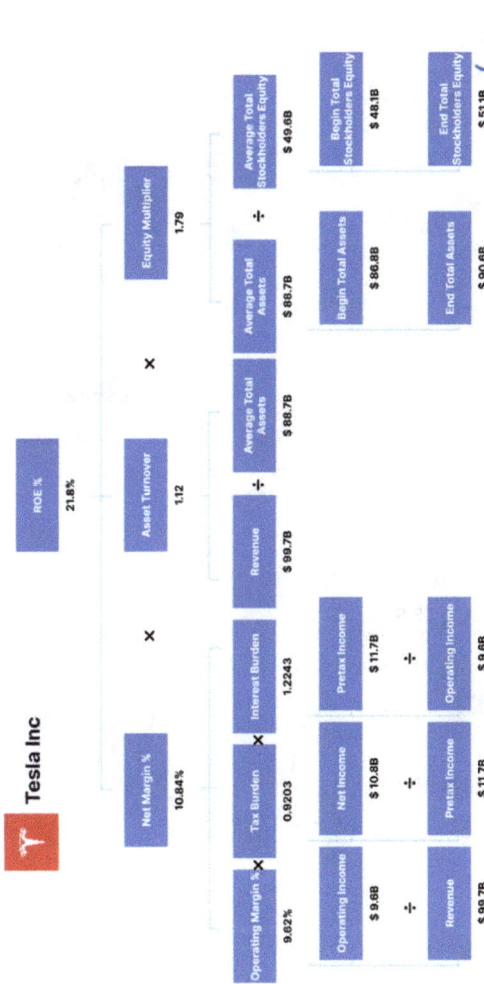

Tesla Inc

ROE %	21.8%

Net Margin %	10.84%

× **Asset Turnover** 1.12

× **Equity Multiplier** 1.79

Operating Margin % 9.62%
× **Tax Burden** 0.9203
× **Interest Burden** 1.2243
× **Revenue** $99.7B
÷ **Average Total Assets** $88.7B
× **Average Total Assets** $88.7B
÷ **Average Total Stockholders Equity** $49.6B

Operating Income $9.6B
÷ **Net Income** $10.8B
÷ **Pretax Income** $11.7B

Revenue $99.7B
Pretax Income $11.7B
Operating Income $9.6B

Begin Total Assets $86.8B
End Total Assets $90.6B
Begin Total Stockholders Equity $48.1B
End Total Stockholders Equity $51B

GURUFOCUS

Exhibit 39: Tesla DuPont Analysis
Source: Guru Focus

1) The net income data used here is the annualized data, which is calculated by multiplying the quarterly net income data by 4. The same rule applies to revenue, pre-tax income and operating income.
2) Asset turnover here is the annualized asset turnover.

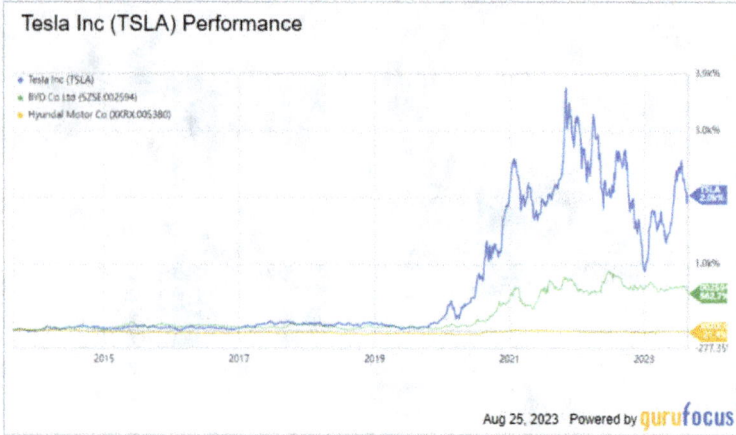

Exhibit 40: Tesla Performance Graphic
Source: Guru Focus

Exhibit 41: Tesla long-term stock performance
Source: Guru Focus

Exhibit 42: Tesla Stock Price
Source: Guru Focus

Exhibit 43: Tesla Technical Analysis
Source: Guru Focus

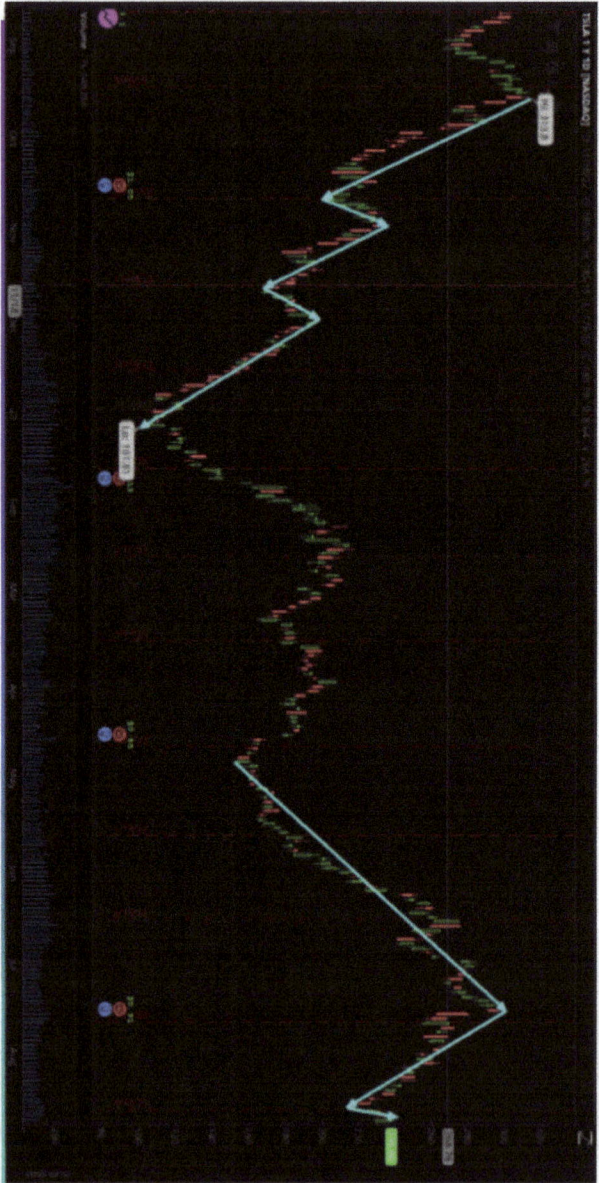

Exhibit 44: Tesla Technical Analysis (Elliot pattern)
Source: Nasdaq

References

Abheey (2023). *S&P 500 Companies with Financials (Updated List 2023).* [online] Finasko. Available at: https://finasko.com/sp-500-companies/ [Accessed 29 Aug. 2023].

Alvarez, S. (2022). *Tesla shareholders to vote on TSLA stock split in annual shareholders meeting.* [online] TESLARATI. Available at: https://www.teslarati.com/tesla-tsla-stock-split-2022-date/ [Accessed 29 Aug. 2023].

Chartmill.com. (2020). Available at: https://www.chartmill.com/stock/quote/TSLA/fundamental-analysis.

Chen, J. (2019). *Elliott Wave Theory Definition.* [online] Investopedia. Available at: https://www.investopedia.com/terms/e/elliottwavetheory.asp.

Chen, J. (2021). *Dividend Per Share (DPS).* [online] Investopedia. Available at: https://www.investopedia.com/terms/d/dividend-per-share.asp.

Corporate Governance Guidelines. (n.d.). Available at: https://digitalassets.tesla.com/tesla-contents/image/upload/IR-Corporate-Governance-Guidelines.

Editor, C.S., SA News (2022). *Electric vehicle roundup: Tesla preps for big step in Germany, Chinese names fall | Seeking Alpha.* [online] seekingalpha.com. Available at: https://seekingalpha.com/news/3815380-electric-vehicle-roundup-tesla-preps-for-big-step-in-germany-chinese-names-fall [Accessed 29 Aug. 2023].

Editor, C.S., SA News (2022). *Hertz adds Tesla Model Y to rental fleet (NASDAQ:HTZ) | Seeking Alpha.* [online] seekingalpha.com. Available at: https://seekingalpha.com/news/3816856-hertz-adds-tesla-model-y-to-rental-fleet [Accessed 29 Aug. 2023].

Fernando, J. (2023). *Current Ratio Explained With Formula and Examples.* [online] Investopedia. Available at: https://www.investopedia.com/terms/c/currentratio.asp.

Fernando, J. (2023). *Inventory Turnover Ratio: What It Is, How It Works, and Formula.* [online] Investopedia. Available

at: https://www.investopedia.com/terms/i/inventoryturnover.asp.

Fernando, J. (2023). *P/E Ratio – Price-to-Earnings Ratio Formula, Meaning, and Examples.* [online] Investopedia. Available at: https://www.investopedia.com/terms/p/price-earningsratio.asp.

Fernando, J. (2023). *Return on Equity (ROE) Calculation and What It Means.* [online] Investopedia. Available at: https://www.investopedia.com/terms/r/returnonequity.asp.

finance.yahoo.com. (n.d.). *Ford Motor Company (F) Stock Historical Prices & Data – Yahoo Finance.* [online] Available at:

https://finance.yahoo.com/quote/F/history?period1=1609286400&peri-

od2=1672531200&interval=1d&filter=history&frequency=1d&includeAd-justedClose=true [Accessed 29 Aug. 2023].

finance.yahoo.com. (n.d.). *Tesla, Inc. (TSLA) Stock Historical Prices & Data – Yahoo Finance*. [online] Available at:

https://finance.yahoo.com/quote/TSLA/history?period1=1609286400&peri-od2=1672531200&interval=1d&filter=history&frequency=1d&includeAd-justedClose=true [Accessed 29 Aug. 2023].

finance.yahoo.com. (n.d.). *Tesla, Inc. (TSLA) Stock Major Holders – Yahoo Finance*. [online] Available at: https://finance.yahoo.com/quote/tsla/holders/.

Hargrave, M. (2022). *Return on Assets (ROA): Formula and 'Good' ROA Defined*. [online] Investopedia. Available at: https://www.investopedia.com/terms/r/returnonassets.asp.

Hayes, A. (2020). *Understanding Total-Debt-to-Total-Assets*. [online] Investopedia. Available at: https://www.investopedia.com/terms/t/totaldebttototalassets.asp.

Hayes, A. (2021). *How Working Capital Turnover Works*. [online] Investopedia. Available at: https://www.investopedia.com/terms/w/workingcapitalturnover.asp.

Hayes, A. (2022). *Asset Turnover Ratio*. [online] Investopedia. Available at: https://www.investopedia.com/terms/a/assetturnover.asp.

Hayes, A. (2022). *Operating Margin: What It Is and the Formula for Calculating It, With Examples*. [online] Investopedia. Available at: https://www.investopedia.com/terms/o/operatingmargin.asp.

https://www.facebook.com/sim.alva (2019). *Tesla is one of the world's Most Innovative Companies, says noted consulting firm*. [online] TESLARATI. Available at: https://www.teslarati.com/tesla-most-innovative-companies-in-2019-ranking/.

If Tesla Isn't Good Enough for an ESG Index, Then Who Is? (2022). *Bloomberg.com*. [online] 19 May. Available at: https://www.bloomberg.com/news/articles/2022-05-19/tesla-creates-awkward-esg-questions-with-ejection-from-s-p-index?in_source=embedded-checkout-banner [Accessed 29 Aug. 2023].

Investopedia (2022). *What is considered a good net debt-to-equity ratio?* [online] Investopedia. Available at: https://www.investopedia.com/ask/answers/040915/what-considered-good-net-debttoequity-ratio.asp.

Kerber, R. and Jin, H. (2022). Tesla cut from S&P 500 ESG Index, and Elon Musk tweets his fury. *Reuters*. [online] 19 May. Available at: https://www.reuters.com/business/sustainable-business/tesla-removed-sp-500-esg-index-autopilot-discrimination-concerns-2022-05-18/.

Macrotrends (2010). *Tesla – 9 Year Stock Price History | TSLA*. [online] Macrotrends.net. Available at: https://www.macrotrends.net/stocks/charts/TSLA/tesla/stock-price-history.

Maverick, J.B. (2021). *What Is a Good Interest Coverage Ratio?* [online] Investopedia. Available at: https://www.investopedia.com/ask/answers/121814/what-good-interest-coverage-ratio.asp.

MAXIMIZE MARKET RESEARCH. (n.d.). *Automotive Market in US: Industry Analysis & Key Trends Forecast 2027.* [online] Available at: https://www.maximizemarketresearch.com/market-report/automotive-market-in-us/86405/.

Morningstar, Inc. (2023). *TSLA – Tesla Inc Sustainability – NASDAQ | Morningstar.* [online] Available at: https://www.morningstar.com/stocks/xnas/tsla/sustainability [Accessed 29 Aug. 2023].

Murphy, C. (2022). *What is Net Profit Margin? Formula for calculation and examples.* [online] Investopedia. Available at: https://www.investopedia.com/terms/n/net_margin.asp.

Murphy, C. (2023). *Why the Receivables Turnover Ratio Matters.* [online] Investopedia. Available at: https://www.investopedia.com/terms/r/receivableturnoverratio.asp.

NASDAQ (2019). *TSLA.* [online] Nasdaq.com. Available at: https://www.nasdaq.com/market-activity/stocks/tsla.

Nasdaq.com. (2023). *Tesla Plans To Request Stockholder Approval For Stock Split.* [online] Available at: https://www.nasdaq.com/articles/tesla-plans-to-request-stockholder-approval-for-stock-split [Accessed 29 Aug. 2023].

Nasdaq.com. (2023). *Will Tesla (TSLA) Regain Its Highs? If so, When?* [online] Available at: https://www.nasdaq.com/articles/will-tesla-tsla-regain-its-highs-if-so-when [Accessed 29 Aug. 2023].

Oboolo (2022). *Tesla – BCG Matrix.* [online] www.oboolo.com. Available at: https://www.oboolo.com/blog/our-tips/tesla-bcg-matrix-02-03-2022.html.

Pavelescu, O. (n.d.). *Moment istoric pentru Tesla. Intră în indicele bursier S&P 500.* [online] www.dcbusiness.ro. Available at: https://www.dcbusiness.ro/moment-istoric-pentru-tesla-dupa-ce-a-intrat-in-calcularea-coeficientului-s-p-500_622208.html#google_vignette [Accessed 29 Aug. 2023].

Profile TSLA F GM TM DDAIF NIO. (n.d.). Available at: https://files.cdn.thinkific.com/file_uploads/666838/attachments/886/03b/ec1/Patreon_only_(1).pdf [Accessed 29 Aug. 2023].

Reeth, M. (2022). *Tesla Competitors: 6 Rival Electric Vehicle Stocks.* [online] US News & World Report. Available at: https://money.usnews.com/investing/stock-market-news/slideshows/upstart-tesla-competitors-to-watch

Seth, S. (2023). *Quick Ratio Formula With Examples, Pros and Cons.* [online] Investopedia. Available at: https://www.investopedia.com/terms/q/quickratio.asp.

shareholder.ford.com. (n.d.). *Ford Motor Company – Investors – Reports & Filings.* [online] Available at: https://shareholder.ford.com/Investors/financials/default.aspx#annual-reports.

Statista. (2017). *U.S. car sales by year 1951-2017 | Statistic.* [online] Available at: https://www.statista.com/statistics/199974/us-car-sales-since-1951/.

Stock Analysis on Net. (n.d.). *Tesla Inc. (NASDAQ:TSLA) | Balance Sheet: Assets.* [online] Available at: https://www.stock-analysis-on.net/NASDAQ/Company/Tesla-Inc/Financial-Statement/Assets.

Stock Analysis. (n.d.). Ford Motor Company (F) Financial Ratios and Metrics. [online] Available at: https://stockanalysis.com/stocks/f/financials/ratios/.

Stock Analysis. (n.d.). Tesla, Inc. (TSLA) Financial Ratios and Metrics. [online] Available at: https://stockanalysis.com/stocks/tsla/financials/ratios/.

sustainalytics.com. (n.d.). *Company ESG Risk Rating – Sustainalytics.* [online] Available at: https://www.sustainalytics.com/esg-rating/tesla-inc/1035322998.

Tesla (2021). *UNITED STATES SECURITIES AND EXCHANGE COMMISSION.* [online] Available at: https://ir.tesla.com/_flysystem/s3/sec/000156459021004599/tsla-10k_20201231-gen.pdf.

Tesla (2022). *Corporate Governance | Tesla Investor Relations.* [online] ir.tesla.com. Available at: https://ir.tesla.com/corporate.

Tesla (2023). *Artificial Intelligence & Autopilot.* [online] Tesla. Available at: https://www.tesla.com/AI.

Washington, D. (2022). *UNITED STATES SECURITIES AND EXCHANGE COMMISSION.* [online] Available at: https://ir.tesla.com/_flysystem/s3/sec/000009501702300149/tsla-20221231-gen.pdf.

Washington, D. (2022). *UNITED STATES SECURITIES AND EXCHANGE COMMISSION.* [online] Available at: https://ir.tesla.com/_flysystem/s3/sec/000009501702300149/tsla-20221231-gen.pdf.

Williams2019-09-17T17:37:00+01:00, M. (n.d.). *US automotive market to struggle against backdrop of global challenges.* [online] Automotive Logistics. Available at: https://www.automotivelogistics.media/electric-vehicles/us-automotive-market-to-struggle-against-backdrop-of-global-challenges/39141.article [Accessed 29 Aug. 2023].

Willing, N. (2023). *Tesla Shareholders | Who Owns The Most Shares in Tesla?* [online] capital.com. Available at: https://capital.com/tesla-shareholder-who-owns-the-most-tsla-stock.

www.chartmill.com. (n.d.). Stock Price, News, Quote and Profile of FORD MOTOR COMPANY – F 6.2 06/01/59(NYSE:F-B) stock. [online] Available at: https://www.chartmill.com/stock/quote/F-B/profile [Accessed 8 Sep. 2023].

www.ey.com. (n.d.). *EY x Tesla Networking Event.* [online] Available at: https://www.ey.com/en_ch/location-events/2022/06/ey-x-tesla-networking-event [Accessed 29 Aug. 2023].

www.growyourwealth.ro. (n.d.). *Grow Your Wealth.* [online] Available at: https://www.growyourwealth.ro/products/grow-your-wealth/categories/2151509009/posts/2162404571 [Accessed 29 Aug. 2023].

www.gurufocus.com. (n.d.). *Tesla Inc Stock Rating and Data | – GuruFocus.com.* [online] Available at: https://www.gurufocus.com/stock/TSLA/summary.

www.msci.com. (n.d.). *ESG Ratings & Climate Search Tool.* [online] Available at: https://www.msci.com/our-solutions/esg-investing/esg-ratings-climate-search-tool/issuer/tesla-inc/IID000000002594878.

www.readyratios.com. (n.d.). *Top U.S. Companies by Revenue for the Manufacturing Industry.* [online] Available at: https://www.readyratios.com/sec/rating/D/ [Accessed 29 Aug. 2023].

www.sec.gov. (n.d.). *10-K.* [online] Available at: https://www.sec.gov/Archives/edgar/data/1318605/000095017022000796/tsla-20211231.htm#item_10.

www.wsj.com. (n.d.). *TSLA | Tesla Inc. Company Profile & Executives – WSJ.* [online] Available at: https://www.wsj.com/market-data/quotes/TSLA/company-people.

*Appendixes are available upon requested in order to better understand the financial analysis done by the author.

Alexandru–Romulus Harbuzaru

From Mad Men to Sad Men: A Self-Reflexive Case Study of a Toxic Triumvirate in a Small Advertising Agency

EMBA Module: Leadership and Organisational Change

Assessment task: *Identify a real leadership or managerial problem that you or your organisation has recently faced. It can be a major organisational-wide issue, or a smaller issue that you or your team have faced personally in recent months. Discuss, with reference to leadership & change theories learned in this module, how effectively you/your team/organisation successfully tackled this problem. Then critically evaluate the response to this problem, as taken by you/ your team/organisation as a failure/negative, or a success/positive.*

Introduction

The following is a self-reflexive case study of a toxic leadership environment at Fortin Agency, a digital advertising agency established in August 2015 by Robert P (then 34), Alexandru Harbuzaru (then 25), and Mihai B (then 23). The three stakeholders behind this Bucharest-based advertising agency all used to work together at the same company before beginning their own businesses. They each owned 33,33% of the company, with equal equity ownership.

They used passion and youth energy as an effective engine to build a team of both creative and technical individuals who served different departments and managed to build several successful projects over the course of four years. After the initial excitement died out, selfishness and chaos took over, and the organisation was plagued by several toxic and disruptive leadership models. This resulted in the founders breaking up, as well as the departure of most of the employees, collaborators, and customers.

The public annual reports described in Appendix 1 show that there has been a decrease in employee numbers from 2018 to 2019. It has been previously stated that a significant number of them were subcontractors, a common practise amongst IT companies in Romania that provided continual services to Fortin Agency and its customers. Unfortunately, the author's lack of access to the company's records prevents us from presenting proof of the involvement or exit of the agency's collaborators or sibling contractors from the organisation.

This study uses prospective participant observations to investigate toxic leadership and its consequences. The author of this paper is also one of the three stakeholders, and as part of the issue, he plays a major role in the organisation's demise. This paper's author also attempts to provide an honest self-reflection, and even self-reflexivity, on his previous behaviour and a fresh perspective on toxic leadership. As Jan Deckers points out in his article *The Value of Autoethnography in Leadership Studies, and its Pitfalls*, published in Philosophy of Management, "The fact that there is a dearth of such studies may be related to the fact that unethical leaders are unlikely to grant their permission to being observed by an external party, fearing public disclosure." (Deckers, 2020)

Researchers' reflexivity entails self-awareness and self-examination of subjective experiences and prejudices that may influence their research. It is a self-aware and critical research approach that is particularly helpful when studying complex and sensitive issues such as toxic leadership. Autoethnography, for example, requires researchers to reflect on their personal relationship with the subject as well as their effect on it. The process of reflecting on knowledge is known as self-reflection, whereas reflexivity is the ability to evaluate oneself while knowing. As Bogdan Popoveniuc (2014) notes in his research on *"Self-Reflexivity: The Ultimate End of Knowledge,"*. While they are linked, reflexivity is more complex and requires continuous self-consciousness. Reflexivity encompasses the researchers socially created experience and necessitates continuous self-critique and assessment throughout the research process.

This qualitative study was designed to examine the processes and practises that occurred prior to, during, and after team consolidation, analyse the leaders' internal dialogues, and identify toxic leadership behaviours. Individually (heterogeneous) and collectively (homogeneous), with a unified voice. The author endeavours to conduct research using autoethnography due to the nature of the available evidence. The majority of the evidence provided consists of the author's personal notes and pictures from 2016, 2017, and 2018, as well as the organisations previously published annual reports.

History, background, and context

Three former coworkers founded the company in August 2015, with the intention of assisting existing clients as well as attracting many more in the years to come. Along with the sudden increase in clients, the team expanded very quickly, adding a total of approximately 12 members (employees and full-time collaborators) to serve departments including SEO, web design, web development, Google Ads, social media, and, later, video production and events, as displayed in Figure 2. Several photographs from 2016 were added to Appendix 2, exhibiting members of the team back then.

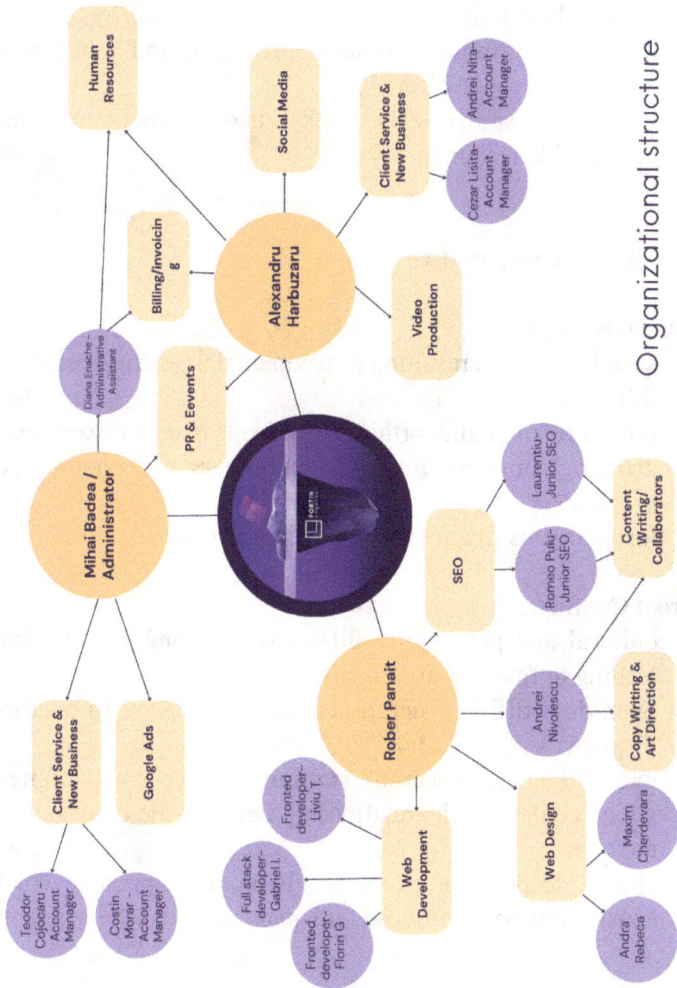

Figure 1: The Organisational chart of Fortin Agency in 2016. Source: Created by the author.

Initial plan, and business goals

To be competitive, the strategy was to:

- provide services with small to medium budgets.
- paying as little as possible for employees and reinvesting the profits.
- to provide the best possible customer service experience.

- to get one senior in each department—"someone smarter than us"—to help train juniors.
- to create reusable resources, products, and ready-made services to reduce effort.
- obtain the greatest possible market share within the constraints of available resources.

After four years, reality

Financial Struggles:
- cash flow issues resulting in payment delays and operational difficulties.
- utilisation of creditworthiness for loans to cover expenses.
- growing tensions among stakeholders due to financial problems.
- losing clients frequently, impacting revenue streams.

Internal Conflicts:
- cultural and personality differences among stakeholders, leading to frequent arguments.
- open-door office structure, causing employees to overhear disputes.
- one of the parties secretly starting a business with a client, which could hurt the relationship between the company and the client.
- chaotic leadership, a lack of vision, and opposing voices causing employees to lose faith and leave for other agencies.

Advertising in Romania

The private sector in Romania is still relatively young, particularly when considering the companies operating prior to the ascension of the Communist Party in 1948. According to Radu Mihaela's (2018) research, we have a 33-year history in the private sector. The accomplishments of businesses during the interwar period have largely gone undocumented and are not illustrated by current education programs. Consequently, a limited number of Romanian entrepreneurs possess the ability to capitalise on a shared business history for the purpose of learning.

According to Chirila and Rabontu (2010), because of the disappearance of state and socialist economic monopolies, Romanians were forced to reinvent advertising and marketing communications. This resulted in a rapid combustion process, leading to spectacular economic growth for the industry and awards for local creations at international festivals. TV spots, radio spots, posters, big billboards, and press designs have become some of the most eye-catching parts of modern culture.

Bucharest, Romania's capital, is the tenth most popular city in Europe for setting up a startup venture. According to Romania Insider (Chirileasa, 2022), a financial technology company that runs credit card payment services for small and medium-sized businesses, there were 402,428 startup businesses in the country from 2015 to 2019, with a large number of them in the software sector. In the first five years, startups in Romania have a survival rate of 51.8%, ranking the country ninth out of 30 studied nations.

Starting a new company is a difficult and risky endeavour. It is interesting to consider that according to global statistics, only 18% of startups survive past their first year, suggesting the formidable odds that entrepreneurs face.

However, nobody begins a business expecting it to fail. This is a frequent error with disastrous consequences. Most large law firms, like Exit Advisory Group (Bedard, 2022) advise that before beginning a business relationship with someone, you should have a written exit strategy in hand. Company dissolution happens not only in unsuccessful but also in successful businesses. Too many businesses are started without proper bylaws, operating agreements, stakeholder agreements, or partnership agreements.

In many cases, it can be difficult to effectively manage decision-making and leadership styles in a company with three owners, especially when the owners' interests shift towards their own personal goals. This can result in ownership disagreements and authority rivalries, as well as a lack of a clear chain of command or leadership structure, all of which can quickly devolve into a toxic and disruptive leadership model.

Toxic leadership can harm a company's success by creating a hostile work atmosphere, undermining employee morale and motivation, and impeding productivity and performance. Leadership has always been associated with positivity, but few studies have investigated the dark side of leadership. Dr. Marcia Lynn Whicker was the first to link toxicity with leadership and discussed three types of leaders within workplaces: trustworthy (green light), transitional (yellow light), and toxic (red light). The repertoire of toxic leaders covers a broad spectrum, and it is difficult to craft a differentiation between destructive leaders that are genuinely toxic, bad leaders that are not toxic but are incompetent only in managerial skills, and good leaders that are wicked people (Rosenthal, 1995).

Introducing the Triumvirate

Individually (heterogeneous) Toxicity

Robert P (then 34) was the eldest partner, the only one with a family at the time, and the only one with a child. He has a background in IT and is an experienced SEO (search engine optimisation) expert with over 7 years of experience. It is important to address family background in this context because one of the problems that caused the differences between the three leaders was a lack of commitment to the company's obligations and day-to-day managerial duties.

Based on the author's personal notes, the following traits were associated with Robert's behaviour and work ethics during their nearly 7-year working relationship (at Fortin Agency and prior to Fortin, when they were colleagues in their previous job):
- unapologetic self-promotion and self-aggrandizing.
- low self-steam, and verbally aggressive behaviour.
- not willing to accept accountability.
- frequent irritation with how slowly others moves.
- disregard for the values or requirements of others.
- objectifies and exploits others.
- come across as distant and unapproachable.

Alexandru H. (then 25) studied visual arts and had 5 years of sales and marketing experience at the time. For almost the entire time he was with Fortin Agency, he was involved in artistic collaborations, acting as an agent for two painters. It is also important to highlight his side projects, which, from the very beginning to the very end, were the source of a great deal of conflict and controversy.

With the qualitative personal notes from 2016, 2017, and 2018 that were made by the author himself, we will conduct a more in-depth analysis of this specific member of the squad. Alcohol abuse represented another significant challenge, resulting in an abundance of additional difficulties for all three executives. The findings in Appendix 3 suggest that Alexandru was in a state of perpetual guilt, which, against his own willpower, resulted in a slew of poor decisions. This also resulted in a decrease in his authority, as well as the loss of his voting power.

The following traits were correlated with Alexandru's behaviour and work ethics:

- not willing to accept accountability.
- want to be the "nice" or "good" one.
- a burning desire to be loved, accepted, and included.
- lack of focus: being distracted, demotivated, and procrastinating.
- selfishness: may prioritise his own interests and goals over the objectives of the company and its team members.
- inability to manage conflict: difficulties in resolving disputes within the company, which may result in a toxic work environment.
- poor emotional regulation – struggles to control his emotions and may respond impulsively, resulting in embarrassing or regrettable circumstances.

Mihai B (then 23), the youngest founder, is an economist with 5 years of sales expertise. Based on his educational qualifications and professional ethics, he was appointed administrator of the business. He was also the most devoted member during the first 3 years.

It's essential to note that in the fourth year, Mihai launched a side business with one of the company's customers, using shady and deceptive tactics with his partners throughout and after the event, even after his statements were ultimately discredited by subsequent events. Because of this, the group eventually broke up, with Alexandru leaving the endeavour and, roughly, 90% of the team following suit.

Mihai's behaviour and work ethic were found to be associated with the following traits:

- exaggeration of reality to the point of fiction.
- excessive speech to gain control of others.
- self-promoting and self-aggrandisement without remorse.
- extensive story pontification, and fabrication.
- disdain for authority figures.

- reject all ideas from others right away.
- dismissing others as unimportant in the pursuit of their objective.
- objectifies others and exploits them for personal gain.
- demands for unconditional loyalty in return for protection.

It is worth noting that none of the subjects had any previous business experience before enrolling at Fortin Agency. It was observed that a deficiency in financial knowledge was a general problem amongst the trio.

Collectively (homogeneous) Toxicity

Northouse (2012) defines leadership broadly as "a process whereby an individual influences a group of individuals to achieve a common goal." Other authors, on the other hand, attempted to expand on this statement and clarify the idea of leadership. According to Cook (1998), leadership is "the act of giving directions, energising others, and obtaining voluntary commitment to the leader's goal." Katz (2009), In turn, he concentrates on a leader (or so-called administrator) rather than a process and describes him as someone who leads the activities of others and accepts responsibility for accomplishing specific goals through these efforts.

In the presented case, we are facing a different type of leadership, which was called a "triumvirate." A triumvirate is a group of three people who share power. In ancient Rome, a group of three notable or powerful people with the most important positions were called a "triumvirate, like Julius Cesar, Crassus, and Pompey in 60 BC. Together, they ruled the Roman Empire. In America's early days, George Washington, Thomas Jefferson, and James Madison were also a triumvirate. It concerns a unique situation, where three people share the same amount of power.

The "Triumvirate of Google," illustrated in Organizational Behaviour: Foundations, Realities, and Challenges, by Nelson and Quick (1997), is possibly the most important case study of a triumvirate in contemporary times, focusing on the ideologies, philosophies, and behaviours of Google's three major figures, Sergey Brin, Larry Page, and Eric Schmidt. The case illustrates the distinctions between managerial and leadership responsibilities, as well as how they are distributed within the business. When it comes to leadership and management, the distinctions go beyond their definitions. In this instance, the managerial and leadership traits are joined in the company's triumvirate.

The triumvirate was established in 2001, and by 2007, when Schmidt was elected chairman, it was fully operational. The main turning point can be seen in the company's transformation from being simply a leader in innovative technologies to a corporation with its own culture, behaviour, and policies. In this respect, the transformation can be seen in the separation of functions among the organisation's key figures. Furthermore, the timeline of Google's accomplishments with Schmidt on board included several acquisitions that enraged the global business community. Acquisitions such as eBay and YouTube, as well as entry into the markets of desktop software and Wi-Fi services, may suggest that the triumvirate's created organisational strategy does not appear to work outside of the company.

According to Ostrom (1998), power triangles function best when there is specialisation. When many people compete for the same position, the outcome favours only one winner. Consider instead how power should be distributed among individuals with various primary responsibilities.

In a qualitative study called "One Member, Two Leaders: Extending Leader–Member Exchange Theory to a Dual Leadership Context", published by Vidyarthi *et al.* (2014) the authors research another phenomenon called "Dual Leadership.", People have used terms like shared leadership, divided responsibilities, and cooperation. This study applies leader–member exchange (LMX) theory to dual leadership. According to relative deprivation theory, workers who work for two leaders have two relationships. Thus, job happiness and voluntary turnover depend on how well the two relationships align. Polynomial regression on time-lagged data from 159 information technology consultants nested in 26 client projects showed that employee outcomes are affected by the quality of the relationship with both agency and client leaders. The degree of alignment between the 2 LMXs explained variance in outcomes beyond that explained by both LMXs. Results also showed that a lack of alignment in the 2 LMXs had asymmetric impacts on outcomes, with agency leaders mattering more than client leaders. Finally, in the low client LMX condition, agency LMX impacted job satisfaction based on agency leader communication frequency.

The toxic triangle

In the case study, according to Appendix 4, the toxic behaviour of the manager towards the team can be explained by the toxic triangle, comprised of three distinct factors. The manager had an authoritative position, which allowed them to exercise control over the team and their working environment. This presented them with the chance to engage in harmful behaviour towards other employees.

The manager might have attempted to justify their toxic behaviour as a necessary means to accomplish the task, or to inspire their subordinates. It is possible that they believed that their methodology was the most efficacious means of attaining success.

The manager might have been subject to pressure to produce results, meet deadlines, or exceed expectations. The pressure may have caused them to adopt toxic behaviours to motivate their team members to work harder or quicker.

The toxic actions of the manager in the case study can be attributed to the convergence of opportunity, rationalization, and pressure, commonly referred to as the "toxic triangle." Gaining comprehension of this system enables one to recognise and grapple with the essential elements that lead to detrimental actions within a work environment.

Overall, the toxic behaviour of the leaders in the case study can be explained by the existence of all three toxic triangle factors: opportunity, rationalisation, and pressure. Understanding this framework allows you to spot and address the underlying factors that contribute to toxic behaviour in the workplace.

Conclusions

The unplanned exit was one of the most frustrating parts of the scenario. It was a very painful and expensive mistake that could have been avoided. According to an article published by Entrepreneur Mascari (2023), business exit planning is important for any transformative business decision and should not be delayed. Executives and business owners may not plan ahead for a business exit strategy because they are too focused on the present and immediate future of their organisation. However, it is important to focus on strategies that will ensure growth, profitability, and stability in the near term. Planning your exit is a good business strategy whether you intend to sell or not, as it sets up your company to maximise growth and profits by creating an organisation that can run independently of you with top talent, a solid foundation, financial stability, and a competitive advantage. Business exit planning should begin during the startup or early growth stages of a business to ensure that all future decisions are made with the long term in mind.

To reduce the risk of toxic leadership, businesses should prioritise effective communication, transparency, and accountability, as well as create a positive work culture that values collaboration and cooperation. Donald Sull and Charles Sull (2022), the authors of the research titled "How to Fix a Toxic Culture," suggest that this strategy will help to promote a healthy workplace environment and ensure that bad leadership does not jeopardise their success.

At the outset of a business partnership, crucial factors such as shared culture, interests, goals, and a unified business vision are typically in sync. However, over time, shared experiences can mold the founders in distinct ways, causing divergent values and potentially even a disparate vision for the enterprise.

References:

Bedard, S. (2022) *Reasons Why Company Founders Break Up With Their Business Partner, Exit Advisory Group.* Available at: https://exitadvisory.com.au/reasons-why-company-founders-break-up-with-their-business-partner/ (Accessed: March 26, 2023).

Bennis, W. (1989) *On Becoming a Leader.* Addison-Wesley Longman. doi:10.1604/9780201080599.

Burns, J.M. (1982) *Leadership.* doi:10.1604/9780061319754.

Cook, T. (1998) *Management Organizational Behavior.* Irwin Professional Publishing.

Chirila, S. and Rabontu, C.-I. (2010) "Analysis of the Romanian Advertising Market," *Annals – Economy Series,* 4, pp. 65–80. Available at: https://ideas.repec.org/s/cbu/jrnlec.html.

Chirileasa, Mr.A. (2022) *Data shows Romania as 10th largest startup location in Europe, Romania Insider.* Available at: https://www.romania-insider.com/paymentsense-ro-startup-sept-2022 (Accessed: March 25, 2023).

Deckers, J. (2020) "The Value of Autoethnography in Leadership Studies, and its Pitfalls," *Philosophy of Management*, 20(1), pp. 75–91. doi:10.1007/s40926-020-00146-w.

Genome, Mr.S. (2019) *Startup Genome, Startup Genome*. Available at: https://startupgenome.com/reports/global-startup-ecosystem-report-2019 (Accessed: March 22, 2023).

Jessica, E., Hongling, X. and Ingrid, R.Olson. "Understanding social hierarchies: T. neural and psychological foundations of status perception (2015) "Social neuroscience 10 no."

Katz, R.L. (2009) *Skills of an Effective Administrator*. (Harvard Business Review Classics: Ser.), pp. 34–42.

Laszlo, K.C. (2012) "From systems thinking to systems being: The embodiment of evolutionary leadership," *Journal of Organisational Transformation & Social Change*, 9(2), pp. 95–108. doi:10.1386/jots.9.2.95_1.

Mascari, N. (2023) *When Should Business Owners Start Developing an Exit Plan?* | *Entrepreneur, Entrepreneur*. Available at: https://www.entrepreneur.com/leadership/when-should-business-owners-start-developing-an-exit-plan/442711 (Accessed: March 27, 2023).

Nelson, D.L. and Quick, J.C. (1997) *Organizational Behavior, Foundations, Realities and Challenges*. doi:10.1604/9780314205674.

Northouse, P.G. (2012) *Leadership, Theory and Practice*.

Ostrom, E. (1998) *A Behavioral Approach to the Rational Choice Theory of Collective Action: Presidential Address, American Political Science Association, 1997*. American Political Science Association (The American Political Science Review), pp. 1–22. Available at: https://www.jstor.org/stable/2585925.

Popoveniuc, B. (2014) "Self Reflexivity. The Ultimate End of Knowledge," *Procedia – Social and Behavioral Sciences*, 163, pp. 204–213. doi:10.1016/j.sbspro.2014.12.308.

Popoveniuc, B. (2014) "Self Reflexivity. The Ultimate End of Knowledge," *Procedia – Social and Behavioral Sciences*, 163, pp. 204–213. doi:10.1016/j.sbspro.2014.12.308.

Radu Mihaela, B. (2018) "Analysis of the Evolution of the Private Sector in Romania after 1990," *Athenaeum University of Bucharest*, pp. 44–52. Available at: https://ideas.repec.org/s/ath/journl.html.

Rosenthal, A. (1995) "Legislative Leadership in the American States.Malcolm E. Jewell , Marcia Lynn Whicker," *The Journal of Politics*, 57(4), pp. 1176–1177. doi:10.2307/2960409.

Santoshi, S. and Santosh, D. (2018) *Toxic leadership The most menacing form of leadership*. Dark sides of organizational behavior and leadership.

Sull, D., Sull, C. and of Technology, M.I. (2022) *How to Fix a Toxic Culture, MIT*

Sloan Management Review. Available at: https://sloanreview.mit.edu/article/
how-to-fix-a-toxic-culture/ (Accessed: March 27, 2023).

Vidyarthi, P.R., Erdogan , errin, Anand, S. and Liden, R.C. (2014) "One Member,
Two Leaders: Extending Leader–Member Exchange Theory to a Dual
Leadership Context," *Journal of Applied Psychology* [Preprint]. doi:10.1037/
a0035466.

Nicolae Moldovan

Employee Engagement. A Study in a Corporate Organisation

EMBA Module: People and Performance. Talent Management in Action

Assignment task: This assignment is a 3000-word people management research case analysis. You will choose an organisation with which you are familiar with. You will investigate a critical HR practice implemented by that organisation and its consequences on individual and organisational outcomes. You will use an appropriate theory to critically evaluate and address the identified practical HRM function, and the challenges faced.

Introduction

Employee Engagement is a topic that sparked a lot of debates among scholars in the last two decades. The purpose of this paper is to study employee engagement in a corporate organization that recently went through a pandemic, material supply shortage, increase in remote work and internal reorganization. Due to internal retention policies the study was done on a small sample of 28 subjects representing employees in the Project Management Department from a multinational organization. This company, operating in the technology and engineering sector, provides innovative solutions to clients across various industries worldwide.

Known for its focus on advancing industrial performance and efficiency, the company supports businesses through specialised software, hardware, and automation technologies.

In Romania, the company operates a major development center that contributes to global research, software engineering, and product innovation. The facility includes laboratories for testing and development, as well as training spaces used to support both internal teams and external collaborators. Since its launch, the center has steadily expanded and plays a strategic role in the company's broader technological initiatives.

Employee engagement is a key factor in the success of any business organization. Engaged employees are more productive, engaged, and more loyal to their company. They are also more inclined to continue working for a longer duration and make valuable contributions towards the growth of the organization (e.g., Harter et al., 2009; Kruse, 2012; Schatz & Reilly, 2014). Therefore, companies should understand employee engagement and take appropriate actions to improve it.

Early scholars were unable to agree on what engagement implies. In other words, engagement lacks a clear agreed-upon definition and "is subject to a number of variations, including 'work engagement', 'personal engagement', 'job engagement', 'staff engagement', 'employee engagement', and just simply 'engagement', each leading itself to a range of different definitions" (Truss et al., 2014). As a result of the lack of consensus regarding a standardised characterization of engagement, a second issue that scholars were unable to reconcile pertains to the most effective way to implement engagement. Scholars have defined engagement by depicting it into three distinct components that collectively constitute a motivational framework (Rich et al., 2010), a work attitude (Harter et al., 2002; Harter et al., 2009), or an opposite to burnout (Maslach & Leiter, 1997). The third source of ambiguity in engagement research is the existence of multiple theoretical frameworks, each with its unique interpretation, implementation, components, and explanatory relationships. The lack of a prevailing model governing the research of engagement is not intrinsically problematic; the existence of a disparate conceptual foundation has obstructed the integration of research findings and hindered the advancement of both conceptual understanding and practical application. For this reason, this essay will only make a brief introduction in the three most widely used frameworks of engagement: Kahn (1990), Schaufeli et al. (2002) and Gallup (e.g. Harter et al., 2002; Harter et al., 2009) and draw some critical thinking from each one.

In his article published in Academy of Management Journals, Kahn (1990: 694) defines engagement as the "harnessing of organization members' selves to their work roles; in engagement, people employ and express themselves physically, cognitively, and emotionally during role performances". In essence, Kahn (1990; 1992) has presented a conceptual structure that defines employee engagement as the measure to which individuals are compelled to invest their material, mental, and psychological assets in the active expression and demonstration of their favored persona within the organizational context. The degree of employee engagement is probably to be impacted by an assortment of elements, encompassing the characteristics of job assignments, atmosphere, and personal attributes. These factors contribute to the cognitive emotions of value, security, and accessibility. Unfortunately, this conceptual framework does not provide a clear set of guidelines regarding the operationalization of employee engagement, thereby resulting in diverse interpretations and understandings of the construct (e.g., Rich et al., 2010).

UWES was developed as the antipode of burnout, as a conceptualisation of employee engagement in response to the limitations in operationalizing engagement (Schaufeli et al., 2002). The original version of the UWES consisted of 17 items, divided into three subscales: vigor (6 items), dedication (5 items), and absorption (6 items). The vigor subscale assesses employees' feelings of liveliness, excitement, and capacity to overcome work-related obstacles. The dedication subscale evaluates employees' sense of importance, fulfillment, and incentive to invest effort in their work. Lastly, the absorption subscale examines employees' immersion, focus, and contentment in their work, potentially leading to time distortion and difficulty in disengaging from work-related activities. However, recent studies have posited that there exists a notable correlation between the dimensions of work engagement and burnout, raising concerns about the potential misalignment between theoretical frameworks and measurement practices. The substantial association observed between these constructs implies a risk of conceptual overlap, warranting a reevaluation of existing theoretical frameworks and assessment methods (Cole et al., 2012).

The definition of employee engagement, as outlined by Harter et al. (2002), offers insights into the concept as put forth by the Gallup Organization. Employee engagement encompasses an individual's deep involvement, satisfaction, and enthusiasm towards their work. It represents the cognitive, emotional, and behavioral aspects that characterise an employee's connection and commitment to their organizational role. It signifies the level of dedication, vigor, and absorption exhibited by employees, indicative of their active participation, positive effect, and sense of fulfillment in the work domain. The Gallup Organization's definition emphasises the significance of individuals' subjective experiences, reflecting their level of investment, contentment, and fervor in relation to their work. This comprehensive understanding of employee engagement serves as a foundational framework for comprehending and evaluating the intricate nature of employees' attitudes and involvement in the workplace. It's noteworthy that Q12, the measure of Gallup's conceptualization of engagement, was designed as a practical instrument to enhance job quality and increase employee satisfaction. Despite the proven efficacy of Gallup's engagement model and its corresponding assessment instrument in forecasting positive job-related disposition like work fulfillment, there were concerns raised regarding the model's conceptual rationality. The utilization of the Gallup measure to examine employee engagement has played a crucial role in the widespread acceptance and recognition of this concept. Nevertheless, academic research, as emphasised by Harter et al. (2002), has identified a potential concern regarding the distinctiveness of the Q12 engagement metric in comparison to well-established frameworks. Consequently, while Q12 can serve as a valuable criterion for evaluating human resource-related policies and practices, its applicability within research aimed at comprehending nature and dynamics of the engagement construct itself may pose challenges. Therefore, caution should be exercised when employing the Q12 measure in such research contexts. Further exploration and refinement of engagement measurement tools are warranted to better understand and assess the multifaceted nature of the engagement construct in specific research settings.

Employee Engagement Study

For this study, the author applied an alternative to Gallup's Q12 survey that will be referred to as Engagement Index, a tool used by many organizations to measure the level of employee engagement. The construction of an Engagement Index typically involves the development of a questionnaire or survey instrument that includes various items or statements related to the different aspects of engagement. Respondents are then asked to rate their agreement or level of endorsement with each item on a scale. By analyzing the responses, an overall engagement score or index can be derived, providing insights into the level of engagement within the studied population. The questions are designed to assess key factors related to employee engagement, such as having the necessary resources, feeling valued and recognised, having supportive relationships at work, opportunities for growth and development, and a sense of purpose and meaningful work. The Engagement Index results provide valuable insight into the overall health of the organization. Companies with high engagement scores tend to have low turnover, high productivity levels, and high customer satisfaction (Harter et al., 2002; Harter et al., 2009). On the other hand, companies with low engagement scores may suffer from employee retention, lower productivity, and lower profitability (De Meuse and Dai, 2012; McMahan et al., 2012). It's important for organizations to not only measure their engagement index but also take action to address their concerns. Offering opportunities for skill enhancement and professional growth, fostering a conducive work atmosphere, and providing enticing remuneration and perks are among the diverse approaches that organizations employ to enhance levels of employee engagement. According to Saks (2006: 603) "the amount of cognitive, emotional, and physical resources that an individual is prepared to devote in the performance of one's work roles is contingent on the economic and socioemotional resources received from the organization."

The results of the Engagement Index were obtained via a questionnaire administered to a number of 28 employees of the Project Management Department. The graphical representations present the proportional breakdowns, classified into distinctive categories denoting various degrees of agreement, encompassing responses to statements pertaining to the organizational work environment. These percentages have been segmented into five discrete classifications, each indicative of a specific level of agreement. The outcomes may be comprehended as a quantitative assessment of employee engagement and job satisfaction within the company. Specifically, a higher proportion of responses categorised as "Strongly Agree" or "Agree" signifies an elevated level of employee engagement and satisfaction with both their work responsibilities and the organization as a whole. Conversely, a greater percentage of responses categorised as "Disagree" or "Strongly Disagree" suggests a reduced level of employee engagement and satisfaction in relation to their work and the company.

Alignment Questions

Alignment questions serve as a tool to assess the extent to which an individual's or team's objectives and actions align with the organization's overall strategy and goals. Such inquiries help pinpoint areas that may require improved coordination and provide valuable insights on optimizing performance and productivity. Commonly used alignment questions can revolve around communication, decision-making, collaboration, and overall comprehension of the organization's mission and values.

As depicted in Fig. 1, based on the survey responses, most employees demonstrate an understanding of how their work contributes to the success of the company and 86% agree or strongly agree that their work provides them with a sense of personal confidence. A broad spectrum of responses was elicited concerning whether employees' skills and abilities are fully utilised at work and whether the work environment enables them to execute their responsibilities efficiently. Additionally, 53% of employees feel that they receive consistent feedback on their performance, and a percentage of 43% agree and strongly agree that their accomplishments are adequately acknowledged. Lastly, most of the employees agree the company's purpose and values are motivating for them.

These findings suggest that employees who feel their job is meaningful and aligned with the company's values are more likely to experience job satisfaction and perform better in their role. Therefore, it is crucial for organizations to prioritise employee engagement and alignment with company values to foster a positive work environment and enhance overall performance.

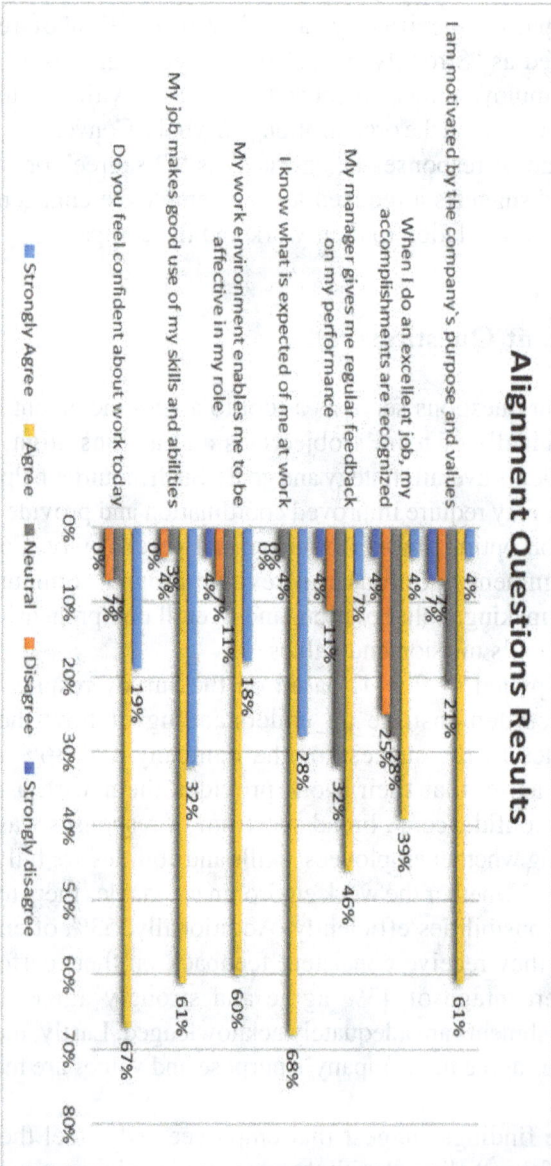

Alignment Questions Results

Question	Strongly Agree	Agree	Neutral	Disagree	Strongly disagree
I am motivated by the company's purpose and values	4%	7%	21%	61%	
When I do an excellent job, my accomplishments are recognized	4%	7%	25%	28%	39%
My manager gives me regular feedback on my performance	4%	7%	11%	32%	46%
I know what is expected of me at work	0%	4%	11%	32%	46%
My work environment enables me to be affective in my role	0%	4%	7%	11%	18% 68%
My job makes good use of my skills and abilities	0%	4%	11%	32%	61%
Do you feel confident about work today	0%	7%	4%	19%	67%

Figure 1. Alignment Questions Results

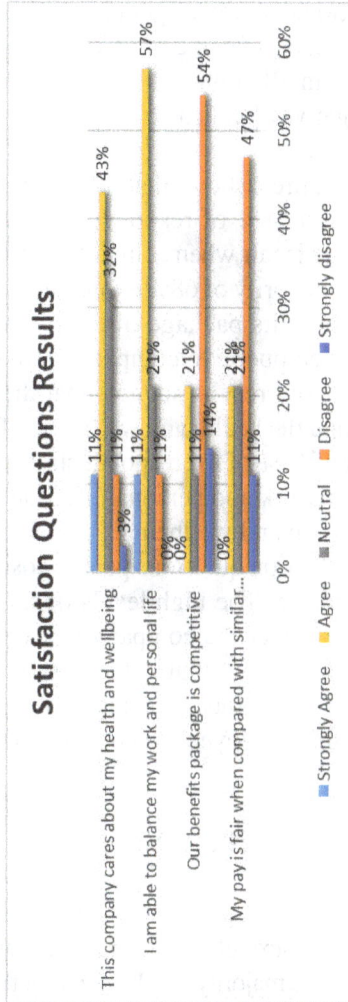

Figure 2. Satisfaction Questions Results

Satisfaction Questions

Despite the many benefits of having a job, many people struggle with job satisfaction. Some common reasons for this include feeling undervalued, not being paid enough, having a poor relationship with one's boss or colleagues, feeling bored or unchallenged by the work, or feeling like the job doesn't align with one's values or interests. Additionally, many people struggle with work-life balance, which can lead to feeling burnt out and unfulfilled in their job. These factors can all contribute to a lack of job satisfaction, which can have negative effects on both mental and physical health (Piening et al., 2013).

The chart from Figure 2 shows that the company is a great place to work, even though 58% of respondents disagree or strongly disagree that their pay is fair when compared with similar positions. Additionally, a vast majority of 68% expressed disagreement when asked about their benefits package offered by the company that they consider is not competitive compared with other companies. Furthermore, the survey results suggest that the company values work-life balance and the health and wellbeing of its employees. A significant number of 68% of the respondents reported that they are able to balance their work and personal life, and that the company cares about their health and wellbeing.

Overall, the satisfaction questions paint a positive picture of the company and its culture. The high levels of satisfaction reported by employees suggest that the company is successful in creating a positive work environment that values its employees and their needs. On the other hand, the company should revise its benefit package and align the employee's income to a market level.

ENGAGEMENT QUESTIONS

As depicted in Figure 3, the Engagement Index results indicate that 68% of the employees either strongly agree or agree that the company is a great place to work, and a majority of 89% consider that their work gives them a sense of personal accomplishment. The finding that a significant proportion of 47 % of respondents disagree or strongly disagree with the statement "I intend to stay with this company for at least the next 12 months" suggests that there may be factors contributing to employee turnover that the company should address. The organization might contemplate integrating employee retention tactics, such as providing remuneration and incentives that are competitive with the market and creating pathways for growth and career advancement.

The comprehensive engagement survey outcomes collectively suggest that the company demonstrates commendable achievements in terms of promoting employee satisfaction and retention. This auspicious trajectory holds promising prospects for the company's future success, as it signifies a workforce that is content and committed to their roles.

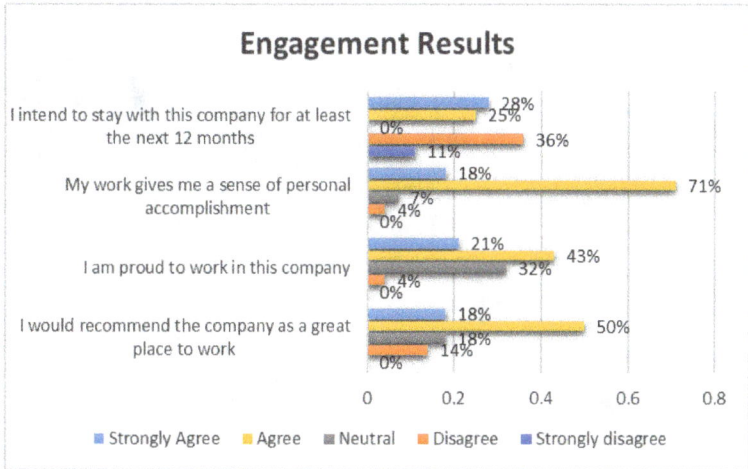

Figure 3. Engagement Results

Future Orientation Questions

The survey data presented in Figure 4 suggests that employees feel confident in their ability to achieve their career goals at the company, with 43% of respondents either agreeing or strongly agreeing with this statement. This indicates that the company's training and development programs may be effective in helping employees advance in their careers. The survey results also reveal that a portion of employees feel that they have been provided with the necessary training, tools, and information to perform their jobs safely and effectively. 68% of respondents either agreed or strongly agreed with this statement. This suggests that the company is investing in training and development programs to ensure that all employees feel adequately prepared to perform their job duties.

Overall, the survey results suggest that the company has been successful in creating a positive work environment that encourages employee loyalty and investing in company training and programs for its employees to be able to perform well on their job.

Future Orientation Questions

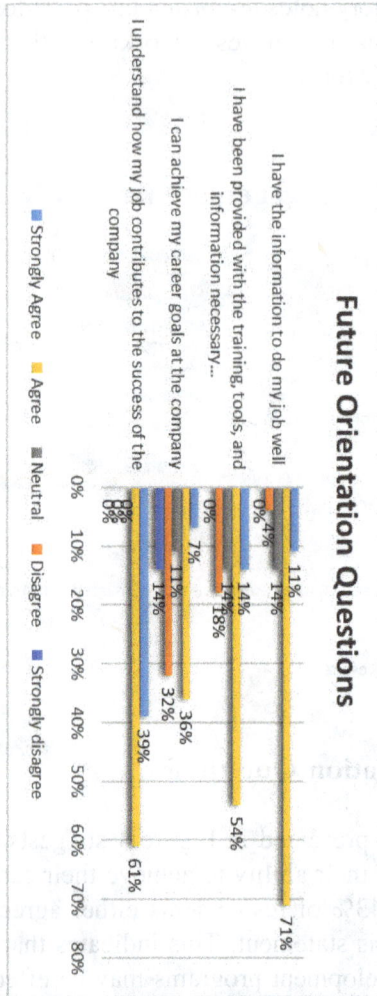

Figure 4. Future orientation questions Results

Open Questions

The survey concludes with two open-ended questions, depicted in Figure 5 and Figure 6, aiming to assess employees' perspectives on potential enhancements in the organization. Based on the graphical representations below, it is evident that 14% of the total respondents express the need for recognition of their accomplishments, while an additional 11% advocate for increased transparency and empowerment of employees.

In terms of strategies to enhance employee engagement within the workplace, 18% of respondents emphasise the importance of recognizing their merits, 14% highlight the significance of augmenting financial benefits, 7% indicate the desire for the creation of new opportunities, and 4% underscores the necessity for transparency.

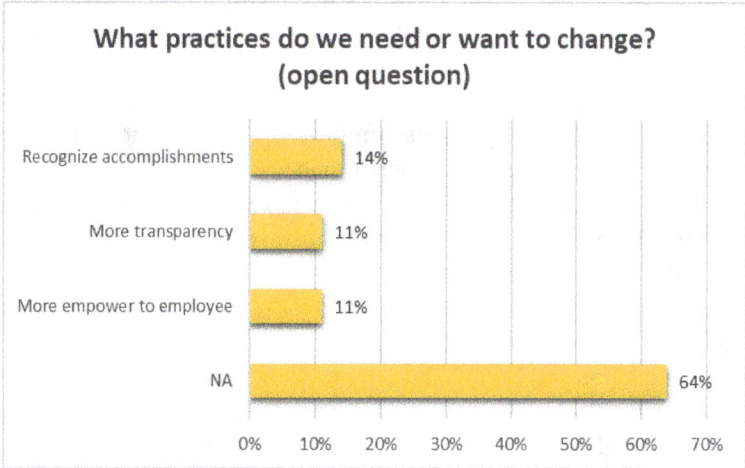

Figure 5. First Open Question

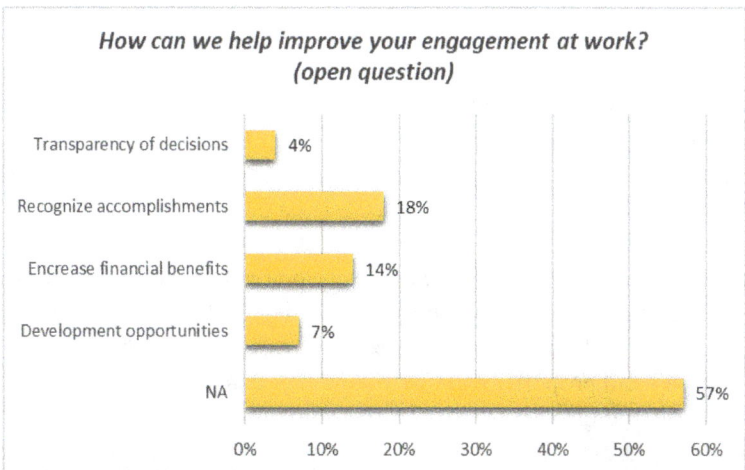

Figure 6. Second Open Question

Conclusions

Based on the findings presented in this study, it can be concluded that employees' perspectives and opinions regarding their work environment, engagement, and desired improvements within the company are as follows:

Meaningful work and alignment with company values positively impact job satisfaction and performance: The study indicates that employees who perceive their work as meaningful and aligned with the values of the company are more likely to experience job satisfaction and perform better in their roles. This suggests that organizations should prioritise employee engagement and value alignment to enhance overall performance.

Positive work environment and employee satisfaction: The survey results demonstrate that the company has created a positive work environment that values employee well-being and work-life balance. The high levels of employee satisfaction indicate that the company is successful in prioritizing its employees and their needs, which contributes to a positive work environment.

Consideration of revising benefits package: While employees reported high levels of satisfaction, concerns regarding pay and benefits were expressed. It suggests that the company may want to consider revising its benefits package to align with market standards, which could further enhance employee satisfaction.

Employee retention challenges: While a substantial segment of the workforce expressed contentment with their job and regarded the organization as an excellent working environment, nearly half of the survey participants indicated a lack of commitment to continuing their employment with the organization over the next 12 months. This indicates potential factors contributing to employee turnover that need to be addressed, such as offering competitive remuneration and providing career growth.

Effectiveness of training and development programs: The study reveals that the company's training and development programs are perceived as effective in helping employees advance in their careers. A significant proportion of respondents felt confident in their ability to achieve their career goals at the company, suggesting that the investment in training and development programs is commendable and contributes to employee satisfaction.

In summary, this study provides valuable insights into various aspects of employee satisfaction and engagement within the multinational company. The findings highlight the importance of employees recognizing the significance of their work, the utilization of their skills and abilities, the acknowledgment of their achievements, and the alignment of their values with the organization's purpose. Additionally, the study emphasises the need for the organization to address concerns related to compensation and benefits, as well as employee retention, in order to foster a positive work environment and enhance overall employee satisfaction and engagement.

References

Cole, M.S., Walter, F., Bedeian, A.G. & O`Boyle, E.H., (2012) *Job Burnout and Employee Engagement: A Meta-Analytic Examination of Construct Proliferation.* Journal of Management, 38, pp. 1550-1581.

De Meuse, K. P. & Dai, G. (2012) *Reducing costs and improving efficiency or damaging the company?*, in C. L. Cooper, A. Pandey and J. C. Quick (eds), *Downsizing: Is less still more?* Cambridge: Cambridge University Press, pp. 258–290.

Harter, J.K., Schmidt, F.L. & Hayes, T.L. (2002) *Business-Unit-Level Relationship between Employee Satisfaction, Employee Engagement, and Business Outcomes: A Meta-Analysis.* Journal of Applied Psychology, 87, pp. 268-279.

Harter, J.K., Schmidt, F.L., Killhan, E.A. and Agrawal, S. (2009) *Q12 meta-analysis: The Relationship between Engagement at Work and Organizational Outcomes.* The Gallup Organization.

Kahn, W.A. (1990) *Psychological conditions of personal engagement and disengagement at work.* Academy of Management Journal, 33, pp. 692-724.

Kahn, W.A. (1992) *To be fully there: Psychological presence at work.* Human Relations, 45, pp. 321-349.

Kruse, K. (2012) *What is employee engagement?* Available online: https://www. forbes.com /sites/kevinkruse. [Accessed April 29, 2023].

McMahan, G., Pandey, A., & Martinson, B. (2012) *To downsize human capital: a strategic human perspective on the disparate outcomes of downsizing*, in C. Cooper, A. Pandey and J. Quick (eds), *Downsizing: Is less still more?* Cambridge University Press, pp. 134–167.

Maslach, C. & Leiter, M.P. (1997) *The truth about burnout: how organizations cause personal stress and what to do about it.* San Francisco, Calif.: Jossey-Bass.

Piening, E. P., Baluch, A. M., & Salge, T. O. (2013) *The relationship between* employees' perceptions of human resource systems and organizational performance: Examining mediating mechanisms and temporal dynamics. Journal of Applied Psychology, 98(6), p. 926.

Rich, B.L., Lepine, J.A., & Crawford, E.R. (2010) *Job Engagement: Antecedents and Effects on Job Performance.* Academy of Management Journal, 53, pp. 617-635.

Saks, A.M. (2006). *Antecedents and Consequences of Employee Engagement.* Journal of Managerial Psychology, 21, pp. 600-619.

Schaufeli, W., Salanova, M., Gonzalez-Roma, V. & Bakker, A.B. (2002). *The Measurement of Engagement and Burnout: A Two Sample Confirmatory Factor Analytic Approach.* Journal of Happiness Studies, 3, pp. 71-92.

Schatz, J. & Reilly, R. (2014). Five Ways to Improve Employee Engagement Now. *Gallup Business Journal.* January 7, 2014, Available online: https://www.gallup.com/workplace/231581/five-ways-improve-employee-engagement.aspx. Accessed May 10, 2023.

Truss, C., Alfes, K., Delbridge, R., Shantz, A. & Soane, E. (2014). *Employee Engagement in Theory and Practice.* New York: Routledge.

Horaţiu-Adrian Pop

Should We or Should We Not Monitor Our Software Development Team Members?

EMBA Module: People and Performance: Talent Management in Action

Assignment task: This assignment is a 3000-word people management research case analysis. You will choose an organisation with which you are familiar. You will investigate a critical HR practice implemented by that organisation and its consequences on individual and organisational outcomes. You will use an appropriate theory to critically evaluate and address the identified practical HRM function, and the challenges faced.

Introduction

Employee engagement is an essential factor in the success of any business. It refers to the level of emotional and intellectual commitment that an employee has toward their job and organization (Kahn, 1990). Employees actively involved in their work are more productive, happier professionally, and more likely to stay with the same company for a long time. On the other hand, monitoring employees refers to tracking and measuring their performance and behavior in the workplace. Although monitoring employees can be an effective way of ensuring the achievement of organizational goals, this practice can have negative consequences, such as reducing employee autonomy, increasing stress and anxiety, and leading to feelings of mistrust and violation (Alder et al., 2007).

This paper will examine the relationship between employee engagement and employee monitoring in a software development company. It will examine the impact of monitoring employees on their engagement and provide recommendations on whether and how software development companies should use this practice to promote engagement and overall organizational success.

Context and Framing the Problem

The author has built a case study around a software development company referred to in this paper as SDC due to confidentiality reasons. SDC comprises two major divisions: IT Products and Software Services. After a few acquisitions in the Romanian market by December 2022, the company had surpassed 1,000 employees. The employees work in multiple major cities in Romania and Chisinau, the capital of the Republic of Moldova. According to Mintzberg (1979, pp. 380-430), the software services division was a "divisional" organization with several business units, given that each of these units is specialised in a specific industry and with high operational and decision-making autonomy, supervised by a central core represented by the Executive Director and the CEO. Each business unit covers domains from Automotive, Life Sciences, Travel and Hospitality, Enterprise Solutions, and Fintech. Each business group is led and managed by a Business Group Manager (BGM), who reports to the division's Executive Director, who in turn reports to the CEO.

After two hard years during the COVID-19 pandemic in 2020 and 2021, when the company worked hard to maintain a solid collaboration with its clients and keep its employees engaged in a remote work environment, in late 2022, it was clear that a hybrid work approach would likely become permanent (Iqbal et al., 2021). The upper management of SDC was concerned that clients might worry about the efficiency of the time SDC's employees spend on tasks, given the hourly-based rates in the Time & Materials contracts and the flexible job controls in remote working. They recommended that SDC management explore ways to monitor employees utilizing technology-enabled tools. Their rationale was that if a customer has any queries about the time spent on tasks, the SDC management can provide metrics showing the daily hours spent on hardware and software tools required for the project's software development. A few BGMs reacted promptly, considering the impact on employee engagement by applying such practice in a culture of mutual trust, well-being, job satisfaction, and work-life balance. Considering the company's publicly spoken "Employee first" business motto, they questioned how this monitoring would feel. Before making a final decision, the upper management asked one of the BGMs to experiment with the monitoring tool provided by the IT department to a small number of people to understand what the monitoring software offers and the feelings and opinions of the monitored people. The tool of choice was Cyclope, available at https://www.cyclope-series.com/.

The BGM selected three trustworthy, open-minded people from his team: two software developers and one functional tester. They agreed to test the tool and provide transparent feedback, keeping this matter confidential among the four of them and the IT department. The BGM synchronised with the IT department and the three subjects for monitoring, determining when to install the software and when the monitoring would take place. The tool ran for a whole working week.

The BGM, as monitor, analyzed Cyclope's dashboard to understand what information he could see and what conclusions he could draw. The most important observations were:

The tool sees only 50% of the time as productive time, given the standard monitoring configuration, while performed on known highly productive people.

Each project and collaboration have its specific necessary tools to perform the tasks, resulting in an enormous overhead for each project, team, and person to configure and maintain the used applications, which means productive time.

In web software development, browser applications are among the essential tools for software developers and testers. The standard configuration sees the browser as non-productive, but if you set it as a productive time, then the person can do anything they want in the browser besides work, and data is no longer relevant.

Time spent in meetings is captured as non-productive since the tool doesn't know whether you are in a meeting or just sitting there in front of the computer.

The BGM provided a feedback form to the employees to capture their feelings, thoughts, and possible recommendations about such a practice. They also had full access to the captured information to know what the tool recorded about their activities. Appendix 1 offers a centralised view of the questions and answers from the feedback form, translated from Romanian. As we can see there, all three confirmed that Cyclope does its job and captures all their activity on their working stations. Yet, data categorization is irrelevant to what it is supposed to do because many required actions and tools for their daily duties are marked as non-productive by this tool. The primary aspect of their feedback is the negative message the company would send to its employees about mutual trust. There were also positive points, like the fact that they could see how they spend their time and try to improve their focus, or if they identify a low performer, to be able to monitor that person for a while.

The consequences of this practice have more profound implications for the company and its employees' engagement. We should dig deeper into what Human Resource Management (HRM) literature says about this before making some conclusions and recommendations about what SDC management should do.

HRM Literature Review

Employee Engagement

Many people talk about employee engagement, which sounds good when mentioned in conversations, but Storey (2008, p. 300) says that "many consultants, companies, and researchers have developed their own definitions of engagement, resulting in confusion of meanings and of approaches". Beardwell and Thompson (2017, p.391) say that employee engagement is employees' commitment and involvement in their work and their organization, directly impacting their job satisfaction and personal growth. Engaged staff members are more productive, innovative, and likely to stick with the company (Harter et al., 2003), positively impacting profitability, performance, and client satisfaction. HR managers and line managers in the case of SDC must develop or continue to foster a work environment that supports and stimulates employees to increase their engagement by generating opportunities for personal and professional growth, meaningful recognition, and incentives (Cao et al., 2013) and encouraging open communication and collaboration. Effective communication and the extent to which workers believe their company cares about their development and well-being are among the critical elements, according to Beardwell and Thompson (2017). To do this, a company must offer a secure and healthy work environment, opportunities for professional development, and an ongoing commitment to diversity and inclusion (El-Amin, 2022).

In the software development industry, highly engaged employees are more likely to deliver high-quality software products, stay with the organization long-term, advance their careers, keep up with new technologies, and continuously improve their technical and soft skills. In this sector, employee engagement is critical because it directly impacts on the quality and timeliness of software products. Given the highly competitive labor market, information technology companies go the extra mile to support, train, and retain their employees. According to Gallup (2017), many other sectors, like manufacturing, are behind and need to catch up to the software development sector when talking about the needs and goals of each employee in the company culture. Employees staying long-term in a company have a significant financial impact, considering also the cost of turnover, which is very high in software development. It can take months to train new hires and get them up to speed; therefore, when an employee leaves, the cost can be about 33% of their annual earnings (Agovino, 2019). According to Gallup (2022), Romanian employees are among the most engaged in Europe. This finding suggests that Romanian organizations have created a positive work environment supporting employee engagement. However, it is important to note that employee engagement is dynamic and requires continuous monitoring and improvement to maintain its effectiveness.

Monitoring employees

Software development is a challenging process that requires knowledge, experience, and innovation. Yet, some employers feel they need to monitor their software developers to ensure they are working effectively and efficiently (Pokojski et al., 2022). Electronic monitoring refers to using technology to track and record employee behavior in the workplace, and it has become increasingly prevalent in recent years. Still, this practice is raising many ethical and legal concerns (Moussa, 2015). Keystroke logging, video surveillance, GPS tracking, and Internet monitoring are all examples of monitoring techniques. The latter involves keeping an eye on how employees use social networking sites, email, and the internet to browse the web so that when the analysis is performed by the monitors, they understand how much work-related is.

Employers have a range of reasons for monitoring their employees. Besides productivity and efficiency, another primary reason would be to protect against security threats by monitoring cyberattacks or physical security breaches (Jiang et al., 2020). By monitoring employee activity, employers can identify and address inefficiencies in the workplace. For example, they may identify employees who spend too much time on non-work-related activities, such as social media, and take steps to reduce these distractions. Additionally, monitoring can help employers discover areas where employees could have more training or support. Another reason for monitoring employees is to ensure company policies and regulations compliance (D'Arcy et al., 2009). Employers may monitor their employees to ensure they are not engaging in illegal or unethical behavior, such as stealing company property or engaging in illegal activities. Related to software development, monitoring code reviews could ensure developers follow the coding guidelines and standards and are not introducing vulnerabilities or malicious code into the software, and the list could go on.

Soft and Hard HRM

Soft HR is a people-oriented approach to human resource management that highlights the value of employee engagement, job satisfaction, and work-life balance. Employee development, training and mentorship, recognition programs, and employee feedback systems are examples of soft HR practices in software development. Soft HR seeks to create an environment where employees feel valued and supported. Research has shown that employees who feel valued and supported are prone to be motivated, productive, and committed to their work (Goleman et al., 2013). Creating an enjoyable work environment is an essential aspect of soft HR. This can include giving employees the opportunity to learn and grow, supporting work-life balance, and encouraging teamwork and collaboration (Armstrong and Taylor, 2014, p. 189). Employees who feel valued and supported tend to be motivated and involved in their jobs, resulting in higher productivity and overall company performance.

Hard HR is a traditional method of managing human resources that focuses on managing people as resources or assets, and monitoring employees is an important aspect of this practice. The focus is on achieving measurable outcomes, such as productivity, efficiency, and meeting organizational goals (Armstrong and Taylor, 2014, p. 197). These practices in software development could include performance appraisals, job analysis, job design, and high pay and rewards systems. These practices also aim to ensure that employees meet organizational goals and objectives, and their performance is closely monitored and evaluated. Hard HR methods involve a more complex comprehension and interpretation of cost-cutting methods. For instance, it acknowledges low salaries, limited training, strict supervision, monitoring, evaluation, reward, and deficient productivity levels like labor intensification and downsizing (Beardwell and Claydon, 2007). In hard HRM, the focus is on ensuring that employees have the necessary skills, knowledge, and abilities to carry out their job duties effectively. The approach tends to emphasise objective, measurable criteria for evaluating employee performance and productivity and is often associated with a more authoritarian management style.

Pros and Cons

Pros

A software development business like SDC may benefit from monitoring personnel in a few ways, including increased security, better work quality, and increased productivity:

Internet monitoring can help SDC detect and prevent security breaches, such as cyberattacks or data breaches, which can protect sensitive information and prevent financial losses (Jiang et al.,

2020). A survey by IBM found that for companies that experienced data breaches in 2020, 21% of them were caused by employees or contractors, and the average ransomware attack cost was USD 4.54 million (IBM, 2022, p.32). Monitoring can help identify potential security risks and prevent data breaches by monitoring employee activity and detecting unusual behavior.

Ball (2021, p.71) argues that electronic monitoring can improve productivity and efficiency by providing real-time data on employee performance and identifying areas where SDC management can act to improve. Organizational internet monitoring can help reduce non-work-related internet usage, increase productivity and diminish the time wasted on non-work activities (Jiang et al., 2020).

Ball (2021, p.33) and Jiang et al. (2020) agree that monitoring internet activities can help organizations like SDC ensure compliance with regulations, such as data protection or comply with ISO certification and GDPR, which can mitigate legal risks.

Cons

Given the pros above, monitoring software developers might seem like a good idea, but many aspects contradict this statement, and some are a real concern regarding employee engagement. The most important are:

Monitoring software developers has some serious downsides, including, probably the most important one, the potential employees' loss of trust in the company. Employees may start to believe that their employer doesn't trust them if they feel like they are being monitored (Jiang et al., 2020). Employee morale and productivity may suffer since they could feel less motivated to complete their work. Additionally, keeping an eye on software developers may be perceived as violating their privacy (Alder et al., 2007), which could further damage the relationship of trust between the company and employees.

Depending on the configuration of monitoring, this practice may negatively affect the autonomy and creativity of the employees, as well as conceptions of procedural, distributive, and privacy fairness (Ball, 2021), leading to decreased job satisfaction, lower motivation, and higher turnover rates (Jiang et al., 2020).

Alder et al. (2007) argue that monitoring can have unintended consequences, such as increased employee stress or anxiety, resulting in decreased mental well-being. Employees may become distracted and spend more time worrying about their work habits than doing their work, or they may be less likely to take risks or try out new ideas.

Internet monitoring software is not always accurate and can generate false positives (Ball, 2021), leading to misunderstandings and mistrust between employees and management or raising ethical concerns about employees' rights.

Recommendations and Conclusions

SDC needs to thoroughly evaluate the potential negative consequences of employee monitoring on future employee engagement within the organization and determine whether the advantages of doing so outweigh the negative impact on long-lasting company culture, "Employee first".

Ball (2021) recommends using electronic monitoring only for legitimate business purposes and avoiding invasive or unnecessary monitoring that could create a sense of mistrust and undermine employee morale. As suggested by one employee in Appendix 1, SDC should electronically monitor a potential low performer, but only after being transparent with that particular person and trying other soft methods to bring them back on a standard professional path. Or, as another one said, let employees monitor as they want on their own to improve themselves. If SDC management concludes to monitor all their employees, Ball (2021) emphasises the importance of developing explicit policies and procedures for electronic monitoring that the company communicates to employees, being fully transparent, and respecting their rights to privacy and autonomy (Alder et al., 2007).

Instead of monitoring employees, SDC should focus more on soft HRM practices and not change its people-oriented company culture. It should continue building trust through communication and collaboration, maintaining a positive work environment, and increasing well-being and productivity. SDC management should provide clear expectations for all its IT professionals and regular feedback on their work, helping employees understand what the company expects from them and helping them stay focused on their work. Provide training to improve all employees' skills and abilities, as Guest (1997) emphasised in his research. SDC managers can use metrics to evaluate the performance of software developers and testers without monitoring them directly. Metrics can include things like the number of bugs generated, fixed, found, or time spent on tasks, so that managers can understand how their team members perform without invading their privacy. Software development is a complex and challenging process that needs a high level of commitment from all team members. SDC cannot achieve this high employee commitment without being highly compatible with its employees' values (Meyer et al., 2004).

According to Collins (2021, p. 60), the stories people tell and retell about the company greatly impact organizational culture and people's thoughts, feelings, and actions both inside and outside the company. So, what would the new stories say about SDC once monitoring its employees starts? The author judges that monitoring employees would trigger negative stories about SDC with a high impact on all employees, but also on future recruitment for the company, given that this practice is missing in all other major competitors of SDC in the labor market.

References

Agovino, T. (2019). *To Have and to Hold*. [online] SHRM. Available at: https://www.shrm.org/hr-today/news/all-things-work/Pages/to-have-and-to-hold.aspx. (Accessed: 15 April 2023)

Alder, G.S., Schminke, M., Noel, T.W. and Kuenzi, M. (2007). Employee Reactions to Internet Monitoring: The Moderating Role of Ethical Orientation. *Journal of Business Ethics*, 80(3), pp.481–498. Available at: https://doi.org/10.1007/s10551-007-9432-2. (Accessed: 27 April 2023)

Armstrong, M. and Taylor, S. (2014). *Armstrong's handbook of human resource management practice*. 13th ed. Philadelphia, Pa: Kogan Page Ltd.

Ball, K. (2021) *Electronic monitoring and surveillance in the workplace: literature review and policy recommendations*. Luxembourg: Publications Office of the European Union. Available at: https://publications.jrc.ec.europa.eu/repository/handle/JRC125716. (Accessed: 23 April 2023)

Beardwell, J. and Claydon, T. (2007). *Human resource management: a contemporary approach*. Harlow, England; New York: Prentice Hall Financial Times.

Beardwell, J. and Thompson, A. (2017). *Human Resource Management: a Contemporary Approach*. 8th ed. Harlow: Pearson

Cao, Z., Chen, J. and Song, Y. (2013). Does Total Rewards Reduce the Core Employees' Turnover Intention? *International Journal of Business and*

Management, [online] 8(20). Available at: https://doi.org/10.5539/ijbm.v8n20p62. (Accessed: 21 April 2023)

Collins, D. (2021). *Rethinking Organizational Culture*. Routledge.

D'Arcy, J., Hovav, A. and Galletta, D. (2009). User Awareness of Security Countermeasures and Its Impact on Information Systems Misuse: A Deterrence Approach. *Information Systems Research*, 20(1), pp.79–98. Available at: https://doi.org/10.1287/isre.1070.0160. (Accessed: 4 April 2023)

El-Amin, A. (2022). FHSU Scholars Repository FHSU Scholars Repository Management Faculty Publications Management. [online] Available at: https://doi.org/10.4018/978-1-7998-8479-8.ch010. (Accessed: 14 April 2023)

Guest, D.E. (1997). Human resource management and performance: a review and research agenda. *The International Journal of Human Resource Management*, [online] 8(3), pp.263–276. Available at: https://doi.org/10.1080/095851997341630. (Accessed: 24 April 2023)

Harter, J.K., Schmidt, F.L. and Keyes, C.L.M. (2003). Well-being in the workplace and its relationship to business outcomes: A review of the Gallup studies. *Flourishing: Positive psychology and the life well-lived.*, pp.205–224. Available at: https://doi.org/10.1037/10594-009. (Accessed: 24 April 2023)

Iqbal, K.M.J., Khalid, F. and Barykin, S.Y. (2021). Hybrid Workplace. *Handbook of Research on Future Opportunities for Technology Management Education*, [online] pp.28–48. Available at: https://doi.org/10.4018/978-1-7998-8327-2.ch003. (Accessed: 4 May 2023)

Jiang, H., Tsohou, A., Siponen, M. and Li, Y. (2020). Examining the side effects of organizational Internet monitoring on employees. *Internet Research*, ahead-of-print(ahead-of-print). Available at: https://doi.org/10.1108/intr-08-2019-0360. (Accessed: 12 April 2023)

Gallup (2017). *State of the global workplace.* New York, NY: Gallup Press. Available at: https://www.slideshare.net/adrianboucek/state-of-the-global-workplace-gallup-report-2017. (Accessed: 15 April 2023)

Gallup (2022). *State of the global workplace.* Available at: https://www.gallup.com/workplace/349484/state-of-the-global-workplace-2022-report.aspx. (Accessed: 15 April 2023)

Goleman, D., Boyatzis, R.E. and Mckee, A. (2013). *Primal leadership: Learning to lead with emotional intelligence*. Boston, Mass.: Harvard Business School Press.

IBM (2022). *Cost of a Data Breach Report 2022 2*. [online] Available at: https://www.ibm.com/downloads/cas/3R8N1DZJ. (Accessed: 19 April 2023)

Kahn, W.A. (1990). Psychological conditions of personal engagement and disengagement at work. *Academy of Management Journal*, 33(4), pp. 692–724. Available at: https://www.jstor.org/stable/256287. (Accessed: 12 April 2023)

Meyer, J.P., Becker, T.E. and Vandenberghe, C. (2004). Employee Commitment and Motivation: A Conceptual Analysis and Integrative Model. *Journal of Applied Psychology*, 89(6), pp.991–1007. Available at: https://doi.org/10.1037/0021-9010.89.6.991. (Accessed: 26 April 2023)

Mintzberg, H. (1979). *The structuring of organizations*. Englewood Cliffs, N.J.: Prentice-Hall.

Moussa, M. (2015). Monitoring Employee Behavior Through the Use of Technology and Issues of Employee Privacy in America. *SAGE Open*, 5(2), p.215824401558016. Available at: https://doi.org/10.1177/2158244015580168. (Accessed: 29 April 2023)

Pokojski, Z., Kister, A. and Lipowski, M. (2022). Remote Work Efficiency from the Employers' Perspective—What's Next? *Sustainability*, 14(7), p.4220. Available at: https://doi.org/10.3390/su14074220. (Accessed: 29 April 2023)

Storey, J., Wright, P. and Ulrich, D. eds., (2008). Chapter: Employee Engagement. *The Routledge Companion to Strategic Human Resource Management*. [online] Routledge. Available at: https://doi.org/10.4324/9780203889015 (Accessed: 30 April 2023)

Annexes

Appendix 1

Feedback form

Please fill out this brief feedback form about your recent experience with Cyclope.

1. What do you think about Cyclope as a monitoring tool?

Answers:
- Software Developer 1: *"It does its job quite well. The margin of error must be set at Idle Time when reading the reports. It considers you idle after a minute, so you end up seeing in the report that you were idle for quite a while, even if you were in a meeting. Otherwise, it's cool; it's not intrusive."*
- Software Developer 2: *"From what I've seen, it does what the IT people say. It records the active windows and groups the information as productive, neutral, or distractive. You can see which sites you have entered, and depending on the messenger application, maybe also with whom you are chatting, if the person's name appears in the window's title."*
- Functional Tester: *"It sees Skype and Teams as productive activities (which is okay, taking into account that Skype and Teams and other apps of the sort are the links that keep the team and projects cohesive in cases of WFH), but the web application I work on is a neutral activity, Jira is neutral, other applications that I need for the main app are also neutral, and if I look at Desktop, that's a distracting activity. It doesn't see everything well... it gave me some name that has nothing to do with reality for a .net domain where I would have stayed for 1 hour... but I don't understand what it is referring to. Besides all that, it's interesting to see what consumed the most of your time that day."*

2. How would you feel working in a company while being monitored with tools like Cyclope?

Answers:

- Software Developer 1: *"Personally, I have nothing against it, but for sure, most of the team will strongly disagree with it. Some might even leave the company."*
- Software developer 2: *"I'd leave!"*
- Functional Tester: *"It is absurd and dangerous to demand such things, dangerous for the employee's mental health, but also for the company's – imposing the use of such an application comes with the ideas of mistrust and distrust that won't forge no solid and healthy connection + people will talk and will leave if such a measure is to become a standard (some will leave, some will get used to it, some will stay and will hate it)."*

3. Would you recommend using Cyclope to be used? If yes, please provide more details.

Answers:

- Software Developer 1: *"I'd say no, but maybe it would be useful to monitor low-performers, hoping they can correctly do their job again."*
- Software developer 2: *"No."*
- Functional Tester: *"Absolutely not!!! Discussions with – Software Developer 1 – using the Cyclope as the last measure to recover a low performer -> The idea sounds good in the books, but in practice, I don't think it can bring many benefits. A man put against the wall (as such a low-performer would be, I imagine) will either step up his game, and this thing will be obvious (colleagues will see, the team lead will see, the PO will see, Jira will see, you'll see), without the need for any other coercive measure, he will install this application, open the appropriate applications nicely and move the mouse all day long, without really doing anything -> Cyclope will say that our man is efficient and productive, colleagues will know that it is not so."*

Andrei–Adrian Racu

The Company Information Technology – Software services Financial Analysis

EMBA Module: Finance and Accounting for Business

Assignment task: Assess the financial performance of a listed company of your choice. Produce a written research report, basing your analysis on the company's most recent financial reports (for the past 3 years) using the financial ratios discussed during the module.

Company Overview

The IT Company (the Company) is a prominent IT company in Romania and is the most important technology company listed on the Romanian Stock Exchange.

Since its start in 1998 as an IT outsourcing entity, the Company has witnessed consistent growth. Presently, the Company boasts software development teams and offices spanning nine nations in Europe, America, and Asia. Furthermore, the Company also possesses a portfolio of software products that find application in enterprises across Central Eastern Europe and Asia.

More than 75% of its earnings are derived from service-related activities, encompassing the development of integrated software solutions. Approximately 20% of its income is from product sales, primarily in fleet management and enterprise software. The remaining portion of its revenue is derived from software integration and hardware resale. Notably, the Company excels in developing embedded software for the automotive sector, a highly profitable segment characterised by enduring client partnerships. Additionally, the Company has leveraged M&A to extend its expertise into the aerospace and life science domains.

In October 2021, the Company raised approx. 15 mil EUR, in a private placement on Romania's AeRO Market, and will be transferred to the Main Market of Bucharest Stock Exchange in September, 2023.

Since its initial public offering in late 2021, the Company has unveiled nine acquisitions, strategically assembling development teams primarily located in Romania. This strategic move reflects their confidence in the rising demand for increasingly intelligent and "autonomous" systems across various industries.

Industry overview and competitive positioning

Romania's information technology (IT) sector stands out as one of the most dynamic segments in the country. According to Wood & Company (2023), from 2015 to 2021, it exhibited a Compound Annual Growth Rate (CAGR) of approximately 17% in terms of Gross Value Added (GVA) in EUR, totaling around EUR 11.2 billion. This accounted for 4.6% of the country's GDP. GVA growth during this period ranked second only to the healthcare sector, with a growth rate of around 18%, significantly surpassing the country's average of 7.6%.

Compared to our group of similar Central and Southeastern European (CEE/SEE) peers, including Portugal, approximately 7% of Romanian college graduates have pursued studies in Information Technology and Communications (ITC). Furthermore, the proportion of young individuals (aged 15-34 years) with ITC qualifications in the Romanian workforce is notably substantial, standing at 79% compared to the peer median of approximately 72%. This suggests that graduates tend to remain in their home country for employment opportunities.

With a workforce that ranks as the second largest in the region, numbering 7.7 million at the end of 2022 (second only to Poland's 16.3 million), the Romanian IT market naturally possesses a critical mass.

Finally, the competitive wages offered in the Romanian IT sector give The Company a good positioning in customer negotiations. In 2020, the average annual salary in this sector was EUR 27.2k, nearly 20% lower than that of regional peers and 56% below the EU27 average. This wage structure likely contributes to the sector's high relative profitability.

In its historical trajectory, the company initially concentrated its efforts on the automotive sector. However, it has since broadened its horizons, venturing into the life sciences, aerospace, marine electronic systems, and securing new automotive contracts, all achieved through recent M&A. Since becoming publicly listed, the Company has made significant strides with nine acquisitions. This strategic move reflects their confidence in the increasing demand for more intelligent and autonomous systems.

In September 2023, the company's stock is scheduled to transition to the Bucharest Stock Exchange's primary market, where it is expected to rank among the most extensive listings initiated by entrepreneur-founders. Furthermore, the CEO and principal shareholder have publicly expressed intentions to create a Secondary Public Offering (SPO) in the months ahead, to raise funds for further acquisition.

Financial Analysis

3.1 Activity Ratio

3.1.1 Days of Sales Outstanding (DSO)

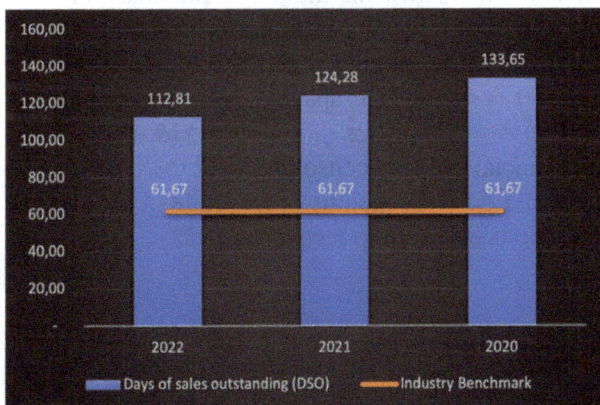

Figure 1. Days of Sales Outstanding

The Days of Sales Outstanding (DSO) ratio improved significantly from 133.65 in 2020 to 112.81 in 2022. This reduction indicates a more efficient accounts receivable management, although it still exceeds the industry benchmark of 61.67, suggesting room for further optimization in cash flow and customer credit policies.

3.1.2 Total Asset Turnover

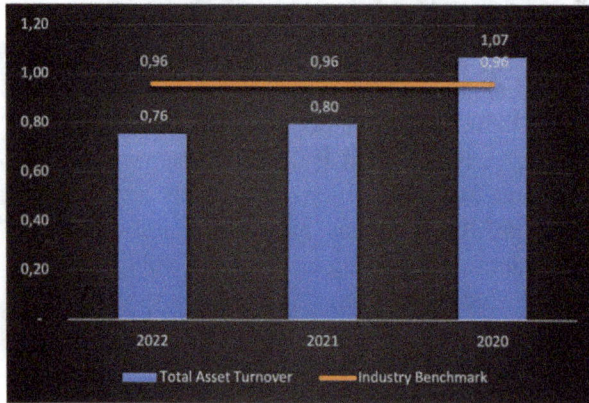

Figure 2. Total Asset Turnover

The company's Total Asset Turnover decreased from 1.07 in 2020 to 0.76 in 2022, indicating a decline in its ability to generate sales from its assets. This falls below the industry benchmark of 0.96, suggesting potential inefficiencies in asset utilization that may require attention to improve profitability and operational efficiency.

Nevertheless, this is not The Company's case, considering that in 2022, it acquired two companies through the M&A processes, and the current financial position consolidates all the functions on the balance sheet and only six months of Revenue in the Income Statement. This ratio is expected to recover in 2023.

3.1.3 Fixed Asset Turnover

The Fixed Asset Turnover ratio declined from 3.59 in 2020 to 1.57 in 2022, signaling a decreased efficiency in generating revenue from its fixed assets. This figure must meet the industry benchmark of 2.48, highlighting the potential underutilization of assets that warrants evaluation and optimization for enhanced operational performance.

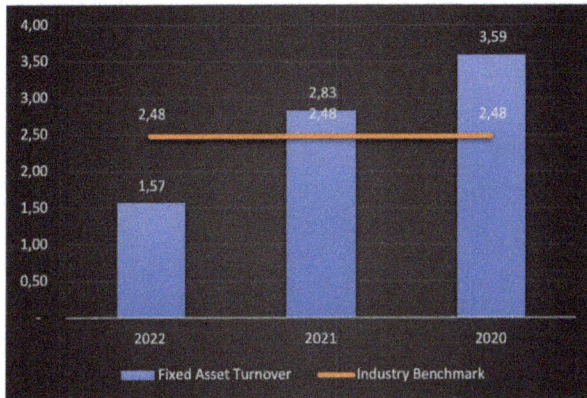

Figure 3. Fixed Asset Turnover

Also, this ratio is heavily influenced by the M&A Processes, considering a 290% increase in Fixed Assets Value in 2022 vs 2020 and only a 70% increase in Revenue during the same period.

3.1.4 Working Capital Turnover

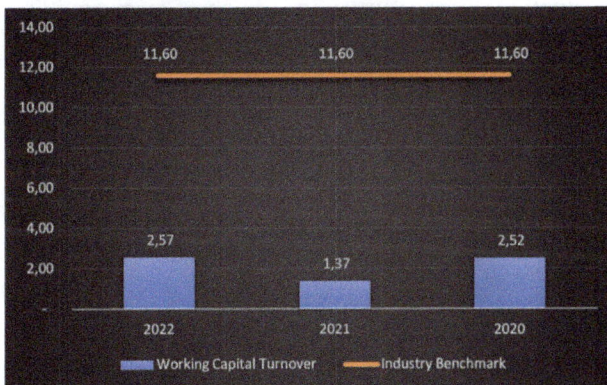

Figure 4. Working Capital Turnover

The company's Working Capital Turnover ratio increased from 2.52 in 2020 to 2.57 in 2022, indicating a modest improvement in its ability to generate revenue relative to its working capital. However, this figure remains notably lower than the industry benchmark 11.6, suggesting potential opportunities for more efficient capital utilization.

3.2 Liquidity Ratios

3.2.1 Current Ratio

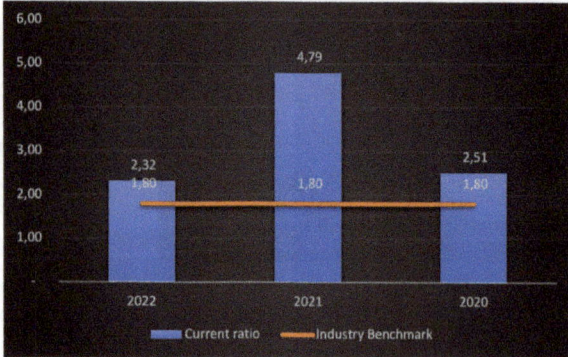

Figure 5. Current Ratio

The company's Current Ratio showed fluctuations over two years, declining from 2.51 in 2020 to 2.32 in 2022, with an unusual spike at 4.79 in 2021. While it remains above the industry benchmark of 1.80, these fluctuations suggest variations in short-term liquidity. It's essential to analyze the factors behind these changes to maintain a healthy balance between assets and liabilities.

3.2.2 Quick Ratio

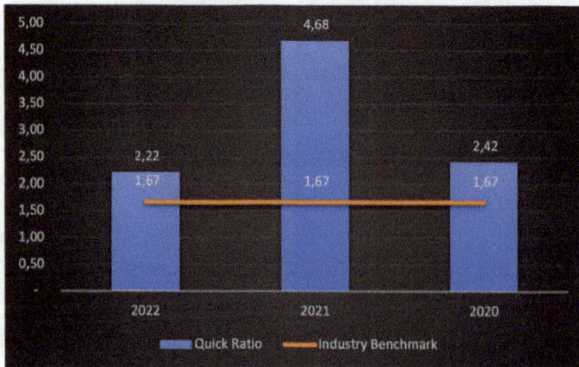

Figure 6. Quick Ratio

The Quick Ratio displayed variations over three years, dropping from 2.42 in 2020 to 2.22 in 2022, with an unusual spike at 4.68 in 2021. Although it consistently outperforms the industry benchmark of 1.67, these fluctuations suggest potential challenges in meeting short-term obligations. A closer examination of these anomalies can help ensure continued financial stability and liquidity management.

Considering that The Company's principal activity is software services and analyzing the current and quick ratios, we can conclude that the business does not hold high-value inventories compared to its Total Current Assets.

3.3 Solvency Ratios

3.3.1 Debt to Equity Ratio

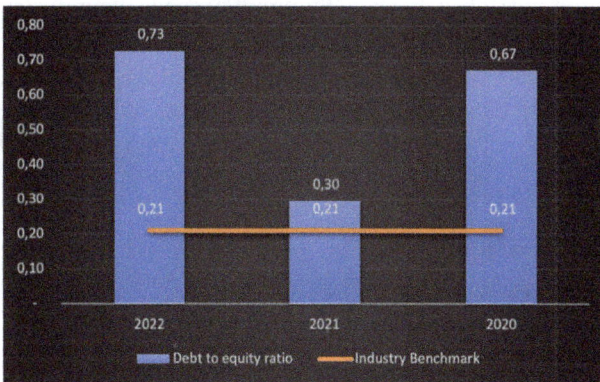

Figure 7. Debt to Equity Ratio

The Debt-to-Equity Ratio increased from 0.67 in 2020 to 0.73 in 2022, indicating a rise in its reliance on debt relative to equity. Despite this increase, it remains significantly higher than the industry benchmark of 0.21, suggesting a comparatively higher debt burden that may warrant closer scrutiny and debt management efforts.

3.3.2 Debt to Assets Ratio

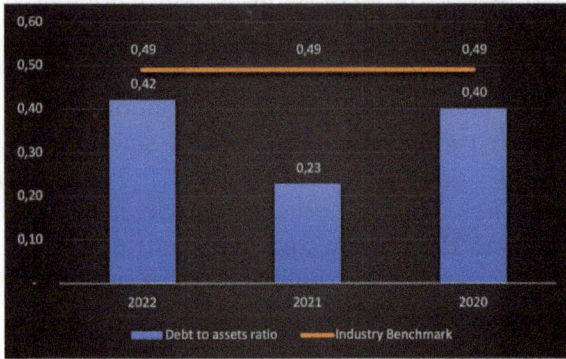

Figure 8. Debt to Assets Ratio

The company's Debt-to-Assets Ratio showed slight fluctuations over three years, rising from 0.40 in 2020 to 0.42 in 2022, with a notable deviation of 0.23 in 2021. Although it exceeds the industry benchmark of 0.21, these variations suggest changing financial leverage. Careful monitoring and analyzing these shifts are essential to maintain a healthy balance between debt and assets for long-term financial stability.

3.3.3 Financial Leverage Ratio

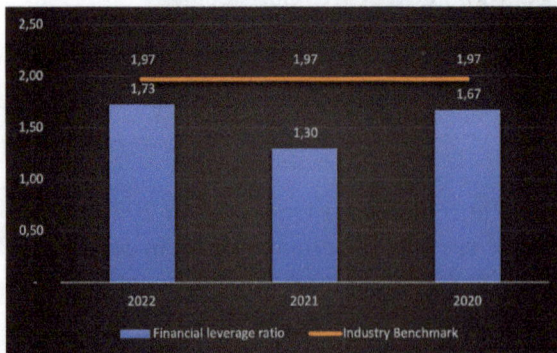

Figure 9. Financial Leverage Ratio

The company's Financial Leverage Ratio increased from 1.67 in 2020 to 1.73 in 2022, indicating a moderate rise in its reliance on debt to finance operations. Despite this increase, it remains below the industry benchmark of 1.97, suggesting a comparatively lower financial risk and debt exposure.

3.4 Profitability Ratios

3.4.1 Net Profit Margin

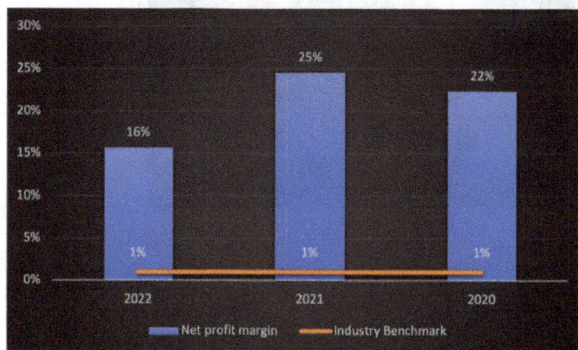

Figure 10. Net Profit Margin

The company's Net Profit Margin decreased from 22% in 2020 to 16% in 2022, reflecting reduced profitability. The declining trend may indicate the need to control costs and enhance operational efficiency to maintain healthy profit margins in the long run. One contributing factor to the profit decrease is the implementation of an Employee Stock Ownership Plan (ESOP), reducing the net profit available for shareholders. On the other hand, this program is expected to increase loyalty and commitment and help the stability of the business, with the employees being the most important asset of The Company.

3.4.2 Operating Profit Margin

The Operating Profit Margin decreased from 26% in 2020 to 18% in 2022, signaling a reduction in profitability from core operations. The main category that led to this decrease, according to THE COMPANY's Annual Report, is the direct employee costs. While still well above the industry benchmark of 3%, this decline may prompt a closer evaluation of cost management and revenue strategies to maintain a healthy margin.

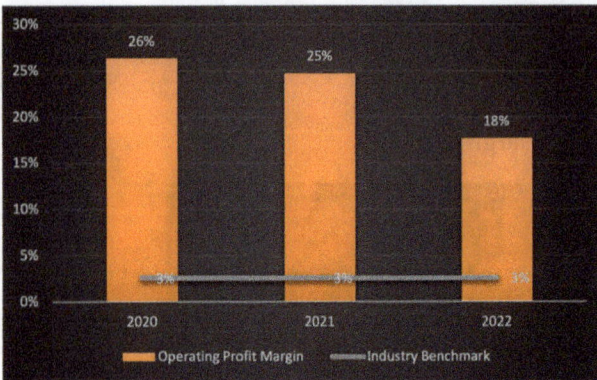

Figure 11. Operating Profit Margin

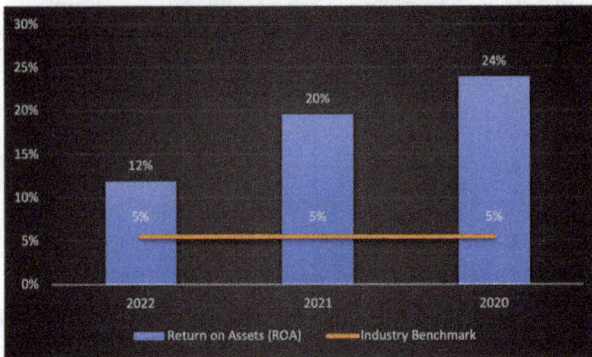

Figure 12. Return on Assets

3.4.3 Return on assets (ROA)

This ratio, Return on Assets, declined from 24% in 2020 to 12% in 2022, indicating a reduced ability to generate profits from its assets. Despite the decrease, it significantly outperforms the industry benchmark of 0.42%, suggesting that the company still efficiently utilises its assets for profitability, although at a lower rate than before.

Figure 13. Return on Equity

3.4.4 Return on equity (ROE)

The company's Return on Equity (ROE) declined from a robust 40% in 2020 to 20% in 2022, indicating a reduced ability to generate shareholder returns. Despite the decrease, it remains significantly higher than the industry benchmark of 2.25%, suggesting continued strength in leveraging equity for profitability, albeit at a lower rate.

3.5 Valuation Ratios

3.5.1 P/E & P/S

The company's P/E ratio saw a marginal increase, rising from 15.63 in 2020 to 15.74 in 2022. This indicates a relatively stable valuation over this period. However, compared to the industry benchmark of 27.63, the company remains undervalued in terms of earnings potential. On the other hand, its P/S ratio declined from 3.5 in 2020 to 2.47 in 2022. This suggests a drop in market price relative to sales, which might signify a reduced revenue outlook.

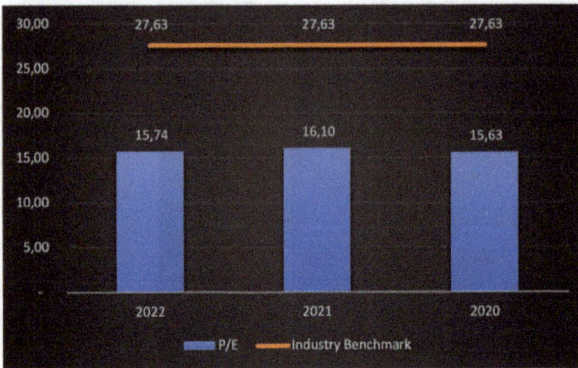

Figure 13. P/E

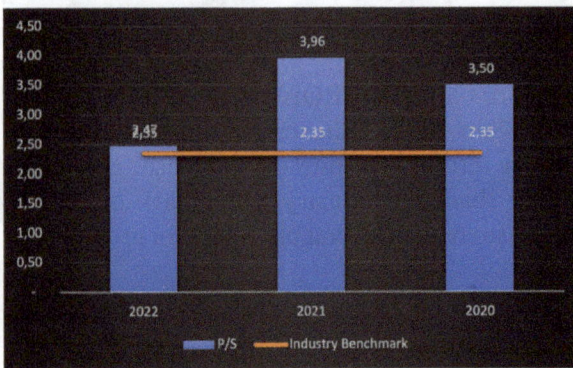

Figure 14. P/S

Still, the company fares slightly better than the industry benchmark of 2.35 for P/S. These metrics collectively suggest the potential for improved profitability but challenges in revenue growth.

Investment Risks

One major risk that the IT Sector is currently facing in Romania is that the government is considering eliminating the tax exception, 10% income tax, for this industry. This will put pressure on the employers to cover the gap in the employees' earnings and, by doing so, increase the company's personnel expense, reducing profitability.

The automotive industry's trend toward in-house software

development may decrease the demand for external suppliers like the Company. This could lead to a company's revenue decline if it cannot adapt to changing customer needs.

Despite a small increase, the Company's P/E ratio has yet to show significant growth. This could indicate earnings volatility or market uncertainty, which can be a risk for investors.

Ultimately, investor sentiment exerts a substantial influence on stock performance. If the Company doesn't effectively communicate its ability to adapt to the changing IT industry landscape, it may face negative sentiment, affecting its stock price.

Environmental, social, and governance

According to the Company's 2022 Annual Report, the company intends to publish a sustainability report by the end of 2023.

Until then, the company had different environmental initiatives in 2022:

- Multiple planting actions are close to Cluj-Napoca, with more than 5,000 trees being planted.
- Energy-saving policies and minimal use of paper.
- Fight for Your Green Cause 2022, internal competition for Green Cause ambassadors
- The company also supports initiatives for the next generation:
- Innovation Labs
- FIX Cluj-Napoca – backing the local entrepreneurship initiative.
- Sustain the Project Management in the IT program and the IoT Lab at Babes Bolyai University.
- Technical articles competition – Writers of the Company
- the Company XMAN Romania – Sports competition

The Company software offerings, including TrackGPS and SASFleet for fleet management, Optimall Logistic for optimizing distribution and production operations, assist companies in achieving fuel efficiency, reducing their carbon footprint, and optimizing routes.

The Company will add two more members to the already existing board of directors in preparation for the transfer to the Main Market of the Bucharest Stock Exchange.

Besides the board of directors, the Company has an advisory

board with three members, an authorised capital market consultant, and a financial auditor, as part of the company's corporate governance.

Conclusions

The company's financial analysis reveals several key points for investors to consider. While specific ratios fluctuate and decrease, they remain above industry benchmarks. The Days of Sales Outstanding (DSO) ratio, Total Asset Turnover, and Fixed Asset Turnover may be temporarily impacted by recent mergers and acquisitions, with expectations for recovery. Liquidity ratios, including the Current and Quick Ratios, are generally healthy, indicating efficient management of short-term assets. Solvency ratios indicate a higher reliance on debt, but it remains manageable. Profitability ratios have decreased, partly due to ESOP, but employee loyalty and stability are expected to benefit. The company exhibits potential but requires careful monitoring, especially post-M&A, to mitigate risks.

Reference list

The IT Company (2022). *2021 Annual Report.* [online] Available at: https://The Company.com/wp-content/uploads/2022/05/THE COMPANY_20220531191449_2021-Annual-Report.pdf [Accessed 25 Aug. 2023].

The IT Company(2023a). *2022 Annual Report.* [online] Available at: https://The Company.com/wp-content/uploads/2023/05/THE COMPANY_20230428181505_EN-THE COMPANY-2022-Annual-Report.pdf [Accessed 1 Sep. 2023].

The IT Company(2023b). *The Company Grup – Situatii financiare consolidate Întocmite în conformitate cu Standardele Internaționale de Raportare adoptate de Uniunea Europeană.* [online] Available at: https://The Company.com/wp-content/uploads/2023/07/The Company-conso-IFRS-December-2022-RO.pdf [Accessed 1 Sep. 2023].

BRK Financial Group (2023). *Raport THE COMPANY Transilvania Software (THE COMPANY) – Initiere acoperire.* [online] Available at: https://www.brk.ro/documente/analize/The Company_initiere_acoperire.pdf [Accessed 4 Sep. 2023].

Bvb.ro. (2023). *BVB – Actiuni THE COMPANY THE COMPANY TRANSILVANIA SOFTWARE.* [online] Available at: https://bvb.ro/FinancialInstruments/ Details/FinancialInstrumentsDetails.aspx?s=The Company [Accessed 11 Sep. 2023].

Wood & Company (2023). *THE COMPANY Transilvania Software Buy Initiation of coverage Rolling up IT development in Romania.* [online] Available at: https://bvbresearch.ro/api/reports/225/attachment [Accessed 25 Aug. 2023].

WSJ. (n.d.). *OSP2 | USU Software AG Stock Price & News.* [online] Available at: https://www.wsj.com/market-data/quotes/XE/XETR/OSP2?mod=quote_ search [Accessed 27 Aug. 2023].

www.gurufocus.com. (n.d.). *USU Software AG (XTER: OSP2) Stock Price, Trades & News | GuruFocus.* [online] Available at: https://www.gurufocus.com/stock/ XTER:OSP2/summary [Accessed 30 Aug. 2023].

Appendix

Appendix 1

Consolidated Balance Sheet – The Company

Consolidated Balance Sheet - AROBS Group			
RON '000	2022	2021	2020
Goodwill	57.763	12.286	775
Other intagible assets	93.318	28.487	21.077
Fixed Assets	19.626	9.045	7.798
Right of use assets for leased assets	12.170	12.147	15.764
Financial Fixed Assets	5.359	1.800	1.854
Deferred Taxes	3.131	2.176	1.930
Total Non-current assets	191.368	65.940	49.199
Inventories	8.923	4.024	4.191
Trade and other receivables	92.660	63.530	64.725
Prepayments	1.947	1.824	1.189
Short-term investments	523	-	-
Cash and Cash equivalents	101.374	102.213	46.401
Total current assets	205.427	171.591	116.507
Held for sale	-	(2.898)	(296)
Total Assets	396.795	234.633	165.409
Share capital	91.139	45.570	100
Issue premium	23.185	68.755	-
Legal Reserves	5.114	2.754	353
Own shares	(7.536)	(4.010)	-
Retained earnings	116.465	73.423	102.400
Other	1.431	(5.453)	(3.570)
Equity Attributable to shareholders	229.799	181.039	99.282
Minority Interests	(76)	58	(312)
Total Equity	229.723	181.098	98.970
Trade and other payables	1.304	5.251	203
Lease debts	7.694	8.620	11.836
Bank loans	55.381	-	2.191
Deferred income tax liabilities	13.078	2.787	2.253
Advance income	801	689	636
Subsidies	185	382	771
Total Long-term liabilities	78.442	17.729	17.891
Trade and other payables	35.804	15.863	12.190
Tax liabilities	235	154	1.199
Lease debts	6.138	5.239	5.201
Bank loans	18.471	2.227	19.067
Dividends payable	667	662	662
Advance income	10.798	10.052	6.502
Subsidies	424	392	394
Provisions	16.093	1.217	1.214
Total short-term liabilities	88.630	35.806	46.430
Held for sale	-	-	2.119
Total Liabilities	167.072	53.535	66.440
Total equity and liabilities	396.795	234.633	165.410
Check	(0)	0	(0)
Number of shares ('000)	911.395	455.697	455.697

https://arobs.com/wp-content/uploads/2023/07/Arobs-conso-IFRS-December-2022-RO.pdf

Appendix 2

Consolidated Income Statement – The Company

Consolidated Income Statement - AROBS Group		
RON '000	2022	2021
Software services revenue	240.119	128.538
Software Products	58.696	48.874
Revenue from the distribution of goods	785	8.315
Other services	215	857
Total Revenues	299.816	186.583
Cost of Sales from software services	164.641	84.713
Cost of sales from software products	27.971	21.376
Cost of distribution of goods	1.446	7.270
Cost of selling other services	207	45
Cost of goods sold	194.265	113.404
Sales and Marketing expenses	8.977	7.477
Admin and general expenses	41.453	18.607
Other revenues/expenses	1.939	907
Operating Profit	53.182	46.189
Financial Income / (expenses) net	82	2.790
Income from Associates	-	2.907
Profit before tax / EBT	53.264	51.886
Income tax	(6.195)	(5.966)
Profit / (Loss) on holdings held for sale	-	(71)
Net profit	47.069	45.850

Consolidated Income Statement - AROBS Group	
RON '000	2020
Production Sold	157.931
Revenue from sale of goods	16.014
Revenue related to the cost of production in progress	(395)
Revenue from the production of intangible and tangible assets	2.404
Trade discounts granted	(841)
Revenue from operating subsidies	182
Other operating income	1.465
Total Revenues	176.761
Expenditure on raw materials and consumables	1.386
Other materials expenses	1.109
Other external expenses (including utilities)	1.383
Expenditure of goods	10.728
Trade discounts received	(287)
Staff expenditure	57.657
Adjustments of tangible and intangible assets	6.141
Adjustments on current assets	139
Other operating expenses	51.450
Adjustments relating to provisions	431
Operating Profit (EBIT)	46.624
Financial Income / (expenses) net	(246)
Profit before tax / EBT	46.378
Income tax	6.811
Net profit	39.567

The Consolidated Income Statement for 2020 is prepared under the Romanian Accounting Standards and in a different format. This is the only Consolidated Income Statement available as of December 31, 2020.

The differences between the Consolidated Income Statement prepared under IFRS for 2021-2022 and the one under RAS (Romanian Accounting Standards) are insignificant; for this reason, I choose to use the data for 2020 in the financial analysis.

Appendix 3

Consolidated Cash Flow Statement – The Company

Consolidated Cash flow statement - AROBS Group		
RON '000	2022	2021
Earnings before taxes	53.264	51.815
Depreciation	16.883	10.359
Benefits granted to SOP employees	3.977	229
Impairments and provisions	8.905	2.521
Interest charges and other financial costs	1.114	472
Interest income and other financial income	(1.969)	(1.589)
Other items	(740)	(1.028)
Operating profit before changes in working capital	81.435	62.779
Change in trade receivables and other receivables	(37.101)	421
Change in trade inventories	(3.977)	548
Change in trade and other payables	42.189	9.461
Change in accrued expenses	(122)	(635)
Change in accrued income	858	3.604
Interest paid	(1.114)	(472)
Interest received	3.561	97
Operating cash generated	85.728	75.801
Income tax paid	(6.276)	(4.920)
Net cash from operating activities	79.452	70.881
Loans (granted)/repaid to affiliates	(1.343)	55
Acquisitions of goodwill	(45.477)	(11.510)
Acquisitions of tangible and intangible assets	(92.357)	(15.076)
(Acquisition)/Sale of own shares	(3.526)	(4.010)
Other investments in financial assets	(523)	-
Proceeds from dividends/financial investments	(2.893)	484
Net cash from investment activities	(146.120)	(30.057)
Proceeds from the share issue	1.810	74.231
Collection/(Repayment) of bank loans	71.625	(19.032)
Payment of debts related to financial leasing	(7.607)	(5.948)
Dividends paid / received	-	(34.263)
Net cash from financing activities	65.829	14.988
Change in cash and cash equivalents	(839)	55.812
Cash and Cash equivalents at the beginning of the financial year	102.213	46.401
Cash and Cash equivalents at the end of the financial year	101.374	102.213

The Company does not have a public Cash Flow Statement as of December 31, 2020.

Appendix 4

Main Financial Ratios

MAIN FINANCIAL RATIOS							
1. Activity Ratios				31.12.2022	31.12.2021	31.12.2020	Industry Benchmark
1.1	Receivables Turnover	=	$\dfrac{\text{Revenue}}{\text{Average Receivables}}$	3,24	2,94	2,73	5,92
	Days of sales outstanding (DSO)	=	$\dfrac{365}{\text{Receivable Turnover}}$	112,81	124,28	153,65	61,67
1.2	Total Asset Turnover	=	$\dfrac{\text{Revenue}}{\text{Average total assets}}$	0,76	0,80	1,07	0,96
1.3	Fixed Asset Turnover	=	$\dfrac{\text{Revenue}}{\text{Average net fixed Assets}}$	1,57	2,83	3,59	2,48
1.4	Working Capital Turnover	=	$\dfrac{\text{Revenue}}{\text{Average Working capital}}$	2,57	1,97	2,52	11,40
2. Liquidity Ratios				31.12.2022	31.12.2021	31.12.2020	Industry Benchmark
2.1	Current ratio	=	$\dfrac{\text{Current Assets}}{\text{Current Liabilities}}$	2,52	4,79	2,51	1,80
2.2	Quick Ratio	=	$\dfrac{\text{Current asset - Inventory}}{\text{Current Liabilities}}$	2,22	4,68	2,42	1,67
3. Solvency Ratios				31.12.2022	31.12.2021	31.12.2020	Industry Benchmark
3.1	Debt to equity ratio	=	$\dfrac{\text{Total debt}}{\text{Total shareholder's equity}}$	0,73	0,30	0,67	0,21
3.2	Debt to assets ratio	=	$\dfrac{\text{Total debt}}{\text{Total Assets}}$	0,42	0,23	0,40	0,49
3.3	Financial leverage ratio	=	$\dfrac{\text{Average total assets}}{\text{Average total equity}}$	1,73	1,30	1,67	1,97
4. Profitability Ratios				31.12.2022	31.12.2021	31.12.2020	Industry Benchmark
4.1	Net profit margin	=	$\dfrac{\text{Net income}}{\text{Revenue}}$	16%	25%	22%	1,02%
4.2	Operating Profit Margin	=	$\dfrac{\text{EBIT}}{\text{Revenue}}$	18%	25%	26%	2,56%
4.3	Return on Assets (ROA)	=	$\dfrac{\text{Net income}}{\text{Average total assets}}$	12%	20%	24%	5%
4.4	Return on Equity (ROE)	=	$\dfrac{\text{Net income}}{\text{Average total equity}}$	20%	25%	40%	11%
5. Valuation Ratios				31.12.2022	31.12.2021	Private placement / IPO	Industry Benchmark
5.1	P/E	=	$\dfrac{\text{Price per share}}{\text{Earnings per share}}$	15,74	16,10	15,63 *Private placement	27,63
5.2	P/S	=	$\dfrac{\text{Price per share}}{\text{Sales per share}}$	2,47	3,96	3,50 *Private placement	2,35

Observations

*Industry benchmark Data Source — https://www.gurufocus.com

* USU Software AG — https://www.gurufocus.com/stock/XTER:OSP2/summary?search=usu

* USU Software AG is operating in the same industry and providing the same services as AROBS, and it has a Market Capitalization and Revenue, similar to our Company. This are the reasons I choose this company as a peer, if the industry benchmark was not available. The peer ratios were calculated by using financial data found on:

https://www.wsj.com/market-data/quotes/XE/XETR/OSP2?mod=quote_search

https://www.gurufocus.com/stock/XTER:OSP2/summary?search=usu

Vasile Rusu

Rethinking Organisational Learning in Software Development: Addressing Gen Z's Career Challenges through Soft Systems Methodology

EMBA module: Systemic Management: Seeing the Bigger Picture

Assignment task: *This assignment is a 3000-word report on a full application of a chosen systemic methodology in the students' business. It will be a 'consulting' type of report, with a briefing to the Board of Directors, providing the results of the systemic analysis undertaken, and the recommendations for improvements resulting from it.*

Introduction

When the COVID-19 pandemic started, the shift to Work-from-Home (WFH) became the norm in the global workplace (Potgieter & Ferreira, 2022). Initially forced by governments because of health and safety concerns (Imtyaz et al., 2020), it has evolved into a new norm, offering insights into the future of work. This new way of working has revealed significant benefits and notable challenges, particularly in career development and work-life balance.

One of the primary advantages of WFH is that employees can now manage their schedules more effectively, balancing work commitments with personal responsibilities (Fried and Heinemeier, 2013). This flexibility often helps employees have a better work-life balance, reduces commute times, and offers a personalised work environment, which can result in increased productivity and overall job satisfaction (Fried and Heinemeier, 2013).

However, along with these benefits, WFH poses distinct challenges, especially concerning career development and employee interactions. The lack of physical interaction with colleagues and mentors can hinder the professional growth of employees, particularly those in the early stages of their careers. Informal learning opportunities, such as shadowing experienced colleagues, spontaneous discussions, and on-the-job learning that typically occur in an office setting, are significantly reduced in a remote work environment, which can lead to isolation and a potential gap in skill development and networking opportunities, which are crucial for career progression.

ABC Context

ABC was founded in 2013 in the heart of Romanian's vibrant tech scene and has embarked on a journey of continuous growth, innovation, and commitment to nurturing talent. In its first years of activity, the company operated as a small-scale venture comprising up to 30 employees. This small team of developers and testers has laid the foundation for a culture of excellence, collaboration, and agility, handling diverse projects that helped grow their skills and expand their expertise. The first seven years were characterised by a strong focus on client-driven solutions, allowing the company to establish a robust portfolio and a reputation for quality and reliability.

The arrival of the COVID-19 pandemic marked a turning point for the company. ABC responded with remarkable adaptability and vision as the world rapidly shifted towards digital solutions to handle new challenges better. The company expanded its workforce to 140 employees, transitioning from a small company to a medium-sized one. This growth was not just in numbers but also in the scope of our services and the depth of our technical expertise. Embracing the changing landscape, we diversified our offerings and began to venture into developing our proprietary products, signalling a new era of innovation and creating freedom.

Recognizing the importance of nurturing the next generation of software professionals but also the need to cover the gap left by the high workforce demand in the industry generated by the COVID-19 pandemic, the company launched internship programs to cultivate young talent. These internship programs offered software engineers and developers a unique opportunity to work alongside experienced mentors, gain hands-on experience, and contribute to real-world projects. The scope was not to have just internal learners but to integrate them as integral members of our development team, bringing fresh perspectives and new ideas.

Soft Systems Methodology (SSM)

The Soft System Methodology is an approach used in systemic management to address complex, "messy situations of all kinds" (Checkland & Poulter, 2010). It was developed by Peter Checkland, a British management scientist, in the 1970s (Checkland, 1999). The SSM came as a response to the limitations Checkland observed in the traditional systems engineering approaches, the primary reason being the limitations of Hard Systems Methodology (HSM), which is suited for problems that could be clearly defined and quantified. As this HSM works well for technical or mechanical systems, where one can clearly define objectives and goals, it fails when the nature of the problem is a complex human or organizational one, where multiple interpretations and perspectives exist (Checkland, 1999). Brian Wilson, another important collaborator with Checkland at Lancaster University (Parra-Luna, 2009), extended and applied SSM in various organizational contexts. He is known for his work in Information Systems and for applying SSM to the practical problems of managing change in organizations.

The messy situation that our company is trying to figure out is the challenge of developing newly trained Gen Z employees from an internship program. The challenge is caused mainly by limited interaction with highly skilled, remote-working Millennial employees.

The primary strength of SSM in this context lies in its ability to handle "soft", messy problems involving human factors and social processes (Checkland, 1999). The company's development of Gen Z employees is not just a training issue; it is linked to organizational culture, communication patterns, and inter-generational dynamics.

SSM emphasises understanding the problem from multiple perspectives, which is crucial in solving this challenge. Gen Z employees, Millennials, management, and other stakeholders likely have differing views on remote working, mentorship, and workplace integration. SSM's participatory approach would involve all these groups in defining the problems and exploring solutions, ensuring that any strategies developed are grounded in the reality of their experiences and needs.

Furthermore, SSM's conceptual models can help the company visualise and understand complex relationships and processes, such as remote interactions, knowledge transfer, and employee development. These models can serve as a basis for discussions and brainstorming, leading to innovative solutions that might not emerge from traditional, linear problem-solving methods.

Lastly, the qualitative nature of SSM is well-suited for a problem that is more about human interaction and perception than quantifiable metrics. In this scenario, where the challenge is deeply rooted in human behaviours and organizational culture, SSM's qualitative, holistic approach can provide sustainable solutions.

Objectives

This paper aims to leverage the use of Soft System Methodology and (1) *mitigate WFH impact on younger generation's career development*, as studies have shown that Gen Z professionals often feel isolated in remote work settings, leading to dissatisfaction and anxiety(Gofus, 2023); (2) *reduce project responsibility load on Millennials*: alleviate the burden on Millennial professionals who often find themselves shouldering the responsibility of carrying projects, by reevaluating and redistributing roles and responsibilities within teams, ensuring a more balanced workload and fostering a collaborative environment where knowledge and skills are shared across generations; and (3) *enhancing team cohesion to boost customer satisfaction*: working on team cohesion between teams composed of Gen Z and Millennial employees, fostering an environment of mutual understanding and effective collaboration.

SSM Implementation

Unstructured problem situation

The company workforce comprises a mix of Gen Z and Millennial professionals. While Millennials are experienced and often work remotely, Gen Z employees, newer to the work world, are more present in the office environment. This generational mix leads to varied work preferences, expectations, and styles.

With a significant portion of the workforce, especially Millennials, opting for remote work, there are growing concerns about the isolation and career development challenges for the on-site Gen Z employees. Though providing flexibility and autonomy, the WFH model might limit the crucial face-to-face mentorship and networking opportunities, which are essential for the career growth of younger employees.

Millennials, often finding themselves in mid-level positions, are experiencing the pressure of leading and managing projects, which can often lead to stress, burnout, and a potential imbalance in work distribution, raising questions about sustainable work practices and effective project management.

Gen Z and Millennials' different work styles and preferences might impact team cohesion. This lack of cohesion could affect project outcomes and, by extension, customer satisfaction.

The company is navigating an evolving organizational culture influenced by generational shifts, remote work trends, and changing market demands. Balancing traditional work models with emerging trends and ensuring that the organizational culture remains dynamic, inclusive, and conducive to growth is a challenge.

This black-and-white sketch (Figure 1) summarises the various elements of the unstructured problem situation, depicting the contrast in work experiences, the impact of remote work on team cohesion, and the evolving organizational culture influenced by generational shifts and remote work trends.

Figure 1. Rich Picture

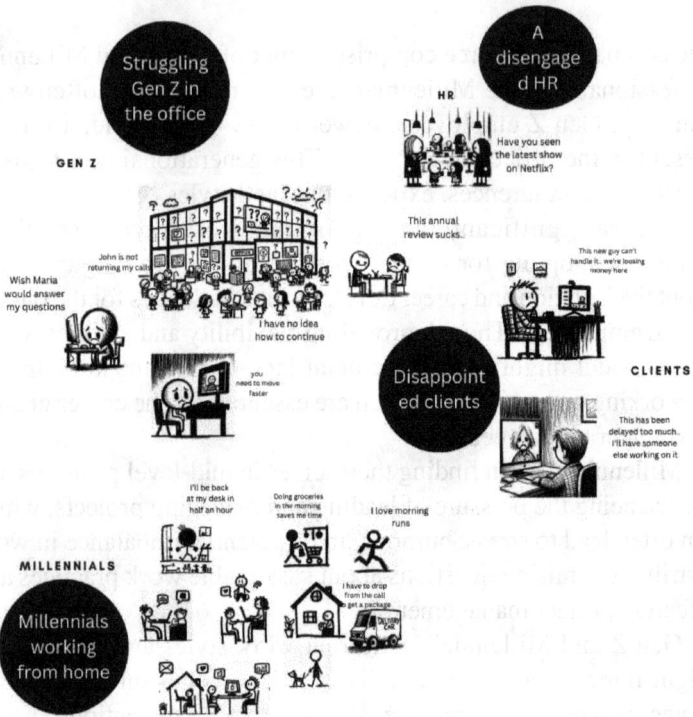

Root definitions and relevant systems

To formulate the root definitions and the relevant systems, the author of this paper will use the BATWOE framework (Checkland & Poulter, 2010).

BATWOE

Beneficiary (B)

The primary beneficiaries are the Gen Z and Millennial employees, who will benefit from improved career development, balanced workload, and enhanced team cohesion. Secondary beneficiaries include the software company itself through improved productivity and customer satisfaction.

Actors(A)
Actors, including HR professionals, team leaders, managers, and employees, will enact the changes. They are responsible for implementing the strategies to address the challenges.

Transformation (T)
The transformation process involves changing work dynamics to a more balanced and supportive environment, which includes enhancing remote work policies for better career development, redistributing project responsibilities, and improving team cohesion between Gen Z and Millennials.

Worldview (W)
The fundamental belief driving these changes is that fostering a workplace environment where every employee feels supported, engaged, and valued, regardless of their generation or work location, is crucial for the long-term success and sustainability of the company. This perspective is rooted in the understanding that when employees, mainly from diverse generational cohorts like Gen Z and Millennials, are given the appropriate resources, mentorship, and collaborative opportunities, it not only enhances their individual career growth and job satisfaction but also leads to higher overall productivity, innovation, and customer satisfaction. The commitment to addressing these challenges stems from a conviction that a harmonious, inclusive, and flexible work culture is essential for attracting and retaining top talent, a key driver for maintaining a competitive edge in the dynamic software industry.

Owners (O)
Owners are those who have the authority to change the system. This case includes top management, department heads, and company shareholders.

Victims (V)
Victims are those who suffer if the changes are not implemented. In this situation, it would be the Gen Z employees facing career development issues, Millennials burdened with excessive project

responsibilities, and potentially the company itself due to reduced employee satisfaction and customer dissatisfaction.

Environment (E)
The environment encompasses the external factors influencing the situation, such as the evolving nature of remote work trends, technological advancements in communication tools, the competitive software industry landscape, and general societal attitudes towards work-life balance.

Root definitions for the challenges

Root definition 1: A system that facilitates effective career development for Gen Z employees in a remote work setup, leveraging technology and mentorship programs to provide the necessary guidance and growth opportunities while respecting individual work preferences and promoting professional networking.

Root definition 2: A system to distribute project responsibilities among employees equitably, reducing the reliance on Millennials to carry the bulk of projects and fostering a culture of shared responsibility, collaboration, and support across generational lines.

Root definition 3: A system to enhance team cohesion and collaboration between Gen Z and Millennials employees, improving customer satisfaction through effective communication, mutual understanding, and leveraging diverse strengths within teams.

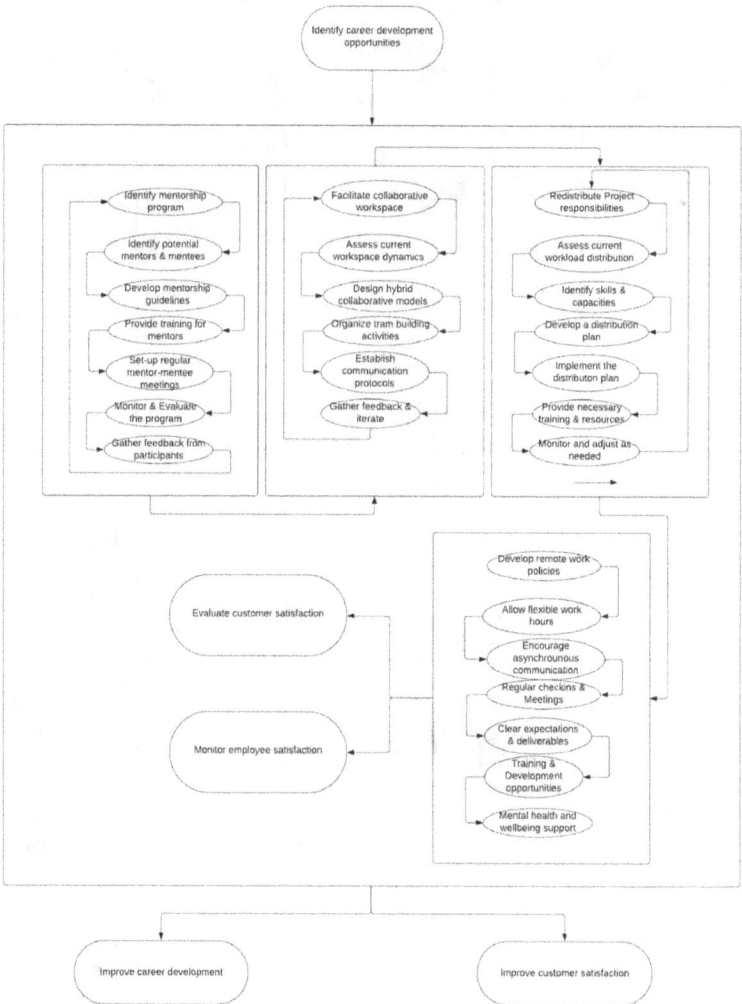

Figure 2. Conceptual models

Table 1. Comparison of models and real–world

Activity	Does it already exist?	How is it done?	How is it evaluated?	Comments
1.1 Identify Potential Mentors & Mentees	Sort of	Each new hire/ intern is assigned a "buddy."	Not evaluated	At the end of the probation period, the "buddy" is supposed to offer a report on the onboarding process and acclimatization of the newly hired. As of now, this is working in a single direction. Feedback should be taken from the person being mentored.
1.2 Develop Mentorship Guidelines	Sort of	The company has an onboarding program that helps new hires get up to speed faster.	Not evaluated	Often times the onboarding program is not followed, as people want to get their "hands dirty" by stepping in to do project-related tasks.
1.3 Provide training for Mentors	No	n/a	n/a	This is a good area of improvement for the company. Many Mentors lack emotional intelligence (Goleman, 1995) capabilities and are not in the right spot to mentor. They are chosen because they are the most experienced people on a team.
1.4 Setup regular Mentor-Mentee meetings	Sort of	One-on-one meetings are often set up.	Not evaluated.	The one-on-one meetings often have no agenda and are shorter than they should be.
1.5 Monitor and evaluate the program	No	n/a	n/a	This is not happening
1.6 Gather feedback from participants	No	n/a	n/a	This is not happening

Activity	Does it already exist?	How is it done?	How is it evaluated?	Comments
2.1 Facilitate collaborative workspace	Yes	The company has an office in 3 cities across Romania and the Republic of Moldova	Not evaluated	Everyone is expected to join the office as often as they can
2.2 Assess current workspace dynamics	Gen Z employees come regularly to the office. Millennials, on the other hand, are not.	At every all-hands meeting, people are reminded about our offices and are encouraged to come more often.	Not evaluated	The company is trying to create a welcoming environment in every location, offering meals for employees who join the office regularly. Snacks and fruits are always available.
2.3 Design hybrid collaboration methods	No	n/a	n/a	Something that the company has thought about implementing, but it never got traction
2.4 Establish communication protocols	Sort of	The company is offering communication tools, like Teams, Zoom, Slack, that people can use to communicate	Not evaluated	Even though there are many tools that can be used to communicate, finding core time with an entire team has become very hard to do. The flexibility offered by the remote work has created many challenges in being able to find everyone at a specific time.
2.5 Gather feedback and iterate	No	n/a	n/a	The company is not getting feedback on this topic
3.1 Redistribute project Responsibilities	No	n/a	n/a	The company often relies on people that have more experi-ence, and are for a longer time with the company, to handle to most difficult projects / tasks.
3.2 Assess current workload distribution	No	n/a	n/a	Some people are overloaded with projects and person-nel to take care of.

Activity	Does it already exist?	How is it done?	How is it evaluated?	Comments
3.3 Identify skills & capacities	No	n/a	n/a	There's no general view on the skills & capacity
3.4 Develop a distribution plan	No	n/a	n/a	This is an important area of focus that the company should address soon
3.5 Implement the distribution plan	No	n/a	n/a	This is an important area of focus that the company should address soon
3.6 Provide necessary training & resources	No	n/a	n/a	Due to COVID-19, conferences and trainings that would happen on site, at the company office, are no longer happening
3.7 Monitor & adjust as needed	No	n/a	n/a	Not happening
4.1 Allow flexible work hours	Yes	Everyone decides on their schedule.	Not evaluated	Due to different clients that are from different time zones, made the company let the employees decide on their schedule. This is creating difficulties in having core time between team members.
4.2 Encourage asynchronous communication	Yes	Async communication can happen using the tools the company has provided	Not evaluated	Async communication is encouraged.
4.3 Regular check-ins & Meetings	Sort of	Regular one-on-one meetings are scheduled	Not evaluated	Each manager should meet with its directs at least 2 times a month. This does not necessarily happen in every team.
4.4 Clear expectations & deliverables	No	n/a	n/a	One of the biggest areas of improvement for the company.
4.5 Training and Development Opportunities	Sort of	Some technical trainings are happening	Being able to get a tech certification is a sort of measuring for training	Often, people lose interest and stop participating in these organised training sessions

Activity	Does it already exist?	How is it done?	How is it evaluated?	Comments
4.6 Mental health and wellbeing support	No	n/a	n/a	Unfortunately, this is not a common practice in Romanian Software companies.
5.1 Monitor Employee Satisfaction	Yes	A survey is being done once a year by the HR department	Sort of. When the survey results are ready, the management team looks over the results and tries to address the critical items.	Often the HR members are very disconnected from what people do every day. Their sense of urgency is sometimes exaggerated or out of context, producing challenges.
6.1 Evaluate customer satisfaction	Yes	A Customer satisfaction survey happens every year.	The management team analyses the results and tries to address critical items.	The company is very reactive to the feedback. An area of improvement is to be more engaged in the relationship with customers and more proactive in gathering feedback from them.

Changes: Systematically desirable and culturally feasible

In the sixth step of SSM, we evaluate the proposed actions' systematic desirability and cultural feasibility. Below is an assessment of each action that the executive team, Engineering Managers, and Project Leads have decided to take actions on.

Tabel 2. Assessment of each action that the executive team have decided to take actions on

Action	Systematically desirable	Implementations	Order
Establish communication protocols	Provides a foundation for effective collaboration, essential for a distributed workforce	Can be implemented right away as it sets the groundwork for other changes	First, as it supports all subsequent actions
Asses current workload distribution	Critical for understanding current challenges and planning workload redistribution	This should be one of the first actions to inform further steps	Second, after establishing communication protocols.
Design hybrid collaboration methods	Essential for balancing the benefits of remote and in-office work, addressing the needs of different generations in the workforce	It should be implemented over time, starting with pilot programs in selected teams.	After establishing communication protocols and assessing the current workload.
Identify skills and capacity	Ensures that the employees are utilised effectively based on their skills and capacities	Concurrently with workload assessment	Alongside or immediately following the assessment of workload distribution
Redistribute project responsibilities	Ensures equitable workload and leverages the strengths of all team members	Gradually, after the assessment of workload distribution and skills	After assessing the workload and identifying skills and capacities
Set clear expectations and deliverables	Ensures clarity in roles and responsibilities, enhancing productivity	It can be initiated right away but refined continuously	In parallel with other actions, as it is crucial for all project-related activities
Develop and implement a distribution plan	Provides a structured approach to redistributing responsibilities	Over time, after thorough assessment and identification of skills and workload	After assessing the workload and identifying skills.

Action to improve the problem situation

Below is a plan detailing the "Who," "How," "When," and "Where" to undertake actions for implementing the changes highlighted above.

Table 3. Action to improve the problem situation

Action	Who	How	When	Where
Design hybrid collaboration methods	IT and HR departments, in collaboration with team leaders	Develop models that combine in-person and virtual collaboration involving agile methodologies as a framework	Initiate development within the next quarter, with a phased rollout	Both in-office and remote environments
Establish communication protocols	HR department with input from employees	Define clear guidelines for communication, including the use of different channels (Zoom, Slack, Microsoft Teams) and response time expectations.	Within one month, followed by regular reviews	Applicable company-wide, both in-office and remotely
Redistribute project responsibilities	Engineering Managers and Team Leads	Reallocate tasks based on current project needs and employee skill sets	Start at the beginning of the next project cycle	Across all teams
Assess current workload distribution	Engineering Managers and Team lead, with support from HR	Use workload assessment tools and employee feedback to analyse the current distribution	Conduct assessments by-annually	Across all teams
Identify Skills and Capacity	The HR department, in collaboration with department heads	Perform skills audits and capacity assessments	Prior to each major project, annually or at hire time.	Company-wide
Develop and implement a distribution plan	Senior Management, Engineering Managers, and HR department	Based on skills and workload assessments, create a plan that distributes responsibilities fairly, with coaching from experienced employees	Implement with the start of new projects	Applicable to all project teams
Set clear expectations and deliverables	Engineering Managers and team leads	Define specific goals, deliverables, and timelines for each team member. Review the goals as often as possible, and provide feedback when necessary	At the start of every task assigned	Applicable to all project teams

Critical reflections

Implementing Soft Systems Methodology (SSM) in the context of a software company dealing with the career development challenges of Gen Z employees, amidst a backdrop of remote work dominated by Millennials, presents a multifaceted case study for the application of this methodology. This extended conclusion delves deeper into the implications, strengths, and weaknesses of using SSM in such a setting.

Synthesis of SSM Application

The application of SSM in the software company scenario involves several key stages, from problem identification to implementing the change. Each stage presents its own set of challenges and opportunities. The methodology's ability to encapsulate the nuances of human-centered problems, like this faced by the Gen Z workforce, is a testament to its design by Checkland and its subsequent refinement by academics like Wilson.

SSM's strengths in addressing complex problems

Comprehensive problem understanding: one of SSM's greatest strengths is its ability to facilitate a comprehensive understanding of complex problems. In our case, it allows for an in-depth exploration of the dynamics between different generations within the workforce (Checkland, 1981). The methodology acknowledges that the issues faced by Gen Z employees extend beyond simple career development challenges and encompass broader organizational culture and communication issues.

Participative approach: SSM's participative nature ensures that multiple perspectives are considered. Involving both the Gen Z and Millennials employees in the problem-solving process helps to identify solutions that are more likely to be accepted and effective (Wilson, 2001).

Iterative and Flexible: the iterative nature of SSM, where understanding evolves with each cycle, is particularly relevant in a fast-changing industry like software development. This flexibility allows the company to adapt and refine its strategies in response to an evolving work environment (Checkland & Poulter, 2006).

Limitations and Challenges in practical implementation

Time and resource intensive: the thoroughness of SSM can also be its drawback. The methodology requires time and resources, both of which are at a premium in fast-paced business environments (Wilson, 2001).

Subjective and Bias: The reliance on subjective interpretations can introduce biases, potentially skewing problem understanding and solution development. This subjectivity necessitates careful management to ensure that all voices are heard and considered equally (Checkland, 1981).

Transition from theory to practice: translating conceptual models into actionable and practical solutions can be challenging. There's often a gap between the idealised models developed during the SSM process and the realities of the organizational setting (Checkland & Scholes, 1990).

Broader implications for Software Companies

In the context of a software company, the challenges of implementing SSM are particularly relevant. The industry is characterised by rapid change, innovation, and a diverse workforce. SSM's ability to handle these dynamics makes it a valuable tool. However, the methodology must be adapted to fit the unique needs of the industry and the specific organizational culture of the company.

To effectively implement SSM in such settings, several adaptations are necessary:
- *Speeding up the process*: Streamlining SSM stages to make them less time-consuming, possibly through the use of technology and more focused workshops.

- *Balancing subjectivity with objectivity*: introducing more quantitative elements into the SSM process to complement the qualitative aspects and provide a more balanced approach.
- *Bridging gap between model and implementation*: developing clearer strategies for translating conceptual models into practical actions within the organization.

Conclusions

In conclusion, while SSM is an effective tool for addressing the complex, human-centered problems faced by software companies, its application in such environments requires careful consideration. The methodology must be adapted to meet the specific needs of the industry and the organizational culture. The challenge lies in maintaining the essence of SSM – its flexibility, participatory nature, and holistic approach – while making it suitable for a fast-paced, innovation-driven industry. As Checkland and Wilson have illustrated through their work, the true strength of SSM lies in its adaptability and its ability to evolve in response to the demands of the problem and the environment. In the case of the software company, adapting SSM to meet the unique challenges of remote work and inter-generational dynamics is crucial for its successful application. This adaptation not only addresses the immediate challenges but also sets a precedent for future problem-solving within the organization.

Personal opinion

In concluding the analysis of applying SSM to address the challenges of the software company, it's crucial to consider the concept of the learning loop within the organization. SSM, as developed by Peter Checkland, is fundamentally a learning system, but its application in this context highlights a critical limitation: the tendency of the company to engage in a single learning loop (Argyris and Schön, 1978).

This single learning loop refers to an organization's approach to problem-solving and learning, where the focus is primarily on finding solutions to immediate problems within the existing framework of norms and objectives. In the context of our company, this manifests as addressing the surface-level issues – such as communication gaps, mentorship needs, and workload distribution – without fundamentally re-evaluating and challenging the underlying assumptions, norms, and objectives that might be contributing to these problems.

Checkland's SSM is designed to promote deeper organizational learning by questioning and rethinking underlying assumptions (Checkland & Poulter, 2006). However, due to time constraints, and difficulties in involving the right stakeholders to this process, the reliance on SSM appears to have fostered a single loop learning process, which might be insufficient for achieving transformative change, especially in dynamic industries like software development where continuous adaptation and innovation are crucial.

References

Argyris, C. and Schön, D.A. (1978). *Organizational Learning: A Theory of Action Perspective*. Reading, Massachusetts: Addison-Wesley.

Checkland, P. (1999). *Soft systems methodology: a 30-year retrospective. Systems thinking, systems practice. Peter Checkland*. Chichester: Wiley.

Checkland, P. (1981). *Systems thinking, systems practise*. Chichester: Wiley.

Checkland, P. and Scholes, J. (1990). *Soft systems methodology: a 30-year retrospective; Soft systems methodology in action / Peter Checkland and Jim Scholes*. Chichester: John Wiley.

Checkland, P.B. and Poulter, J. (2010). *Soft systems methodology. In: Systems Approaches to Managing Change: A Practical Guide* (ed. M. Reynolds and S. Holwell), 191–242. London: Springer.

Checkland, P. and Poulter, J. (2006). *Learning for action a short definitive account of soft systems methodology, and its use for practitioners, teachers and students*. Hoboken, N.J. [U.A.] Wiley.

Fried, J. and David Heinemeier Hansson (2013). *Remote: office not required*. Crown Business, New York

Gofus, A. (2023). *Generation Z Prefers Flexibility Over Fully Remote Work*. [online] www.worldwideerc.org. Available at: https://www.worldwideerc.org/news/global-workforce/generation-z-prefers-flexibility-over-fully-remote-work.

Imtyaz, A., Haleem, A. and Javaid, M. (2020). Analysing governmental response to the COVID-19 pandemic. *Journal of Oral Biology and Craniofacial Research*, [online] 10(4), pp.504–513.

Jackson, M.C. (2019). *Critical systems thinking and the management of complexity.* Hoboken Wiley.

Parra-Luna, F. (2009). *Systems Science and Cybernetics – Volume III.* EOLSS Publications.

Potgieter, I.L. and Ferreira, N. (2022). *Managing human resources: the new normal.* Cham: Springer.

Wilson, B. (2001). *Soft systems methodology: conceptual model building and its contribution.* Chichester: Wiley.

Adrian Sălăjan

Ownership Strategy and Governance Solutions: Transgenerational Continuity

EMBA Module: Governance and Business Ethics

Assignment task: *The assignment is a 3000-word report that will consist of students' own organisations' approaches to corporate governance, with recommendations for improvements. Alternatively, you can choose other business organisations or make a policy proposal.*

Executive summary

Company ABC, a family-owned business that has been operating for 25 years, faces significant challenges in ensuring its continuity into the future. The primary issue is that the next generation is not involved or motivated to assume leadership and ownership roles. Furthermore, there is an ongoing conflict among the current three shareholders regarding ownership battle and decision-making authority, highlighting the need to transition towards a more functional governance model. Lastly, it is essential to establish a structured family governance framework and a long-term ownership strategy to sustain the company's legacy across generations.

Family businesses often encounter a paradox. On one hand, they draw strength from their commitment to preserving a family legacy, fostering a long-term orientation, and aligning familial and business objectives. On the other hand, they frequently struggle with internal power dynamics, conflicts, governance inefficiencies, strategic direction, and succession planning. These challenges can threaten their long-term sustainability and overall business continuity.

In addressing these challenges, this report recommends adopting the four-room governance model and outlines specific strategies for the ownership structure to promote the company's enduring sustainability and ongoing family ownership.

Introduction

Good governance is essential for the sustainability of organisations of all types and all sizes—large, medium, and small, family-owned or not. Family businesses might be perceived as arenas of power struggles, favouritism, and internal conflicts—dynamics that negatively affect both the company and the family owners. From the famous Gucci family to the Murdochs and NewsCorp business, and in this case, Company ABC, there are numerous examples of governance practices failing. In contrast, many businesses draw strength from their commitment to preserving the family legacy. This dedication to ensuring the business's survival across generations, known as transgenerational orientation (TGO), is a central topic in family business research (Chua, 1999; Habbershon, 2003; Lumpkin & Brigham, 2011).

The author poses a hypothetical question: *Can Romanian family businesses face dramatic failures, or will they be enduring enterprises?*

"Governance structures are the continuity engine for family companies" (Lansberg, 1999). Where there is a lack of governance, ownership strategy, and a dysfunctional decision-making model, the family can burden the business heavily and, in extreme cases, risk causing its demise (Baus, 2013). According to McKinsey (2024), family businesses generate an estimated 70% of global GDP. The family business ecosystem in Romania is relatively young, with most companies still in the first generation. Compared to other European states, only a tiny fraction has progressed to the second generation. According to a study by PwC (2023), 58% of Romanian family entrepreneurs aim to retain ownership and management within the family in the long term. Interestingly, the study also reveals that 58% of these entrepreneurs do not have any second-generation family members involved in the company's operations.

Family businesses—where two or more family members exercise control simultaneously or sequentially—can be significantly more fragile or resilient than their counterparts. This duality underscores the need for careful succession planning, developing a continuity governance model, and establishing an ownership strategy to extend transgenerational boundaries.

This report will outline the essential components of Company ABC's continuity governance model, propose solutions, address obstacles discovered, and provide recommendations for extending the business across generations.

Description of the *"status quo"*

Company ABC is a family-owned business founded in 1991. The company produces and distributes products in Romania. The three family shareholders own and govern Company ABC: two brothers each own 33.4%, and one brother-in-law holds 33.2%. The older brother and brother-in-law, both in their 70s, are less proactive in their involvement in the company, while the younger brother is more actively engaged. Over the years, some younger family second-generation members were initially introduced to the business but eventually withdrew due to constant questioning of decisions, ongoing power struggles, and tension among the shareholders. The older shareholders hesitate to hand over the company administration to the younger brother due to trust issues, differing visions, and a lack of collaboration and communication in decision-making. From a succession standpoint, the absence of second-generation involvement in the family business poses a significant challenge and risk.

Operational responsibilities within each business function are determined by the shareholder in charge, but fundamental, strategic, management, and investment decisions require consensus from all three. Due to differing visions, values, and capacities for understanding, daily confrontations arise, ranging from micro issues to strategic and fundamental problems. All these issues fuel ownership battles among current stakeholders for control and power, creating a confrontational and aggressive environment within the company. These disputes often stem from differing visions for the company's future, varying degrees of involvement in the business, and conflicts of interest affecting operational efficiency and ultimately threatening the company's stability. Decision-making lacks a transparent model and structure.

Key Issues for Consideration:

- Ongoing power struggles between the two brothers are severely disrupting daily operations. Frequent invalidation of each other's decisions contributes to a toxic and unstable working environment.
- The management structure lacks formalization, resulting in blurred responsibilities and inefficient operational oversight.
- The absence of clearly defined authority lines among shareholders fosters internal tension, with employees often caught in the crossfire and pressured to take sides.
- Management responsibilities are not defined and inconsistently executed, leading to operational drift and a lack of accountability.
- Strategic investments and critical business decisions are frequently blocked or overturned due to shareholder conflicts, stalling progress and growth.
- Persistent issues with misinformation and miscommunication among staff undermine coordination and trust within the organization.
- One particular shareholder, driven by a need for command and control, routinely invalidates any decision not initiated by him, further destabilizing governance and morale.

Identification of the problems in the *"status quo"*

Drawing on direct experience and direct exposure to the governance challenges faced by ABC company, the author gained valuable insights into the complex interplay and dynamics and identified five key issues related to ownership and governance. Through in-depth analysis of the current situation, these challenges were examined in context, with practical insights into how addressing them can strengthen governance, reduce internal conflict, and ensure sustainable business continuity.

Ownership model

The ownership model plays a vital role in shaping family business governance by setting clear rules on who can be an owner, the roles they assume, and how control is shared. It distinguishes between Operators (active in the business), Governors (involved at board/shareholder level), and Investors (passive owners), each with different implications for decision-making and long-term sustainability (Baron & Lachenauer, 2021). In this context, the case highlights an ownership problem: older shareholders seek to secure the future of the business for the next generation but struggle with trust issues—particularly toward the younger brother—raising concerns about control and involvement. As the family grows, second-generation members often lose identification with the business (Zellweger & Kammerlander, 2015), paving the way for internal conflicts over strategic direction and ownership, potentially undermining sustainability and continuity (Kidwell, 2012).

Governance

"Governance structures are the continuity engine for family companies" (Lansberg, 1999). Where governance models fail, with no ownership strategy and a dysfunctional decision-making model, the family can become a limitation on the business and, in some cases, risk causing its demise (Baus, 2013). In family businesses, success is centered on the family's dynamics and structure (James, 1999), specifically on the family involvement and how it organises, identifies, and relates to the business (Olson et al., 2003).

Company ABC's inability to strike a balance between involvement, relationship, and disengagement has created significant obstacles. Decision-making is centralised and contentious, with shareholders invalidating each other's input, reflected in statements like "No LEU can be spent without my approval." Such behaviour has fostered a toxic culture, as seen in elements of the Dark Triad (Paulhus and Williams, 2002), and led to shareholder inaction, leaving managers uncertain and unable to move forward. A governance approach that fails to prioritise all stakeholders, blocks innovation, and undermines talent retention poses a significant risk to long-term sustainability (Siebels & Knyphausen-Aufseß, 2012).

Fundamentals for value creation

Ownership strategy is essential to a business's long-term success, particularly in family businesses, where owners can define success beyond financial returns, aligning it with shared values and priorities (Frank et al., 2016). While owners have the right to the residual value the business generates, they are also responsible for setting a clear strategic direction. Company ABC's lack of alignment and clarity among shareholders regarding strategy, goals, and profit distribution has resulted in internal conflict and missed opportunities. The absence of shared values and a common vision pose a fundamental risk, undermining the company's purpose and cohesion. Without a unified direction, the business risks reaching a standstill, threatening its continuity and long-term viability.

Communication

Poor communication deepens trust issues among shareholders, fuelling suspicion and resistance to collaboration. This dynamic often creates a toxic environment where decisions are delayed, blocked, or reversed by dissenting voices, leading to operational inefficiencies. Differing visions among shareholders further compound this misalignment, resulting in fragmented actions and undermining strategic coherence. Without open, transparent dialogue, managers are left without direction, paralyzing key initiatives and stalling progress. Effective communication is essential for clarity and building trust and cohesion within the ownership group.

What is missing?

Transgenerational orientation (TGO) reflects a family business's strategic commitment to sustaining the enterprise across multiple generations. In the case of Company ABC, the lack of next-generation involvement poses a critical threat to continuity. Without a clear succession plan or a secure governance mechanism for ownership transfer and/or transformation, the business faces risks such as leadership vacuums, strategic drift, and rising tensions among shareholders and family members.

Fundamental and often difficult questions remain unanswered: *What will happen to the business and the investments we've built? How do we let go, involve the next generation, and transform the company for their future? How do we prepare them for leadership?*

While business governance focuses on strategic oversight and operations and defines and delivers the company's strategic direction and control (Gallo & Kenyon-Rouvinez, 2005), family governance serves a distinct but complementary role. It aims to foster family cohesion, guide the family's influence on the business, and align expectations for its future (Mustakallio et al., 2002).

"It is essential to acknowledge that succession in any aspect is a process, not an event!"

Recommendations for addressing the problems

Setting the Ownership Type for the Future

Given the lack of a clear strategy, the absence of shareholder consensus on the company's future, and the family members' limited interest in actively working within the business, Company ABC would benefit from adopting a distributed ownership model (Baron and Lachenauer, 2021). This approach allows all family members to retain ownership and participate in key decisions, while delegating day-to-day operations to a professional, non-family CEO. Such a structure strengthens governance, supports continuity, and enhances long-term sustainability by preserving family involvement at the ownership level and ensuring effective leadership across generations.

Benefits of Distributed Ownership with a Nonfamily Management:

1. Inclusive Ownership:
Distributed ownership allows any family member to be an owner, which helps keep the family's wealth tied to the business and ensures that all family members have a stake in the company's

success[1]. This inclusive approach can strengthen family unity and commitment to the business, even if they are not actively involved in day-to-day operations.

2. Professional Management:

With a nonfamily CEO, Company ABC can benefit from professional management practices and expertise critical for the company's growth and sustainability. The nonfamily CEO brings objectivity, a focus on operational efficiency, and the ability to implement best practices without being influenced by family dynamics[2].

3. Stability and Continuity:

Distributed ownership provides stability and continuity by preventing the need to buy out non-active family members. Shares are passed down through generations[3], ensuring that the company remains under family ownership while being professionally managed.

Family Governance Development

The Four-Room Governance Model (Baron & Lachenauer, 2021) is recommended to address ABC's company governance challenges and ensure clarity around roles, responsibilities, and decision-making authority. This structured framework helps family businesses navigate the increasing complexity of growth and generational transition. The model promotes transparency, reduces conflict, and supports more effective decision-making by clearly delineating the functions of family, ownership, board, and management (Baron & Lachenauer, 2021).

---

1. See Aronoff, C. and Ward, J. (2016). Family Business Governance: Maximizing Family and Business Potential. [online] Perlego. Palgrave Macmillan. Available at: https://www.perlego.com/book/3478974/family-business-governance-maximizing-family-and-business-potential-pd-f?utm_source=google&utm_medium=cpc&campaignid=20933451054&adgroupid=162926082892&gad_source=1&gclid=Cj0KCQjwwO20BhCJARIsAAnTIVTCoX4FUnxET2h7lT7hWk7jZYPfCpm-PEpK5b-su_KHRylJF7JzsyQAaAjNwEALw_wcB.
2. Sustainable best practices. See Binz Astrachan, Claudia & Waldkirch, Matthias & Michiels, Anneleen & Pieper, Torsten & Bernhard, Fabian. (2020). Professionalizing the Business Family: The Five Pillars of Competent, Committed, and Sustainable Ownership.
3. Business continuity and stability. See Davis, J.A., Hampton, M.M., Lansberg, I. and E, G.K. (1997). Generation to Generation: Life Cycles of the Family Business. Harvard Business Press. Available at: https://books.google.ro/books/about/Generation_to_Generation.html?id=4SmhXxKQ1L4C&redir_esc=y

The Four-Room Governance Model consists of the following components[4], as presented in Figure 1.

The Four-Room Model

Thinking of your business as having a separate room for every group of stakeholders—along with rules about what may be decided in each—clarifies roles and minimizes conflict.

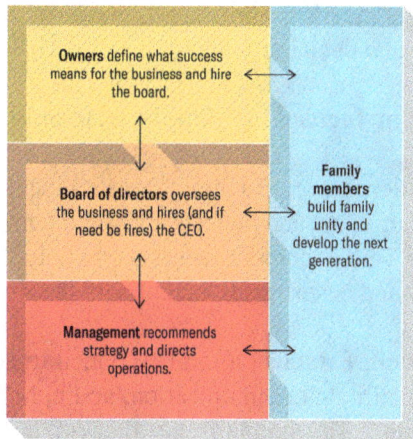

Owners define what success means for the business and hire the board.

Board of directors oversees the business and hires (and if need be fires) the CEO.

Management recommends strategy and directs operations.

Family members build family unity and develop the next generation.

Source: BanyanGlobal

⏱ **HBR**

Figure 1 – 4 Room Governance Model. *Source: Family business handbook (Baron and Lachenauer, 2021)*

1. The Management Room focuses on the company's operations and strategic management.

Management Leadership: The CEO oversees business operations, supported by a professional management team. This ensures that the company is run efficiently and in line with best practices.

Operational Committees: Establish operational committees[5] focused on specific areas such as finance, marketing, production, and quality.

---

4. See Baron, J. and Lachenauer, R. (2021). Build a Family Business That Lasts. [online] Harvard Business Review. Available at: https://hbr.org/2021/01/build-a-family-business-that-lasts.

5. More details on operational committees. See onboard.com (2022). What is an Operating Committee? (Overview, Roles, and Responsibilities). [online] OnBoard Board Management Software | Board Portal | Board Intelligence. Available at: https://www.onboardmeetings.com/blog/operating-committee/.

2. Ownership Room addresses ownership issues and the rights and responsibilities of shareholders.

Distributed Ownership Guidelines: Develop comprehensive guidelines for share distribution, voting rights[6], and succession planning[7]. These guidelines must be documented and communicated clearly to all family members.

Shareholder Meetings: Hold regular shareholder meetings to discuss ownership matters, financial performance, and strategic direction. These meetings provide a platform for transparent communication and decision-making.

3. Family Room focuses on family dynamics, values, and relationships[8].

Family Constitution: Develop a family constitution[9] that outlines the family's values, mission, and policies regarding family involvement in the business. This document serves as a guide for maintaining family harmony and ensuring alignment with the strategic business objectives.

Family Council: Establish a family council to address family-related issues, facilitate communication, and uphold the family's vision and values. The council can also organise educational programs to strengthen family bonds.

4. The Board Room provides strategic oversight and ensures the business achieves its long-term objectives.

Board of Directors: Form a board of directors with a mix of family members and independent professionals. The board's role is to provide strategic guidance, oversee the Management Board, and ensure that the company's actions align with its long-term goals.

Committees: Establish committees comprising industry experts and experienced professionals offering advice on critical issues and enhancing management skills and capabilities.

---

6. See Lake, R. (2021). Explaining the Shareholder Voting Process. [online] SoFi. Available at: https://www.sofi.com/learn/content/shareholder-voting-process/.

7. Succession planning. See www.everwisecu.com. (n.d.). Principles of Business Succession Planning | The Latest Blog | IN, MI Trust Resources | Everwise CU. [online] Available at: https://www.everwisecu.com/about/the-latest-blog/september-2023/principles-of-business-succession-planning

8. Details on the four-room model, See Baron, J., Lachenauer, R. and Ehrensberger, S. (2015). Making Better Decisions in Your Family Business. [online] Harvard Business Review. Available at: https://hbr.org/2015/09/making-better-decisions-in-your-family-business.

9. Family Constitution and By-Laws. See Ward, M. (n.d.). Morgan Stanley. [online] Morgan Stanley. Available at: https://advisor.morganstanley.com/michelle.ward/documents/field/w/wa/ward-sofia-michelle/Family_Constitution_and_Family_By_Laws.pdf.

Implementation Plan for ABC Company Governance

1. Ownership Guidelines:
Develop and document comprehensive guidelines for distributed ownership, including rules for share distribution, voting rights, and passing down shares through generations. Ensure legal compliance and alignment with the family's values.

2. Establish the Family Council:
Form a family council to address family-related issues and facilitate communication. The council should include representatives from different branches of the family and meet regularly to discuss family matters and align on the family's vision for the business.

3. Create the Board of Directors:
Appoint a board of directors with both family members and independent professionals. Define the board's responsibilities and ensure it meets regularly to provide strategic oversight and support to the Management Board.

4. Empower the Nonfamily CEO:
Provide the CEO with the authority and resources needed to manage the business effectively while maintaining accountability to the board of directors.

5. Monitor and Review Governance Practices:
Review and assess the governance model's effectiveness regularly. Adjust as needed to meet the family's and the business's needs.

Strategy for value creation

The Owner Strategy Triangle (Baron and Lachenauer, 2021)—illustrated in Figure 2—is a valuable framework for aligning three critical dimensions of a family business: ownership objectives, business operations, and shareholders' interests. For Company ABC, understanding and applying this model is essential to aligning and developing a coherent strategy and governance structure that supports continuity, long-term sustainability, and future growth.

The Owner Strategy Triangle

Most family businesses choose to prioritize two of the
three main goals depicted here to guide their strategy.

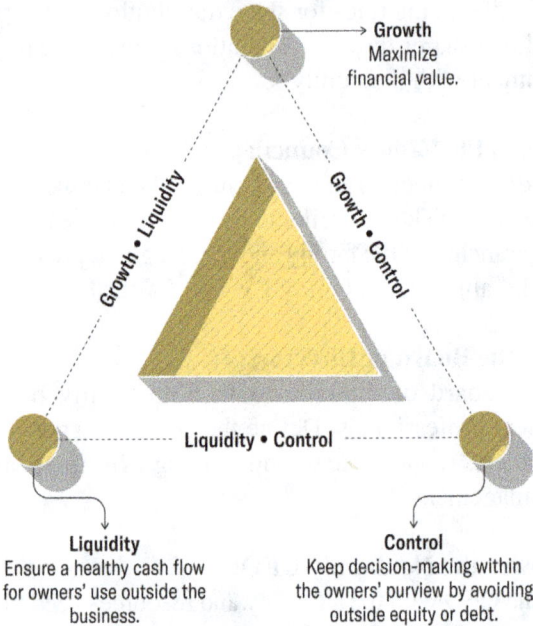

Growth
Maximize
financial value.

Growth • Liquidity

Growth • Control

Liquidity • Control

Liquidity
Ensure a healthy cash flow
for owners' use outside the
business.

Control
Keep decision-making within
the owners' purview by avoiding
outside equity or debt.

Source: BanyanGlobal

⊽ HBR

Figure 2 – Ownership Strategy Triangle. *Source: Family business handbook (Baron and Lachenauer, 2021)*

Given Company ABC's current context—marked by the absence
of a prepared second generation, trust issues among shareholders,
and limited interest from younger family members in active
involvement—the Growth-Liquidity[10] strategy emerges as a highly
suitable option. Aligned with the recommendation to implement a
professional management team, this approach allows the business
to continue expanding under capable leadership while offering
liquidity and financial returns to family shareholders. It balances
the need for professionalization, intending to preserve family wealth
and legacy.

---

10. Owner Strategy. See Baron, J. and Lachenauer, R. (n.d.). Why You Need an Owner Strategy. [online] Banyan Global.
Available at: https://banyan.global/ideas/why-you-need-an-owner-strategy.

Growth-Liquidity Strategy

This strategy drives substantial business growth while delivering meaningful financial returns to shareholders. It is designed to professionalise management, scale operations, and create long-term value—without requiring direct involvement from family members—while ensuring that owners continue to benefit from the company's success through regular distributions or liquidity events.

Characteristics:

External Funding: Use of outside equity or debt to finance growth.

Owner Payouts: Regular payouts to shareholders from the profits, ensuring that owners receive financial benefits while the company grows.

Implementation Plan:

1. Financial Policies:
Develop clear financial policies that define the balance between profit reinvestment and shareholder payouts. These policies should be well-documented and transparently communicated to all family shareholders to ensure alignment and avoid misunderstandings. One practical approach is establishing a fixed percentage of profits for dividends, while allocating the remainder toward reinvestment in the business to support long-term growth and stability.

2. Secure External Funding:
Explore options for external funding through debt to finance growth initiatives. This can include strategic partnerships, venture capital, or loans.

3. Optimise Cash Flow:
Focus on optimizing cash flow by enhancing operational efficiency, reducing unnecessary costs, and boosting overall profitability. To support this, implement clear performance metrics that track cash flow regularly and help ensure the company remains on target with its financial objectives.

5. Regular Review and Communication:
Regularly review the ownership strategy to ensure it stays aligned with the family's long-term goals and the evolving needs of the business. Maintain open and transparent communication among all stakeholders to build trust, encourage collaboration, and support cohesive decision-making.

By adopting the Growth-Liquidity strategy, ABC company can ensure effective governance, continuity, and sustainability, securing its legacy for future generations while maintaining professional management and family involvement.

Transgenerational orientation

The objective is to ensure ABC company's long-term sustainability and continuity by developing a comprehensive transgenerational orientation strategy. This strategy will prepare the next generation for ownership and governance roles without focusing on developing an entrepreneurial mindset[11] within the family. This will secure the family legacy and business success across generations[12], even if the future generation is not actively involved.

Transgenerational orientation relies on three key components: succession planning to ensure a structured transition of ownership and governance; education and training to prepare the next generation for responsible ownership; and engagement and communication to build alignment, trust, and shared purpose across the family.

1. Succession Planning
Create a succession plan detailing the transfer process of ownership and leadership commitments to the next generation. This plan should address successor selection and transition timelines and include contingency measures for unforeseen circumstances.

Identify Potential Successors: Assess family members based on their interests, skills, and commitment to the business.

Establish Criteria: Define clear criteria for successors, including

---

11. TGO without focus on entrepreneurial development. See Habbershon T, Nordqvist M, Zellweger T (2010) Transgenerational entrepreneurship. In: Nordqvist M, Zellweger T (eds) Transgenerational entrepreneurship: Exploring growth and performance in family firms across generations.
12. TGO long-term survival Frank H, Kessler A, Rusch T, Suess J, Weismeier-Sammer D (2016) Capturing the familiness of family businesses: Development of the family influence familiness scale (FIFS).

education, experience, and leadership qualities. Ensure these criteria are communicated and agreed upon by all family stakeholders.

Timeline and Process: Develop a timeline for the succession process, including key milestones and deadlines. Outline the steps involved, from initial assessment to final transition.

2. Education and Training

Invest in the education and training of potential successors to prepare them for future ownership and governance roles. This includes formal education, on-the-job training, and mentorship programs.

Educational Programs: Encourage potential successors to pursue relevant educational programs, such as business degrees or specialised courses in family business management.

On-the-Job Training: Provide opportunities for potential successors to gain practical experience by working in various roles within the company. Rotate them through different departments to build a comprehensive understanding of the business.

Mentorship: Pair potential successors with experienced mentors who can guide them and provide valuable insights into leadership and business management.

3. Engagement and Communication

Maintain regular and open communication with all family members to keep them informed and engaged in the business, even if they are not actively involved. This ensures they remain committed to the family legacy and support the business's goals.

Regular Meetings: Hold family meetings to discuss business performance, strategic plans, and family matters.

Transparent Communication: Foster a culture of transparency by sharing important information about the business's operations, financial performance, and strategic decisions.

Conclusion and Real-World Consequences

This analysis examined and developed solutions for the ABC family business, addressing critical ownership, governance, and continuity issues. A lack of effective corporate governance lies at the core of these challenges.

First, the involvement of multiple shareholders has introduced significant complexity. As Nordqvist (2014) notes, ownership diversity often increases conflict, leading to operational inefficiencies and fragmented decision-making driven by power struggles. A well-functioning board of directors can counterbalance these dynamics by serving the broader interests of the business and improving strategic clarity.

Second, the absence of a formal family constitution or shareholders' agreement has escalated shareholder disputes. Such a document could have served as a governance tool to promote family unity, clarify expectations, and align the family with the business's long-term objectives.

Third, the company's failure to establish a clear transgenerational strategy has left the future of ownership uncertain. With the second generation disengaged and unmotivated to assume leadership, family involvement and ownership continuity are at serious risk.

ABC's continued reluctance to adopt appropriate governance structures and apply key strategic recommendations was central to the company's decline. A once-promising family business built over 25 years unravelled as unresolved tensions, lack of alignment, and the absence of a clear succession plan eroded trust and cohesion. Instead, what could have been managed with foresight and structure deteriorated into irreparable damage. Faced with growing dysfunction and no shared vision for the future, some shareholders chose to sell their participations, resulting in the loss of majority family ownership and control.

As Bammens (2008) highlights, *"the exit or failure of a significant number of these family incidents could be avoided by implementing good-functioning governance mechanisms."* ABC's experience is a powerful example of the risks of inaction and a reminder of the importance of governance in securing continuity and preserving family legacy.

References

Aronoff, C. and Ward, J. (2016). *Family Business Governance: Maximizing Family and Business Potential*. [online] *Perlego*. Palgrave Macmillan. Available at: https://www.perlego.com/book/3478974/family-business-governance-maximizing-family-and-business-potential-pdf

Bammens, Y., Voordeckers, W. and Van Gils, A. (2008), "Boards of directors in family firms: a generational perspective", Small Business Economy, Vol. 31 No. 2, pp. 163-180

Baron, J. and Lachenauer, R. (2021). *Build a Family Business That Lasts.* [online] Harvard Business Review. Available at: https://hbr.org/2021/01/ build-a-family-business-that-lasts.

Baron, J. and Lachenauer, R. (n.d.). *Why You Need an Owner Strategy.* [online] Banyan Global. Available at: https://banyan.global/ideas/ why-you-need-an-owner-strategy/

Baron, J., Lachenauer, R. and Ehrensberger, S. (2015). *Making Better Decisions in Your Family Business.* [online] Harvard Business Review. Available at: https:// hbr.org/2015/09/making -better-decisions-in-your-family-business.

Baus K (2013) Die Familienstrategie. Wie Familien ihr Unternehmen über Generationen sichern, 4. Aufl. Gabler Verlag, Wiesbaden

Binz Astrachan, Claudia & Waldkirch, Matthias & Michiels, Anneleen & Pieper, Torsten & Bernhard, Fabian. (2020). Professionalizing the Business Family: The Five Pillars of Competent, Committed, and Sustainable Ownership.

Brealey, R., Myers, S. and Allen, F. (2013). *Principles of Corporate Finance: Second Edition.* [online] *Google Books.* McGraw-Hill US Higher Ed USE Legacy. Available at: https://books.google.ro/books/about/Principles_of_ Corporate_Finance.html?id=xXQcAAAAQBAJ&redir_esc=y [Accessed 20 Jul. 2024].

Chua JH, Chrisman JJ, Sharma P (1999) Defining the family business by behaviour. Entrep Theory Pract 23:19–39

Davis, J.A., Hampton, M.M., Lansberg, I. and E, G.K. (1997). *Generation to Generation: Life Cycles of the Family Business.* [online] *Google Books.* Harvard Business Press. Available at: https://books.google.ro/books/ about/Generation_to_Generation.html?id=4SmhXxKQ1L4C&redir_esc=y [Accessed 20 Jul. 2024].

Edmondson, A. (2018). *The Fearless Organization: Creating Psychological Safety in the Workplace for Learning, Innovation, and Growth – Book – Faculty & Research – Harvard Business School.* [online] www.hbs.edu.

Frank H, Kessler A, Rusch T, Suess J, Weismeier-Sammer D (2016) Capturing the familiness of family businesses: Development of the family influence familiness scale (FIFS).

Gallo M, Kenyon-Rouvinez D (2005) The importance of family and business governance. In: Kenyon-Rouvinez D, Ward JL (eds) Family business: Key issues. Palgrave/Macmillan, New York, pp 45–57

Ganeshi, S. (2023). *The Dark Triad and Leadership.* [online] Medium. Available at: https://sreekanthganeshi.medium.com/the-dark-triad-and-leadership-52f98c4bbd9#:~:text=These%20three%20personality%20traits%20add%20 up%20to%20bad%20leadership..

Habbershon TG, Williams ML, MacMillan I (2003) A unified systems perspective of family firm performance. J Bus Venturing 18:451–465

Habbershon T, Nordqvist M, Zellweger T (2010) Transgenerational entrepreneurship. In: Nordqvist M, Zellweger T (eds) Transgenerational entrepreneurship: Exploring growth and performance in family firms across generations. Edward Elgar, Cheltenham, pp 1–38

Hartel, C.E.J. (2008). "How to build a healthy emotional culture and avoid a toxic culture." In C.L. Cooper & N.M. AshKanasy (Eds.), Research Companions to Emotion in Organizations

Kidwell RE, Kellermanns FW, Eddleston KA (2012) Harmony, justice, confusion, and conflict in family firms: implications for ethical climate and the "Fredo Effect". J Bus Ethics 106:503–517

Lake, R. (2021). *Explaining the Shareholder Voting Process*. [online] SoFi. Available at: https://www.sofi.com/learn/content/shareholder-voting-process/.

Lansberg I (1999) Succeeding generations: realizing the dream of families in businesses. Harvard University School Press, Boston

LeCouvie, K. and Pendergast, J. (2017). *Family Business Succession: Your Roadmap to Continuity*. [online] *Perlego*. Palgrave Macmillan. Available at: https://www.perlego.com/book/3505979/family-business-succession-your-roadmap-to-continuity-pdf?utm_source=google&utm_medium=cpc&campaignid=20933451054&adgroupid=162926082892&gad_source=1&gclid=Cj0KCQjwwO20BhCJARIsAAnTIVTw0ji7hqkBKWlBVH9DqD26CRynGbLmfwbJdNgH8v9r2FIVMvOHiKoaAnM9EALw_wcB [Accessed 20 Jul. 2024].

London, P., Cheese, P., Thomas, R. and Craig, E. (2008). *Strategies for Globalization, Talent Management and High Performance THE TALENT POWERED ORGANIZATION*. [online] Available at: http://ndl.ethernet.edu.et/bitstream/123456789/32369/1/247. Peter%20Cheese.pdf.

Lumpkin GT, Brigham KH (2011) Long-term orientation and intertemporal choice in family firms. Entrep Theory Pract 35:1149–1169

Mckinsey & Company (2024). *All in the family business*. [online] www.mckinsey.com. Available at: https://www.mckinsey.com/featured-insights/sustainable-inclusive-growth/ chart-of-the-day/all-in-the-family-business.

Nordqvist, M., Sharma, P. and Chirico, F. (2014), "Family firm heterogeneity and governance: a configuration approach", Journal of Small Business Management, Vol. 52 No. 2, pp. 192-209

onboard.com (2022). *What is an Operating Committee? (Overview, Roles, and Responsibilities)*. [online] OnBoard Board Management Software | Board Portal | Board Intelligence. Available at: https://www.onboardmeetings.com/blog/operating-committee/.

Paine, L.S. (2023). *What Does 'Stakeholder Capitalism' Mean to You?*

[online] Harvard Business Review. Available at: https://hbr.org/2023/09/what-does-stakeholder-capitalism-mean-to-you.

PwC Romania (2023). *Principalele rezultate pentru România.* [online] Available at: https://www.pwc.ro/ro/Publicatii/Raport-Family%20Business%20Survey-2023.pdf [Accessed 19 Jul. 2024].

Paulhus, D.L. and Williams, K.M. (2002). The dark triad of personality: Narcissism, machiavellianism, and psychopathy. Journal of Research in Personality, [online] 36(6), pp.556–563. doi:https://doi.org/10.1016/s0092-6566(02)00505-6.

Siebels JF, Knyphausen-Aufseß D (2012) A review of theory in family business research: the implications for corporate governance. Int J Manag Rev 14:280–304

Ward, M. (n.d.). *Morgan Stanley.* [online] Morgan Stanley. Available at: https://advisor.morganstanley.com/michelle.ward/documents/field/w/wa/ward-sofia-michelle/Family_Constitution_and_Family_By_Laws.pdf.

www.everwisecu.com. (n.d.). *Principles of Business Succession Planning | The Latest Blog | IN, MI Trust Resources | Everwise CU.* [online] Available at: https://www.everwisecu.com/about/the-latest-blog/september-2023/principles-of-business-succession-planning [Accessed 21 Jul. 2024].

Zellweger T, Kammerlander N (2015) Family, wealth and governance. An agency account. Entrep Theory Pract 39:1281–1303

Cipriana Stan

Marketing plan to launch "Gelateria Dolce Lusso" into the Romanian marketplace

EMBA Module: Marketing in a Digital World

Assignment task: Create an abridged Marketing plan to launch "ACME Ice Cream" into the Romanian marketplace.

Executive Summary

Marketing Plan for Gelateria Dolce Lusso's Artisanal Gelato

This marketing plan presents a comprehensive strategy for successfully launching Gelateria Dolce Lusso in the competitive gelato market of Cluj-Napoca, encompassing key elements such as target audience insights, unique value proposition (UVP), positioning, marketing channels, launch timeline, budget allocation, and performance evaluation metrics.

The market analysis indicates a favourable environment for artisanal gelato, with a growing demand for premium, health-conscious ice cream experiences.

Gelateria Dolce Lusso has set SMART business goals, including launching the brand by April 2024, maintaining a 30% profitability margin, reaching a revenue of 100,000 euros by the end of 2024, and becoming a recognised and trusted name for artisanal Italian gelato in Cluj-Napoca.

The primary target audience comprises parents aged 30 to 45 years seeking family-friendly outings and wellness seekers with health-conscious preferences. Understanding their needs and preferences is vital to tailor marketing efforts effectively.

Gelateria Dolce Lusso's UVP lies in its commitment to authentic Italian craftsmanship, premium ingredients, health-conscious options, and a customer-centric approach. By positioning itself as the leading solution for indulgent yet health-conscious gelato, the brand aims to create a strong emotional connection with the audience.

The customer journey lies at the heart of this plan, guiding potential customers from awareness to becoming loyal advocates. Through captivating content, engaging social media interactions, and seamless customer experiences, Gelateria Dolce Lusso aims to foster strong customer bonds and create brand advocates.

The marketing mix is designed to create exceptional value for each buyer persona, with a competitive and value-driven pricing strategy. The marketing communication mix comprises digital marketing, local events, content marketing, influencer marketing, direct marketing, and CSR initiatives to position Gelateria Dolce Lusso as the go-to destination for indulgent and health-conscious gelato experiences.

The launch strategy is divided into three phases, focusing on building anticipation through multi-channel marketing, content creation, and influencer marketing. Continuous monitoring of performance indicators will allow for optimization of marketing strategies throughout the launch. This allows for agile adjustments to the marketing strategies, ensuring optimal results.

Introduction

In the pursuit of launching Gelateria Dolce Lusso (*Figure 1*) into the vibrant market of Cluj-Napoca, **this comprehensive marketing plan is crafted with a thorough analysis built on the three levels of the business environment (macro, micro and internal)**.

By considering these dimensions, the gelateria can gain valuable insights into the market landscape, target audience preferences, and competitive forces, enabling the development of a well-informed and successful marketing strategy. Additionally, the plan is enriched with valuable insights based on author's personal experiences as an ice cream consumer and inhabitant of Cluj. This multifaceted research methodology ensures the marketing strategy is rooted in data-driven decision-making and industry best practices.

The customer journey is at the heart of this marketing plan, as it outlines the step-by-step process through which potential customers become aware of Gelateria Dolce Lusso, develop an interest in its offerings, consider and decide to make a purchase, and finally, become loyal advocates of the brand.

In the quest to appeal to **two primary buyer personas, parents and wellness seekers**, the marketing plan will emphasise the value proposition that caters to their specific needs and desires. Specialised content marketing strategies will be employed to create a sense of community around the gelateria, encouraging customers to share their delightful experiences and generate word-of-mouth buzz.

Ongoing training and development for staff members will be prioritised to reinforce the gelateria's commitment to excellence.

By understanding the internal and external business environment, harnessing the power of technology and partnerships, and **focusing on delivering a delightful customer journey**, Gelateria Dolce Lusso is poised to establish itself as the foremost destination for authentic Italian gelato in Cluj-Napoca.

Contextual Analysis

About the company

The new gelateria will be a small-sized enterprise that will operate in the HoReCa industry, in Cluj-Napoca as a SRL. Based on the research, the business will target a medium and high-end maket by serving premium gelato at affordable prices. With a total number of 10 employees, the company will have one central location and two vending selling carts that can be moved around the city, or at private events. The Business Model Canva (Osterwalder et. al., 2010) for the organisation is outlined in *Appendix 1.*

About Gelateria Dolce Lusso

At Gelateria Dolce Lusso, we take immense pride in our **artisanal excellence, crafting authentic Italian gelato** that sets us apart from the mass-produced offerings in the market.
We value your well-being, which is why our focus on health-conscious options shines through in our **reduced sugar, low-calorie, and vegan choices.** As the world prioritiwes healthier lifestyles, **we provide guilt-free indulgence without** compromising dietary preferences and values.

With a deep connection to our Italian heritage, Gelateria Dolce Lusso taps into the **authentic flavours and culinary traditions of Italy,** adding a touch of sophistication and uniqueness to each scoop. You can savour a cultural experience with every delicious bite.

Our commitment to social responsibility and sustainability is at the core of our brand.
We take pride in our **eco-friendly practices and support for local communities,** aligning with the values of socially conscious consumers.
Step into Gelateria Dolce Lusso, and you'll be welcomed by an exquisite ambiance, reflecting our dedication to creating a luxurious and inviting setting. **Our stylish interior and attention to detail elevate your ice cream experience,** making it a memorable outing every time you visit.

We place our customers at the heart of everything we do.
Our diverse array of classic and innovative flavours ensures there's something for everyone, catering to individual tastes and encouraging repeat visits.

Figure 1. About the company. Source: Author's contribution

Smart Objectives, Mission And Vision

The new business objectives are:
1. Launch the new brand by April 2024
2. Maintain a profitability margin of 30% from the launch and onwards.
3. Establish a strong presence in Cluj-Napoca's ice cream market, reaching a revenue of 100.000 euro by the end of 2024.
4. Become a recognisable and trusted name for artisanal Italian gelato in Cluj-Napoca by the end of 2024 and onwards.

Proposed name: Gelateria Dolce Lusso
The name Gelateria Dolce Lusso, as explained in *Figure 2*, has been proposed. It reflects the brand's premium offerings and is suggestive enough to know from the start what it is.

Proposed name:
Gelateria Dolce Lusso

The name exudes luxury and elegance, perfectly reflecting the
brand's premium offerings. "Gelateria" adds an authentic
Italian touch, while "Dolce Lusso" combines the sweetness of
"Dolce" with the sophistication of "Lusso," creating a
memorable and appealing name for the new gelato venture.

Figure 2. The name Gelateria Dolce Lusso. Source: Author's contribution

The Vision

The vision (*Figure 3*) is to provide a unique luxury ice cream
experience at affordable prices that combine the richness of artisanal
Italian gelato with a commitment to health consciousness and
social responsibility. Through our commitment to innovation and
the continuous pursuit of harmony between indulgence and well-
being, we envision inspiring a profound appreciation for the art of
ice cream while promoting a healthier and more conscious lifestyle.

The Mission

Gelateria Dolce Lusso's mission is to bring joy and satisfaction
to its customers through well-being with a captivating culinary
journey through the rich heritage of Italian gelato craftsmanship,
whether it is a moment of indulgence shared with loved ones or
a personal treat.

Vision

Each scoop is carefully prepared with the finest ingredients and skilled craftsmanship, promising a truly delightful, healthy and exquisite taste.

Our vision is to be recognised as the foremost destination for connoisseurs of artisanal ice cream, setting new standards of excellence in taste, quality, offerings and customer experience.

To provide a unique and exceptional ice cream experience that combines the richness of artisanal Italian gelato with a commitment to health-consciousness and social responsibility.

Mission

Create and serve the finest artisanal Italian ice cream

To craft and serve the finest artisanal Italian ice cream that tantalises the taste buds, delights the soul, and embodies the essence of indulgence and well-being.

Our mission is to bring joy and satisfaction to our customers. Whether it's a moment of indulgence shared with loved ones or a personal treat, we seek to enhance the happiness and well-being of our customers through our delectable scoops of our creations that transport them on a captivating culinary journey through the rich heritage of Italian gelato craftsmanship.

Figure 3. The vision and mission of Gelateria Dolce Lusso. Source: Author's contribution

The Brand

The tagline *"Artisanal Indulgence for the Health-Conscious Gourmand"* encapsulates the gelateria's message, inviting customers to savour an ice cream experience that delights their senses while nourishing their well-being. The brand's purpose (*Figure 4*) is to offer a unique gelato experience that combines the richness of artisanal Italian gelato with a commitment to health-consciousness and social responsibility at affordable prices.

Visual Identity

The logo (*Figure 5*) is carefully crafted, **incorporating golden patterns to convey a premium touch**, while a modern font alongside a **handwritten style suggests the artisanal experience**. The iconic ice cream cone instantly communicates the nature of the business, symbolising the delightful gelato offerings.

Dolce Lusso Gelateria

The Purpose

The purpose of Gelateria Dolce Lusso is to provide a unique and exceptional ice cream experience that combines the richness of artisanal Italian gelato with a commitment to health-consciousness and social responsibility at affordable prices.

Artisanal Indulgence for the Health-Conscious Gourmand

Gelateria Dolce Lusso goes beyond offering exclusive Italian ice cream at affordable prices. It stands as a beacon of authenticity, catering to the discerning consumer consciousness towards synthetic ingredients.

Our brand takes pride in delivering high-quality, artisanal ice cream, blending classic flavours with innovative and healthy options.

Recognising the rise of lifestyle diseases like obesity and diabetes, we offer low-calorie alternatives that do not compromise on taste.

Gelateria Dolce Lusso:

Embracing the global trend of veganism, we present a delightful array of vegan ice cream options, celebrating the natural goodness of plant-based ingredients.

Our commitment to using only natural and wholesome components resonates with those seeking authentic and nourishing treats.

With a focus on the growing health concerns, we meticulously craft our ice cream using premium ingredients like whole milk and skim milk, ensuring a guilt-free indulgence.

At Gelateria Dolce Lusso, we invite you to savor the delightful fusion of traditional expertise and contemporary health consciousness, as we curate a unique ice cream experience that indulges your senses while elevating your well-being.

Figure 4. The brand's purpose. *Source: Author's contribution*

The New Brand: Dolce Lusso

Figure 5. The logo. *Source: Author's contribution*

The UVP

Through applying the VRIO analysis (*Figure 6*), Gelateria Dolce Lusso has identified several key strengths underpinning its Unique Value Proposition (UVP). By thoroughly **examining the gelateria's resources and capabilities, valuable insights have been gained,** shedding light on the factors that set it apart and allow for delivering exceptional value to its customers on the factors that set it apart and allow for delivering exceptional value to its customers.

Gelateria Dolce Lusso's Unique Value Proposition sets it apart from competitors in the gelato market. **By highlighting artisanal excellence, health-conscious options, authentic Italian heritage, social responsibility, and an exquisite ambience**, the brand caters to the preferences of a diverse customer base.

This **UVP aligns perfectly with current market trends and customer demands**, positioning Gelateria Dolce Lusso as a leading player in the competitive Cluj-Napoca market. Gelateria Dolce Lusso ensures success through its customer-centric approach and unparalleled ice cream experience.

Gelateria Dolce Lusso's Competitive advantage using VRIO framework

Capability	Valued	Rare	Costly to imitate	Non-substitutable	Competitive advantage
Artisanal Excellence: The dedication to crafting authentic and artisanal Italian gelato using premium ingredients adds value to Gelateria Dolce Lusso. This focus on craftsmanship resonates with customers seeking a high-quality and indulgent ice cream experience.	YES	YES	YES	YES	SUSTAINABLE COMPETITIVE ADVANTAGE
Health-Conscious Options: Offering health-conscious choices with reduced sugar, low-calorie, and vegan options adds value to the brand by catering to the preferences of health-conscious consumers.	YES	YES	YES	YES	SUSTAINABLE COMPETITIVE ADVANTAGE
Social Responsibility: The commitment to social responsibility and sustainability adds value by aligning with the values of socially conscious consumers. Establishing eco-friendly practices and community support can be challenging for competitors to replicate quickly.	YES	YES	YES	YES	SUSTAINABLE COMPETITIVE ADVANTAGE
Customer-Centric Approach: Gelateria Dolce Lusso's customer-centric approach, reflected in the diverse array of flavors and attention to individual preferences, relies on efficient organization and customer feedback management.	YES	YES	YES	YES	SUSTAINABLE COMPETITIVE ADVANTAGE

Figure 6. VRIO framework applied for the new gelateria (Barney, Hesterly, 2011). Source: Author's contribution

Unique Value Proposition

"Indulgence Redefined: Artisanal Italian Gelato for the Health-Conscious Gourmand"

Why?

- **Artisanal Excellence:** Gelateria Dolce Lusso's UVP highlights our commitment to crafting authentic and artisanal Italian gelato. The brand's dedication to the traditional gelato-making process and the use of premium ingredients set it apart from mass-produced ice cream offerings in the market. This focus on craftsmanship resonates with customers seeking a genuinely indulgent and high-quality ice cream experience, and with existing market trends.

- **Health-Conscious Options:** The UVP emphasises Gelateria Dolce Lusso's dedication to health-consciousness, offering options with reduced sugar, low-calorie, and vegan choices. In a world where consumers increasingly prioritise their well-being, this aspect of the brand's UVP appeals to health-conscious gourmets who want to indulge without compromising their dietary preferences and values and with the identified market trends.

- **Authentic Italian Heritage:** By positioning ourselves as an exclusive Italian gelato brand, Gelateria Dolce Lusso taps into the appeal of genuine Italian flavours and culinary traditions. This authentic connection with Italian heritage adds a touch of sophistication and uniqueness to the brand, drawing customers who appreciate the rich cultural experience behind each scoop.

- **Social Responsibility:** The UVP highlights Gelateria Dolce Lusso's commitment to social responsibility and sustainability. As customers become more conscious of the impact of their choices, the brand's eco-friendly practices and support for local communities align with the values of socially conscious consumers from our target audience.

- **Exquisite Ambiance:** The UVP conveys Gelateria Dolce Lusso's dedication to creating a luxurious and inviting ambience. The gelateria's stylish interior and attention to detail in presentation add to the overall experience, making it an ideal destination for those seeking ice cream and a memorable outing.

- **Customer-Centric Approach:** The UVP emphasises Gelateria Dolce Lusso's focus on meeting the preferences and desires of its customers. By offering a diverse array of classic and innovative flavours, the brand ensures something for everyone, catering to individual tastes and encouraging repeat visits.

- **Our authentic Italian gelato, focus on premium quality and dietary choices, commitment to social responsibility, and exquisite ambiance come together to create an unparalleled ice cream experience for our discerning customers.**

Figure 7. Gelateria Dolce Lusso's Unique Value Proposition. *Source: Author's contribution*

External and internal environment

The gelateria's economic environment is crucial in shaping its growth and success. To ensure the gelateria can effectively adapt to the economic landscape, we comprehensively analysed the macro and microeconomic factors using frameworks such as PESTEL (Johnson et al., 2017), Porter's 5 Forces (Porter, 2008), and SWOT (Hill et al., 2017), and by also looking at the general context of the industry global ice cream market (*Figure 8*), European (*Figure 9*) and local market (*Figure 14*).

This strategic approach enables the gelateria to identify and capitalise on opportunities while navigating potential challenges, ensuring sustainable growth in the competitive market. By comprehensively understanding the economic landscape, the gelateria will be well-equipped to make informed decisions that align with its business objectives and drive long-term success.

PESTEL and SWOT Analyses

The ice cream market context analysis, PESTEL analyses (*Figure 10*), and SWOT (*Figure 11*) have provided valuable insights **into identifying SO strategies**. Therefore, the gelateria should invest in targeted marketing and promotional campaigns highlighting health-conscious and vegan gelato options. Collaborating with local health and wellness influencers and organizations will create awareness among the target audience. Special promotions and discounts on vegan gelato flavours will attract new customers and foster repeat visits, solidifying the gelateria's position in the market.

For successful market expansion, conducting thorough market research to identify potential cities or regions in Romania is essential. Strategic partnerships with local tourism boards and events will promote the brand, attracting tourists seeking an authentic Italian gelato experience. **Continuous product innovation, guided by customer feedback, will keep the menu relevant to evolving preferences and demands, sustaining a loyal customer base.**

To implement the ST and WT strategies, Gelateria Dolce Lusso must invest in market research to tailor marketing efforts and product offerings to Cluj-Napoca's specific needs. **Continuously innovating the gelato menu** with unique flavours and seasonal

GLOBAL ICE CREAM MARKET HIGHLIGHTS

CAGR

+4.2%
CAGR 2022-2030

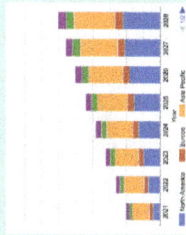

MARKET DRIVERS

- The growing preference for ice cream as a daily post-meal dessert
- Increased urbanisation and rising disposable income made it possible for them to **afford luxury goods and high-quality lifestyles.**
- Due to its portability and growing global popularity, the impulsive ice cream business is the most lucrative in the whole ice cream industry.
- **The rise in house events and parties where ice cream is served as a snack** or dessert (take-home ice cream).
- The creation of an **effective supply chain and technological advancements in deep freezer technology**
- New products: **a low-calorie and low-fat ice cream** for consumers who are concerned about their health

MARKET RESTRAINS

- Ice cream products face hurdles in **storage and transportation** due to the need for low freezing temperatures, resulting in **high costs and energy usage.**
- The market for **organic ice cream** is anticipated to face challenges from strict rules for ingredient standardisation.
- **A steep decline in product demand throughout the winter and monsoon seasons,** which can further impede market expansion.
- The demand for the product is often at its height during the summer.
- The **ice cream industry is highly fragmented and competitive,** with many domestic and foreign rivals.

The increasing **health consciousness** among consumers is **expected to fuel the demand for premium ice creams** in the upcoming years.

AUDIENCE INSIGHTS & BEHAVIOUR

- The growing preference for ice cream as a daily post-meal dessert
- Growing demand for **dairy-free**
- Rise in **health consciousness** among customers
- **Vegan products** would increase as people start to favor healthier choices
- Manufacturers are increasing their product range by including **functional ingredients, organic, herbal, and exotic flavors in product formulations to meet the changing consumer demand.**
- The increasing **trend for natural ingredients**
- Rising consumer consciousness toward synthetic ingredients.
- One of the most well-liked flavours in the world is vanilla.
- **Organic herbal fillings, and exotic flavours in product formulations** to acquire a competitive advantage and appeal to more consumers' inclination for testing out new flavours.

Figure 8. Global Ice Cream Market highlights based on cited sources in references. Author's contribution

EUROPEAN ICE CREAM MARKET HIGHLIGHTS

CAGR

+4.87%
CAGR 2023-2028

Source https://www.businessmarketinsights.com/

MARKET DRIVERS

- **Increasing disposable income** and the introduction of various products in the dessert category to cater to the choices of a vast group of consumers.
- The surge in the consumption of **high-quality frozen desserts** is one of the biggest trends in the food industry.
- The growing trend of consuming frozen desserts after a meal as an effective digestive product
- Increased consumption of **artisanal ice cream**
- Many social changes, such as the growing number of smaller households and the rising millennial population across the region
- New **innovative flavours**, offered by companies.
- One of the popular trends in the European ice cream market is the **premiumisation of ice creams.**
- **The demand for luxury ice cream and regular ice cream** desserts is also rising sharply in the European market due to the continent's rapidly expanding urbanisation and **the dairy industry's improved technological improvements.**
- There has been **an ongoing trend of artisanal ice cream** across European regions like Italy, France, and others regions.
- **Rising demand for healthy Ice Creams.**

AUDIENCE INSIGHTS & BEHAVIOUR

- Demand for ice creams that are **low on fats, made using natural ingredients, yet do not compromise on taste** and indulgence is growing across Europe.
- Europeans prefer **premium ice creams** due to their distinctive flavours and portions.
- Consumers prefer the use of **novel ingredients such as whole milk, skim milk, and sweetening and flavouring agents.**
- Owing to a rise in the lifestyle diseases like obesity, and diabetes, a growing preference for **veganism, and increasing health consciousness among consumers, ice creams without dairy ingredients** are gaining momentum in the European market.
- Non-vegan health-conscious individuals demand **low-calorie and natural ingredients** in ice creams.
- **Demand for non-dairy or "healthier" ice cream** is booming in European countries.

One of the popular trends in the European ice cream market is the **premiumisation of ice creams, and an ongoing trend of artisanal ice cream.**

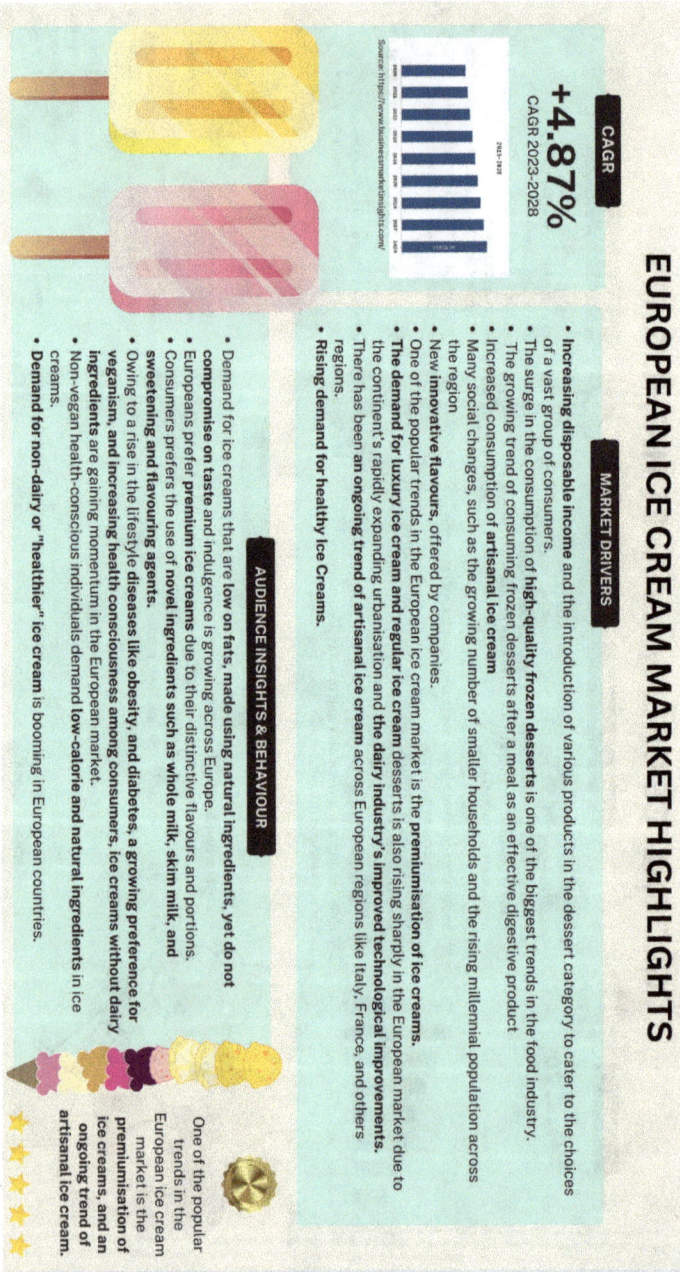

.
Figure 9. European Ice Cream Market highlights based on cited sources in references. Author's contribution

offerings will counter intense competition and solidify the gelateria's brand identity. Engaging the local community through exciting marketing campaigns and events will overcome seasonality challenges, fostering anticipation for new flavours and promotions.

Addressing new market entry and limited distribution channels requires building strong relationships with local businesses and influencers, increasing brand awareness and attracting new customers.

PESTEL Analysis

Political	Economic	Social	Technological	Environmental	Legal
Taxation and Regulations: Changes in tax policies may impact the gelateria's operating costs and pricing strategies.	**Growing market and increased consumer spending:** The overall economic growth and disposable income of Cluj residents will influence their spending on non-essential items like gelato.	**Health and Wellness Trends:** The growing emphasis on health-consciousness and wellness may drive demand for premium gelato options with reduced sugar and natural ingredients.	**Technological Factors:** Digital Marketing: Leveraging digital marketing channels and social media platforms will be essential to reach and engage with the tech-savvy youth demographic.	**Sustainability Practices:** Consumers are increasingly conscious of environmental issues.	**Food Safety and Hygiene Regulations:** Compliance with food safety and hygiene standards is essential for ensuring customer trust and meeting legal requirements.
The Government in Romania is talking about introducing new taxes, which means that the instability will increase.	**Inflation and Currency Fluctuations:** Economic factors such as inflation and currency fluctuations can affect ingredient costs and overall profitability.	The increasing demand for luxury ice cream desserts in Europe.	**Ordering and Delivery Systems:** technological advancements in ordering and delivery systems are better positioned to meet the ever-increasing expectations of modern consumers.	**Energy Consumption:** Energy consumption in gelato production primarily revolves around the equipment and processes involved in creating and storing the frozen dessert.	**Employment Laws:** Local labour laws regarding hiring, working hours and employee rights.
The uncertainty and potential instability resulting from such changes make it challenging for businesses to stick to long-term plans.		The rise of demand for healthy ice cream around the world.		**Environmental Trend -** Sustainable Energy Usage and Transportation	

Figure 10. PESTEL Analysis. Source: Author's contribution

The organisation	Strengths – S	Weaknesses – W
	1. Artisanal Excellence 2. Health-Conscious Options 3. Authentic Italian Heritage 4. Social Responsibility 5. Exquisite Ambiance 6. Customer-Centric Approach	1. New Market Entry: As a new brand, Gelateria Dolce Lusso faces the challenge of building awareness and establishing a customer base in Cluj-Napoca 2. Limited Distribution Channels: The lack of existing distribution channels may hinder initial market penetration and reaching a wider customer base.
Opportunities – O 1. Growing Health-Consciousness 2. Rising Demand for Vegan Choices 3. Market Expansion 4. Growing market & increased consumer spending	**SO Strategies** • **Emphasising the brand's authenticity and Italian heritage in** marketing communications can differentiate it from competitors and appeal to customers seeking genuine Italian gelato experiences. • **Offering reduced sugar, low-calorie, and vegan gelato choices.** Develop and promote a special menu featuring a variety of healthy and indulgent gelato options that cater to the increasing demand from health conscious consumers. Emphasise the use of natural ingredients and the nutritional benefits of these gelato offerings to attract and retain health-conscious customers. • **Expand the range of dairy-free and vegan flavours on the menu to cater to the preferences of vegan and lactose-intolerant consumers.** Develop creative and unique vegan gelato flavours using premium ingredients to differentiate the brand in the market and attract a broader customer base seeking vegan alternatives. • **Understanding Consumer Preferences:** Understanding and adapting to the preferences of the local population, such as flavours, portion sizes, and presentation, are vital for Gelateria Dolce Lusso's success.	**WO Strategies** • should focus on effective marketing and brand building initiatives to create awareness and attract customers in Cluj-Napoca. **Gelateria Dolce Lusso can implement eco-friendly practices**, such as biodegradable packaging and sourcing local ingredients. • Gelateria Dolce Lusso, being a responsible player in the market, should proactively consider the environmental impact of its operations, with a particular focus on refrigeration and transportation. • Engaging in social media marketing, local events, and partnerships can enhance visibility and draw customers to the gelateria. • Explore various distribution channels, such as collaborations with local cafes and restaurants, to expand its reach. Building strategic partnerships with local tourism associations and event organizers can further increase brand exposure and attract a wider audience.
Threats – T 1. Intense Competition 2. Seasonality 3. Evolving Consumer Preferences 4. Taxation & Regulations 5. Energy consumption and environmental impact 6. Political instability – higher taxes for small companies in Romania are announced	**ST Strategies** • Utilise Gelateria Dolce Lusso's strengths in artisanal excellence, health-conscious options, authentic Italian heritage, and exquisite ambiance to differentiate the brand from competitors. Implement loyalty programs and customer engagement initiatives to build a loyal customer base, reducing the risk of losing customers to competitors. • Introduce seasonal promotions and limited-time offers to encourage customer visits during off-peak periods. Create innovative gelato flavours and promotions that align with specific seasons or holidays to maintain customer interest and attract visitors throughout the year.	**WT Strategies** • effective marketing and brand-building initiatives. **Offering special promotions and discounts to first-time customers can incentivise trial and encourage repeat visits.** building strategic partnerships with local cafes, restaurants, and hotels can provide additional points of sale and increase brand exposure. • **introducing takeaway and delivery options to reach customers who may not visit the gelateria in person.** having a buffer at the profit margin to overcome taxes increases and currency fluctuation. • **The gelateria should prioritize eco-friendly options to deliver its delightful gelato to customers.** Embracing electric or hybrid vehicles can substantially decrease emissions associated with transportation, contributing to cleaner air and reduced environmental harm.

Figure 11. SWOT Analysis. Source: Author's contribution

The Internal Environment

The new gelateria's internal environment is characterised by the technical know-how the owner has in the ice cream production, and the validated know-how, and it will be organised as a limited society (SRL), with ten employees for the primary location and the two mobile vending carts.

The presence of ten dedicated employees for the central gelateria location and two mobile vending carts ensures a strong workforce to cater to customer demands effectively. The team's passion and commitment to delivering exceptional customer service contribute to a positive and memorable customer experience, fostering loyalty and repeat business.

INTERNAL ENVIRONMENT

Other assets:

- the new company will open 1 location in Cluj, in a central area, will have two vending carts.
- Dolce Lusso will need to hire 10 people who can serve and prepare the ice cream.

Legal Organisation

SRL

Main capabilities:

- Technical Know-How
- Validated recipe in Italy.

Porters 5 Forces Findings

The Porter 5 Forces analysis (*Figure 12*) pointed out that entering the gelato market in Cluj presents opportunities and challenges for the new Gelateria.

1. **Threats of New Entry:** The gelato industry's specialised knowledge and craftsmanship act as barriers for new entrants without experience. Established competitors like Gioelia Cremeria, Bianco Milano, and Moritz Eis already have a strong brand presence and customer loyalty, making it challenging for newcomers. However, the high demand for gelato and health-conscious options may attract some new entrants.

2. **Buyer Power:** Customers in Cluj have multiple gelato options and can switch based on price, taste, and service. Gelateria Dolce Lusso must be attentive to customer preferences and offer a compelling value proposition to retain and attract buyers amid competition.

3. **Competition:** Rivalry among existing gelato competitors in Cluj is intense. Gelateria Dolce Lusso must focus on its Unique Value Proposition (UVP), offering artisanal gelato and catering to health-conscious consumers.

4. **Supplier Power:** Suppliers of premium ingredients have some bargaining power due to product uniqueness. Gelateria Dolce Lusso can mitigate this by establishing strong relationships with local suppliers and seeking multiple sources.

5. **Threats of Substitution:** Gelateria Dolce Lusso faces competition from other gelaterias and dessert alternatives like frozen yoghurt shops. To differentiate, the gelateria should highlight its unique artisanal gelato, health-conscious options, and captivating flavour combinations.

To conclude, Gelateria Dolce Lusso can leverage premium and health-conscious options demand through strong brand identity, innovative flavours, and exceptional customer service. Active social media presence and addressing competitors' weaknesses will build brand awareness, enabling Gelateria Dolce Lusso to thrive in Cluj's competitive gelato market.

Porters 5 Forces

Threats of new entry

- +Gelato industry requires specialized knowledge and craftsmanship, which can be a barrier for new entrants without prior experience.
- -Existing competitors like Gioelia Cremeria, Bianco Milano, and Moritz Eis already have established brand presence and customer loyalty, making it challenging for new entrants to gain traction.
- +However, the relatively high demand for gelato and the growing trend of premium, health-conscious options may attract some new entrants.

Supplier power

- - Suppliers of premium and natural ingredients might have some bargaining power due to the uniqueness and quality of their products.
- + Gelateria Dolce Lusso can mitigate this by establishing strong relationships with local suppliers, seeking multiple sources, and negotiating favourable terms.

Competition

- -Rivalry among existing competitors in the gelato market in Cluj is intense, with Gioelia Cremeria, Bianco Milano, and Moritz Eis vying for market share and customer attention.
- + To stand out, Gelateria DolceLusso must focus on its Unique Value Proposition (UVP), such as offering artisanal gelato with a luxury touch and catering to the preferences of health-conscious consumers.
- - Many competitors, at similar size and price offering, direct and indirect
- + Weak differentiation in positioning.
- + Better product than the competition

Buyer power

- - Customers in Cluj have multiple options for gelato, and they can easily switch between competitors based on factors like price, taste, and service.
- As Gioelia Cremeria, Bianco Milano, and Moritz Eis are well-established competitors, Gelateria Dolce Lusso needs to be attentive to customer preferences and offer a compelling value proposition to retain and attract buyers.

Threats of substituitons

- - Gelateria Dolce Lusso faces competition not only from other gelaterias but also from various dessert alternatives, such as frozen yogurt shops, pastry stores, and confectioneries.
- To differentiate itself, Gelateria Dolce Lusso should highlight its unique artisanal gelato, health-conscious options, and captivating flavor combinations.

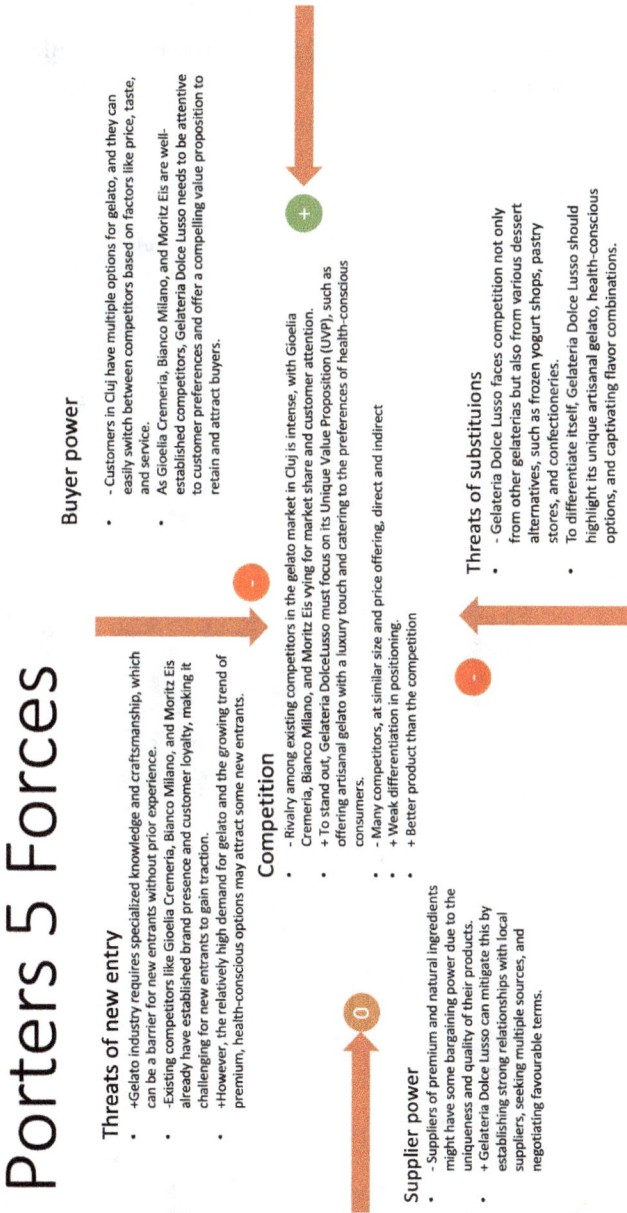

Figure 12. Applying Porters 5 Forces Framework (Porter, 2008). Source: Author's contribution

The Competition

After a comprehensive analysis of the main competitors in the local gelato market, namely Gioelia Cremeria, Bianco Milano, and Moritz Eis, several key findings have been revealed, as pointed out in *Figure 13*.

Competition Analysis

Competitor	Strengths	Weakness
Gioelia Cremeria	- over 80 reviews on Google with a score of 4.5 out of 5 - a franchise from Italy - a good positioning in Iulius Mall - Customers say that the ice cream it is identical to the one in Italy. - They have a variety of desserts, both by the glass, but also wonderful and tasty cakes. - Good ice cream quality - active communication on social media	- customers are complaining that the cups are much smaller than in Bucharest, but they have the same price and that not all the time staff is well prepared and friendly, - the customers complain that the price is very high, similar to the one in Rome. - high prices
Bianco Milano	- over 340 reviews on Google with a score of 4.6 out of 5 - central location in the main market square in Cluj - good ice cream quality and various desserts - not active on social media	- always a long line; people have to wait quite a lot to buy an ice cream - customers are complaining that horrible, rude service not worth the experience " it kills all your appetite for ice cream, the nervous staff raises their voice" - not very active on social media. Just a minimum presence and used for different announcements.
Moritz Eis	- over 433 reviews on Google with a score of 4.7 out of 5 - not active on social media in Romania - good ice cream quality - in Cluj they are making home delivering on all 3 delivery platforms	• the main issues the customers are complaining are the attitude of the personnel: "the worst, careless and arrogant service"

Figure 13. Competition analysis. Source: Author's contribution

Gioelia Cremeria, a well-positioned franchise from Italy, boasts positive online reviews and a variety of desserts. However, **customers have raised concerns about portion sizes, staff friendliness, and high prices**.

Bianco Milano enjoys a central location and positive reviews but **lacks active social media presence and faces criticism for long waiting times and poor service**.

Moritz Eis receives positive reviews for ice cream quality but lacks social media presence and **faces complaints about personnel attitude**.

In conclusion, for the new gelateria, there are opportunities to differentiate itself by **emphasising a strong online presence, providing exceptional customer service, and ensuring product authenticity. Addressing customer concerns and maintaining a competitive pricing strategy** will be crucial for the new brand to thrive in the competitive Cluj gelato market.

The Marketing Strategy

The Buyer Persona

As Gelateria Dolce Lusso prepares to launch its premium artisanal gelato venture in Cluj-Napoca, a comprehensive market and consumer preferences analysis has revealed four distinct buyer personas (*Figure 14*). These buyer personas represent different segments of the target audience, each with unique characteristics and preferences when indulging in delightful gelato experiences. The Buyer Personas are extensively analysed in *Appendix 2*.

While all four buyer personas present exciting opportunities for gelateria's growth and success, **focusing on parents and wellness seekers during the first year after launch is rooted in a strategic approach** to maximise gelateria's impact and establish a strong foundation in the market.

Parents seeking indulgent treats for themselves and their children represent a significant consumer group with the potential for repeat visits, and wellness seekers, who prioritise health-conscious choices, are increasingly seeking guilt-free indulgences.

In preparation for entering the competitive gelato market of Cluj-Napoca, Gelateria Dolce Lusso **should adopt a strategic**

approach to customise its Unique Value Proposition (*Figure 15*) **according to the diverse needs and desires of the target audiences**. This customer-centric approach is intended to foster enduring connections and loyalty with these segments.

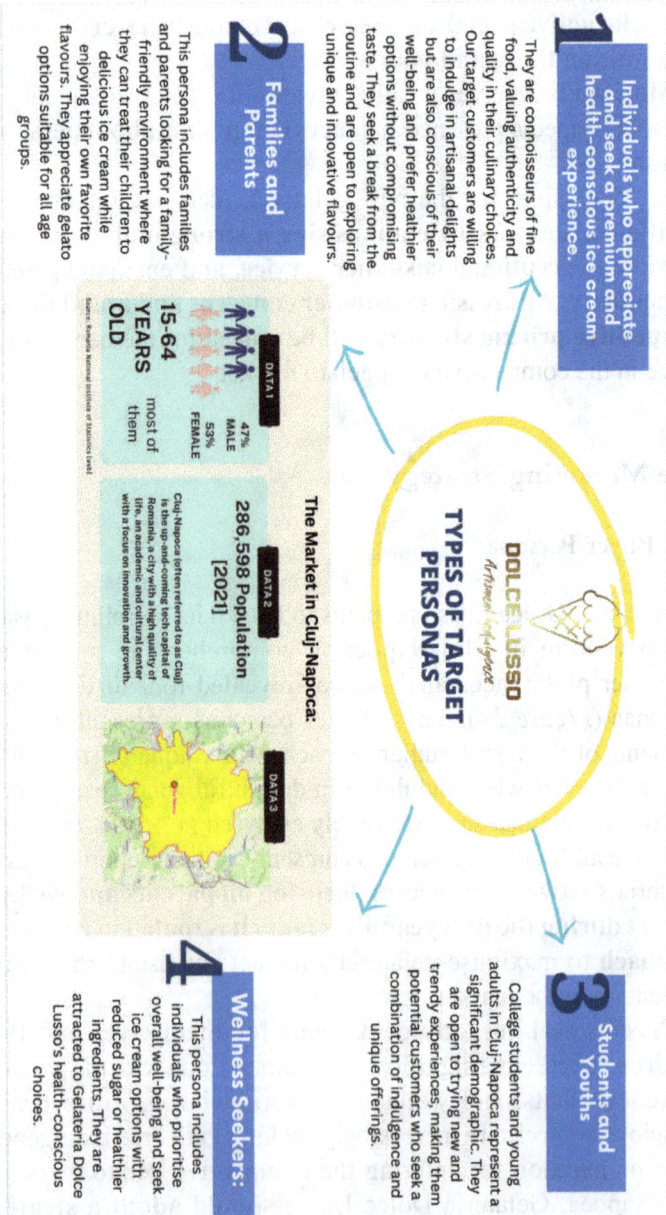

TYPES OF TARGET PERSONAS

DOLCE LUSSO
Artisanal Gelateria

1 Individuals who appreciate and seek a premium and health-conscious ice cream experience.

They are connoisseurs of fine food, valuing authenticity and quality in their culinary choices. Our target customers are willing to indulge in artisanal delights but are also conscious of their well-being and prefer healthier options without compromising taste. They seek a break from the routine and are open to exploring unique and innovative flavours.

2 Families and Parents

This persona includes families and parents looking for a family-friendly environment where they can treat their children to delicious ice cream while enjoying their own favorite flavours. They appreciate gelato options suitable for all age groups.

3 Students and Youths

College students and young adults in Cluj-Napoca represent a significant demographic. They are open to trying new and trendy experiences, making them potential customers who seek a combination of indulgence and unique offerings.

4 Wellness Seekers:

This persona includes individuals who prioritise overall well-being and seek ice cream options with reduced sugar or healthier ingredients. They are attracted to Gelateria Dolce Lusso's health-conscious choices.

The Market in Cluj-Napoca:

DATA 1

15-64 YEARS OLD — most of them

47% MALE
53% FEMALE

Source: Romania National Institute of Statistics (web)

DATA 2

286,598 Population [2021]

Cluj-Napoca (often referred to as Cluj) is the up-and-coming tech capital of Romania, a city with a high quality of life, an academic and cultural center with a focus on innovation and growth.

DATA 3

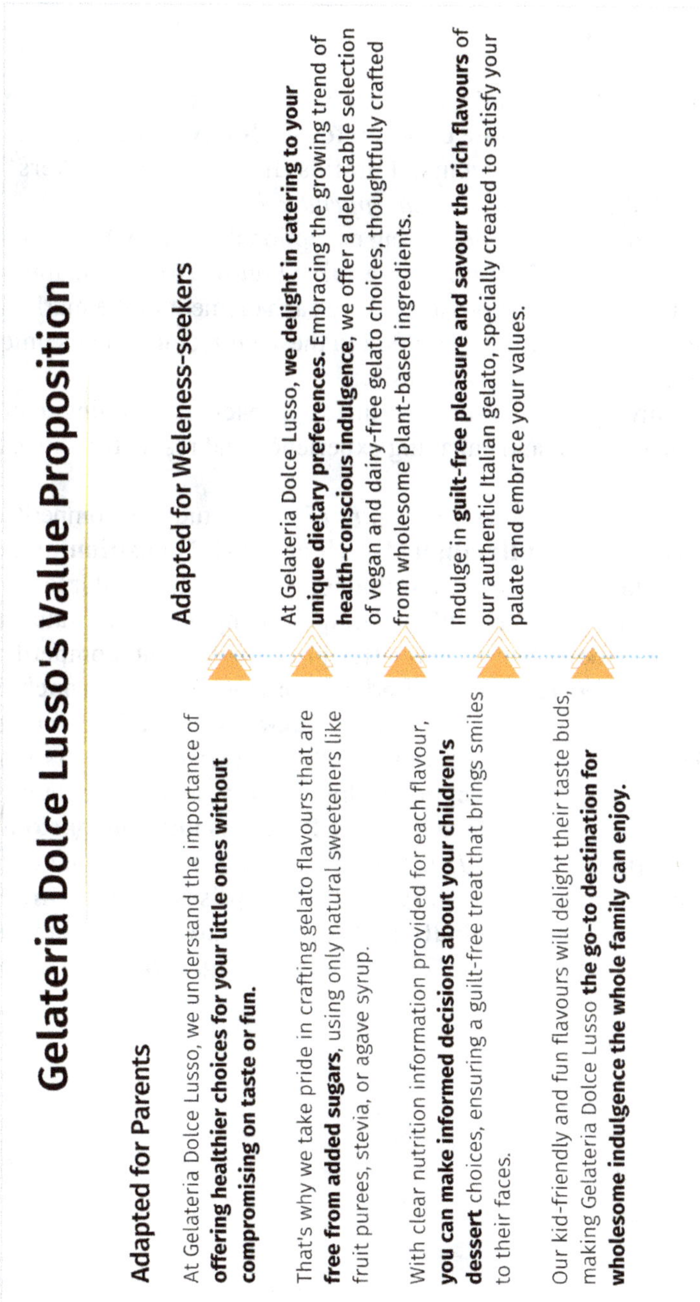

Gelateria Dolce Lusso's Value Proposition

Adapted for Parents

At Gelateria Dolce Lusso, we understand the importance of **offering healthier choices for your little ones without compromising on taste or fun.**

That's why we take pride in crafting gelato flavours that are **free from added sugars,** using only natural sweeteners like fruit purees, stevia, or agave syrup.

With clear nutrition information provided for each flavour, **you can make informed decisions about your children's dessert** choices, ensuring a guilt-free treat that brings smiles to their faces.

Our kid-friendly and fun flavours will delight their taste buds, making Gelateria Dolce Lusso **the go-to destination for wholesome indulgence the whole family can enjoy.**

Adapted for Weleness-seekers

At Gelateria Dolce Lusso, **we delight in catering to your unique dietary preferences.** Embracing the growing trend of **health-conscious indulgence,** we offer a delectable selection of vegan and dairy-free gelato choices, thoughtfully crafted from wholesome plant-based ingredients.

Indulge in **guilt-free pleasure and savour the rich flavours of** our authentic Italian gelato, specially created to satisfy your palate and embrace your values.

Figure 15. The UVP. Source: Author's contribution

The Marketing Mix

The marketing mix is meticulously tailored around the central idea of value creation for each buyer persona within the two main segments: families and wellness seekers, as detailed in *Appendix 3 and Appendix 4*.

In the pursuit of delivering exceptional value to the two main audiences, the **7P marketing mix** (*Figure 16*) was adapted to ensure a tailored approach, where each element of the marketing mix has been carefully crafted to these target audience's unique needs, preferences, and desires.

Through this customer-centric approach, it is aiming to craft a personalised and engaging experience that resonates with each group.

The pricing strategy (*Figure 17*), after studying competitor's prices, **is carefully aligned with gelateria's positioning as a premium yet affordable Italian gelato brand.** To cater to price-sensitive customers without compromising perceived value and quality, the gelateria will offer prices below the competitors, **following a transparent and customer-centric approach**. By adopting this **competitive and value-driven pricing strategy**, Gelateria Dolce Lusso aims to attract diverse customers while maintaining the perception of high-quality artisanal gelato.

Based on the selected Buyer Personas and the marketing objectives (*Figure 18*), Gelateria Dolce Lusso's marketing communications mix (*Figure 19*) comprises a **well-rounded and engaging combination of digital strategies, local events, content marketing, influencer marketing, direct marketing, and CSR initiatives.**

MARKETING MIX

05 People

Well-trained and friendly staff are essential for providing excellent customer service and enhancing the overall customer experience. Employees should be knowledgeable about the gelato flavours, ingredients, and health-conscious options.

06 Process:

The customer's journey and experience when visiting the gelateria. The ordering process should be streamlined and efficient, and the presentation of the gelato should be visually appealing. Maintaining a clean and welcoming ambiance is also crucial.

07 Physical Evidence

Gelateria's interior design, eco-friendly packaging, branding materials, the uniforms, and any other touchpoints that customers interact with.

PRODUCT

1. Artisanal Gelato (main product)
2. Health-Conscious Options Gelatos
3. Gelato Cakes and Specialties
4. Gelato Vending Carts (single servings to on-the-go customers)
5. Customised Gelato Creations (flavours for special occasions or unique taste preferences)

PRICE

Gelateria Dolce Lusso will adopt an affordable pricing strategy to reflect the high-quality and unique offerings. Additionally it may offer promotional pricing during off-peak seasons or for special events.

PLACEMENT

1. Main Gelateria Location strategically located in the center of the city
2. Mobile Vending Carts in key areas with high footfall
3. Online Delivery through delivery apps
4. Strategic Partnerships with cafes, restaurants, and hotels can serve as an additional distribution channel

PROMOTION

1. Digital Marketing: PPC, SEO, email marketing, video
2. Influencer Marketing
3. Content Marketing
4. Local Events
5. Direct Marketing
6. Strategic Partnerships
7. CSR

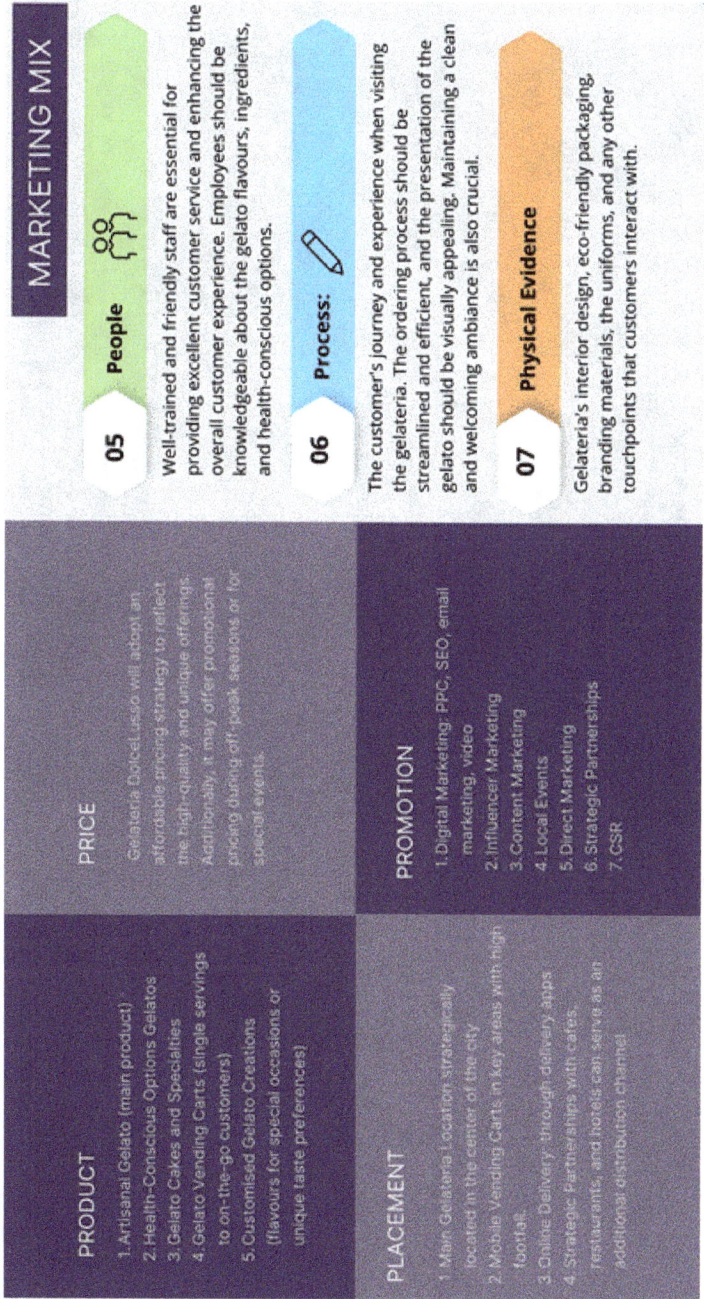

Figure 16. The 7P Marketing Mix. Source: Author's contribution

Competitor's pricing strategy:

Competitor	Price in shop	Price to-go (500 gr) through delivering apps
Gioelia Cremeria	12 lei/ globe	77 lei
Bianco Milano	12 lei/ globe	75 lei
Moritz Eis	12 lei/ globe	65 lei

Pricing Strategy

Price/scoop (in-shop)	Price fro 500 gr (delivery)
9 lei	60 lei

Explanation:

1. A single serving of gelato, priced at 9 lei, provides a budget-friendly option for customers seeking a quick and delicious treat without straining their budget.

2. The 500g gelato container, priced at 60 lei, offers an attractive option for customers who want to indulge in a larger quantity of gelato at a reasonable price. This can be particularly appealing to families or groups looking to enjoy gelato together, encouraging repeat purchases and fostering customer loyalty.

Figure 17. Pricing Strategy. Source: Author's contribution

MARKETING OBJECTIVES

1.RESEARCH

- Validate the current buyer personas
- Continuous feedback collection from users to integrate in product development
- Tight connection with the owner to make sure the products are aligned to the Buyer Persona needs and expectations

2.BRAND AWARENESS

- Finalise the branding process by building a unitary brand identity (logo, website, social media templates, user stories etc.)
- Implement the new branding for Gelateria Dolce Lusso and communicate the new brand and positioning
- Implement the new branding on different social media channels.
- Ensure high top-of-mind recognition for Gelateria Dolce Lusso based on the UVP
- Educate and create awareness in targeted segments, through content marketing (articles, videos, etc.) highlighting the uniqueness of the products
- Support and identify potential partnerships

3.BUSINESS GROWTH

- Support business development through partners (awareness, education, sales support, engagement) and market research.

. 4. CUSTOMER RETENTION & LOYALTY

- Implement engagement campaigns & programs (loyalty programs, reminder emails, motivational emails, summary emails).
- Start building a community around Indulgence Redefined.

5. CUSTOMER JOURNEY

- Mapping the customer journey (identifying all the touch-points, understand how customers interact with the brand, understand the different phases a customer goes through before making the final purchase, find/validate the motivation behind the purchase, identify the pain points and ways to address them to convert potential customers).
- Record the visits with a special heat map tool (ex. Hotjar)

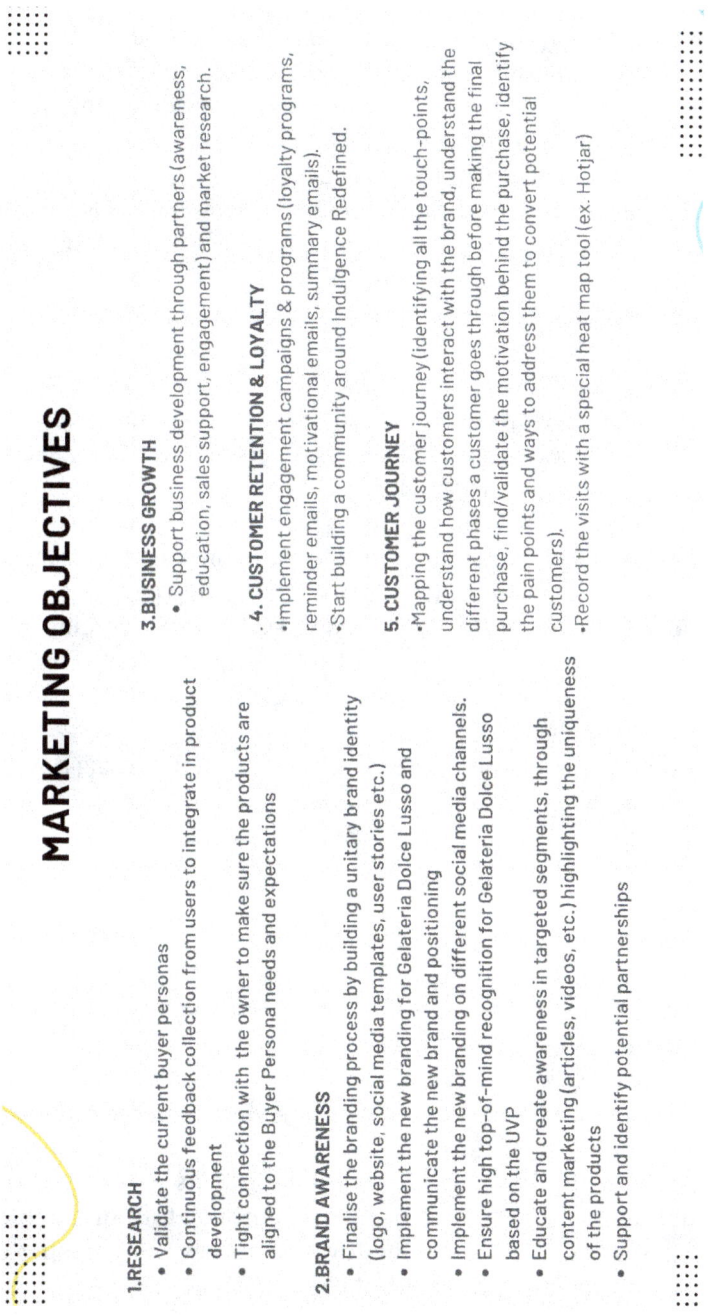

Figure 18. Marketing Objectives cascaded from the Business Objectives. Source: Author's contribution

The marketing communication mix for Gelateria Dolce Lusso consists of several key elements (*Figure 19*):

1. **Digital Marketing:** Utilising visually appealing content, such as enticing images and videos of gelato flavours, to captivate and entice the target audience online.
2. **Local Events:** Engaging in food festivals and gelato-tasting events to create direct interactions with the community, increasing brand exposure.
3. **Content Marketing:** Employing blog posts, videos, customer testimonials, infographics, and e-books to share the gelateria's unique offerings and values.
4. **Influencer Marketing:** Leveraging food bloggers, health influencers, and other relevant personalities to extend the brand's reach and credibility.
5. **Direct Marketing:** Using flyers to offer free tastings or discounts, attracting first-time customers and encouraging them to try the gelateria's delectable gelato creations.
6. **CSR Initiatives:** Showcasing sustainable sourcing, eco-friendly packaging, reduced energy consumption, and employee welfare to appeal to socially conscious consumers.

By skillfully integrating these elements into its marketing strategy, the gelateria can position itself as the ultimate destination for indulgent and health-conscious gelato experiences.

Customer Experience and Journey

To create a seamless and memorable customer experience at each marketing funnel stage, specific actions have been defined to engage and guide customers effectively, as described in *Figure 20*.

Understanding and documenting Gelateria Dolce Lusso's customer journey is absolutely crucial for achieving the business objectives. It allows to gain valuable insights into customers' interactions with the brand at every touchpoint, from the initial awareness stage to becoming loyal advocates. By mapping out the customer journey, the brand can identify pain points, areas of improvement, and opportunities to create delightful experiences for its valued customers.

Recommended Marketing Communications Mix

Digital

(social, PPC, SEO, email marketing, social media: Share visually appealing and mouth-watering images and videos of gelato flavors, new menu items, and special promotions.)

Local Events

(Food Festivals, Seasonal Celebrations, Culinary Workshops for Families, Gelato Tasting Events etc.)

Content Marketing

Blog Posts: gelato recipes, behind-the-scenes stories of gelato-making, health-conscious living tips, and gelato-related news and trends. **Video Content:** short and captivating video content showcasing the gelato-making process. **Customer Testimonials, Infographics, E-books and Guides** etc.

Influencer Marketing

(Food Bloggers and Foodies, Health and Wellness Influencers, Travel Influencers, Local Influencers, Family and Parenting Influencers etc.)

Direct Marketing

(flyers - Offering free tastings or discounts for first-time customers)

CSR

(Sustainable Sourcing, Eco-Friendly Packaging, Reduced Energy Consumption, Health and Well-Being Initiatives , Transparent Communication about CSR efforts, Employee Welfare)

Figure 19. Marketing Communications Mix (Promotion). Source: Author's contribution

Documenting the customer journey **empowers Gelateria Dolce Lusso to be customer-centric, optimise strategies, and achieve business objectives effectively**. It aligns the efforts with customer needs, leading to long-term success and growth.

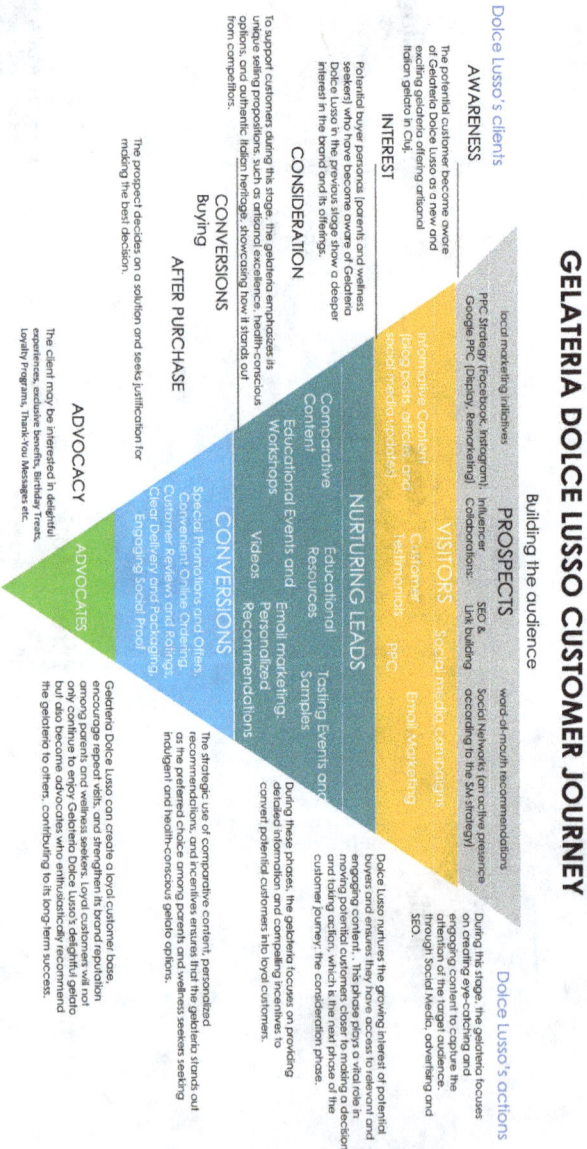

GELATERIA DOLCE LUSSO CUSTOMER JOURNEY

Building the audience

Dolce Lusso's clients

AWARENESS

The potential customer become aware of Gelateria Dolce Lusso as a new and exciting gelateria offering artisanal Italian gelato in Cluj.

INTEREST

Potential buyer personas (parents and wellness seekers) who have become aware of Gelateria Dolce Lusso in the previous stage show a deeper interest in the brand and its offerings.

CONSIDERATION

To support customers during this stage, the gelateria emphasizes its unique selling propositions, such as artisanal excellence, health-conscious options, and authentic Italian heritage, showcasing how it stands out from competitors.

CONVERSIONS
Buying

The prospect decides on a solution and seeks justification for making the best decision.

AFTER PURCHASE

The client may be interested in delightful experiences, exclusive benefits, Birthday Treats, Loyalty Programs, Thank-You Messages etc.

ADVOCACY

PROSPECTS

local marketing initiatives
PPC Strategy (Facebook, Instagram); Influencer Collaborations; Google PPC (Display, Remarketing)

VISITORS
informative Content (blog posts, articles and social media updates)
Customer Testimonials
SEO & Link building
Social media campaign
PPC
Email Marketing

NURTURING LEADS
Comparative Content
Educational Resources
Educational Events and Workshops
Videos
Tasting Events and Samples
Email marketing; Personalized Recommendations

CONVERSIONS
Special Promotions and Offers; Convenient Online Ordering; Customer Reviews and Ratings; Clear Delivery and Packaging; Engaging Social Proof

ADVOCATES

word-of-mouth recommendations
Social Network (an active presence according to the SM strategy)
SEO

During this stage, the gelateria focuses on creating eye-catching and engaging content to capture the attention of the target audience through Social Media, advertising and SEO.

Dolce Lusso nurtures the growing interest of potential buyers and ensures they have access to relevant and engaging content. This stage plays a vital role in moving potential customers closer to making a decision and taking action, which is the next phase of the customer journey, the consideration phase.

During these phases, the gelateria focuses on providing detailed information and compelling incentives to convert potential customers into loyal customers.

The strategic use of comparative content, personalized recommendations, and incentives ensures that the gelateria stands out as the preferred choice among parents and wellness seekers, indulgent and health-conscious gelato options.

Gelateria Dolce Lusso can create a loyal customer base, encourage repeat visits, and strengthen its brand reputation among parents and wellness seekers. Loyal customers will not only continue to enjoy Gelateria Dolce Lusso's delightful gelato but also become advocates who enthusiastically recommend the gelateria to others, contributing to its long-term success.

Dolce Lusso's actions

Figure 20. The Customer Journey. Source: Author's contribution

Launch Strategy

The launch strategy is a carefully crafted marketing plan (*Appendix 6*) and the budget allocation to achieve the business and marketing objectives, presenting Gelateria Dolce Lusso as the ultimate destination for delightful gelato experiences that prioritise well-being and sustainability.

The launch timeline is divided into three phases:

1. **Pre-Launch Preparations (Month 1-2):** Finalizing branding, creating marketing collaterals, conducting buyer persona research, and establishing strategic partnerships.
2. **Launch Preparation (Month 3-4):** Implementing multi-channel marketing, content creation, influencer marketing to build anticipation for our grand opening. An awareness campaign on social media will be running in this period for both audiences. As segmented and proposed for parents în *Appendix 5* will be created an awareness campaign also for the second audience, with specific messages.
3. **Launch and Post-Launch (Month 5-12):** Hosting a grand opening event, offering exclusive deals, free tasting events, engaging customers through loyalty programs and community building, and continuously optimizing the customer journey.

Measuring the Marketing Performance

The performance indicators will be closely monitored throughout the launch, and onwards to assess the success and refine the marketing strategies accordingly. The marketing strategy of Gelateria Dolce Lusso revolves around a comprehensive 5P approach to measure and achieve its objectives, as detailed in *Figure 21*. By evaluating and optimising Positioning, Portfolio, People, Processes, and Performance KPIs, the gelateria aims to deliver an exceptional experience to its valued customers while successfully attaining its business goals.

The Marketing Strategy

Phase 1
Pre-Launch Preparations (Month 1-2):

1.Brand Finalization: The gelateria will finalize its brand identity, including the name, logo, and tagline, reflecting its commitment to artisanal gelato and health-conscious indulgence.

2.Marketing Collaterals: The creation of marketing materials, such as brochures, menus, and signage, will be completed to ensure a cohesive and visually appealing brand representation.

3.Buyer Persona Research: In-depth research will be conducted to understand the preferences and behaviours of the target audiences, parents, and wellness seekers, shaping the marketing strategies accordingly.

4.Strategic Partnerships: The gelateria will establish collaborations with local health and wellness influencers, relevant organizations, and tourism boards to create awareness and attract potential customers.

Phase 2
Launch Preparation (Month 3-4):

1.Multi-Channel Marketing: Implementing a multi-channel marketing strategy to reach the target audiences through various platforms, including social media, local publications, and online advertisements.

2.Content Creation: Developing captivating and informative content that showcases the gelateria's unique features, health-conscious options, and artisanal gelato craftsmanship.

3.Influencer Marketing: Collaborating with health and wellness influencers and food bloggers to endorse Gelateria Dolce Lusso and create buzz among the target audience.

4.Awareness Campaign: Running an awareness campaign on social media and other digital platforms, highlighting the gelateria's offerings and its commitment to providing delightful and health-conscious gelato experiences.

5.Exclusive Offers: Offering exclusive deals and promotions to early customers during the grand opening to attract a large number of visitors and create a sense of urgency.

6.Loyalty Programs: Planning loyalty programs to reward and retain customers, encouraging repeat visits and fostering brand loyalty.

Phase 3
Launch and Post-Launch (Month 5-12)

1.Grand Opening Event: Host a captivating grand opening event to attract customers and generate media coverage.

2.Exclusive Deals and Offers: Offer promotions to drive sales and incentivise visits.

3.Continuous Marketing: Sustain marketing efforts to maintain brand visibility and engagement.

4.Customer Engagement: Implement loyalty programs and gather customer feedback.

5.Seasonal Offerings: Introduce innovative gelato flavors based on customer feedback.

6.Community Building: Strengthen ties with the local community and participate in events.

7.Customer Experience: Optimize the customer journey for seamless experiences.

8.Monitoring and Metrics: Track KPIs to evaluate marketing success.

9.Influencer Campaigns: Collaborate with influencers to reach new audiences.

10.Product Innovation: Experiment with new gelato flavors and offerings.

Figure 21. The Marketing Strategy summary. Source: Author's contribution

Recommendations

1. **Act promptly:** Launch Gelateria Dolce Lusso swiftly to establish itself as a market leader in Cluj-Napoca's gelato market, offering authentic Italian gelato experiences.
2. **Define a captivating brand:** Craft a unique brand identity and name that resonates with artisanal gelato craftsmanship, health-conscious options, and luxury indulgence.
3. **Consistency is key:** Maintain consistent quality and branding across all aspects, from gelato taste to packaging and marketing materials.
4. **Focus on customers:** Prioritise customer satisfaction by understanding their needs and feedback and continuously gathering insights to improve offerings.
5. **Build a loyal community:** Engage customers through social media, loyalty programs, and exclusive offers to foster brand advocacy and word-of-mouth marketing.
6. **Embrace digital marketing:** Leverage digital platforms, including social media and content marketing, to reach a broader audience and showcase Gelateria Dolce Lusso's uniqueness.
7. **Promote health-conscious choices:** Highlight reduced sugar, low-calorie, and vegan options to attract health-conscious consumers seeking guilt-free indulgence.
8. **Family-friendly environment:** Create a welcoming atmosphere for families with kid-sized portions and child-friendly gelato flavours.
9. **Embrace innovation:** Introduce innovative gelato flavours and seasonal offerings to surprise and delight customers.
10. **Validate the market:** Consider launching an MVP version to test market interest and validate the business model before a full-scale launch.
11. **Form strategic partnerships:** Collaborate with local tourism associations, event organisers, and influential bloggers to increase brand visibility.
12. **Invest in staff training:** Empower staff to deliver excellent customer service and align with the brand's values for a memorable customer experience.
13. **Emphasise sustainability:** Showcase eco-friendly practices

and social responsibility efforts to appeal to socially conscious consumers.

14. **Monitor performance and adapt:** Continuously track KPIs and be agile in adapting strategies based on feedback and market trends.

SMART KPIS FOR THE MARKETING OBJECTIVES

Positioning

- Increase brand recognition by 20% within the target market segment over the next 12 months.
- Clearly differentiate the brand by highlighting its unique features, benefits, and values in comparison to competitors using social media campaigns over the next 12 months.
- Implement marketing strategies according to the marketing plan to enhance brand visibility and reach the target audience effectively.
- Enhance brand awareness through targeted marketing campaigns, resulting in a 10% increase in brand recall within the next 6 months.

Portfolio

- Create innovative gelato flavours and other desserts by end of 2024 that can overcome the seasonality in Romania.
- Conduct a market research to identify customer preferences and trends in Cluj-Napoca by end of 2023.
- Strengthen the commitment to social responsibility and sustainability. Implement eco-friendly practices, such as using biodegradable packaging and supporting local initiatives, to resonate with socially conscious consumers by end of 2023.

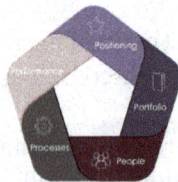

How do we measure?

People

- Team consolidation and specialisation by end of Q3 2024 based on business needs, as proposed in the first year.
- Introducing an Employer Branding strategy (align on organisational culture, align leadership, measuring employee engagement etc.) by end of 2024.
- Introducing a Performance Management process – by the end of Q3 2024 (setting objectives, measuring objectives, reporting & rewarding them).

Processes

- Validate the current buyer personas or assumptions about the new business model within 6 -12 months after launch.
- Continuous feedback collection from customers & integrate the feedback in product development – ongoing
- Documenting the customer journey and all the touch points by end of 2024 and proposing ways to improve it.
- Create a process to create ongoing partnerships (strategic partnerships with local businesses, event organisers, and tourism associations to increase brand exposure and tap into new customer segments) by end of 2023.

How do we measure?

Performance

- Profitability and Financial Growth: Revenue of min 100K eur in the first year and increase with 20 % in the second year.
- Increase brand recognition and awareness through marketing and promotional activities within Cluj area.
- Generate at least 100 customers /day within 6 month after launch
- 1000 website visits/ month on the website by end of 2024 and onwards
- Reach 3000 followers on social media channels by end of 2024, and increase by 20% monthly onwards

How do we measure?

By executing these strategies diligently, the brand will reach its objectives to create an enduring brand presence, drive sales growth, and establish Gelateria Dolce Lusso as a trusted name in the Cluj-Napoca ice cream landscape.

Reference list

Chen, F. and Kodono, Y. (2014) 'Fuzzy VRIO and SWOT Analysis of Chery Automobile', *Journal of Advanced Computational Intelligence and Intelligent Informatics*, 18(3), pp. 429–434. Available at: https://doi.org/10.20965/jaciii.2014.p0429.

Cluj-Napoca (Cluj, Romania) – Population Statistics, Charts, Map, Location, Weather and Web Information (2023) *www.citypopulation.de*. Available at: https://www.citypopulation.de/en/romania/cluj/_/054975__cluj_napoca/.

Europe Ice Cream Market (2020) *www.businessmarketinsights.com*. Available at: https://www.businessmarketinsights.com/reports/europe-ice-cream-market#:~:text=The%20Europe%20ice%20cream%20market (Accessed: 29 July 2023).

Europe Ice Cream Market | Growth | Trends | Forecasts (2018) *www.mordorintelligence.com*. Available at: https://www.mordorintelligence.com/industry-reports/europe-ice-cream-market (Accessed: 29 July 2023).

Hill, C.W.L., Schilling, M.A. and Jones, G.R. (2017) *Strategic Management : an Integrated Approach : Theory & Cases*. Boston, Ma: Cengage Learning.

Ice Cream – Romania | Statista Market Forecast (2018) *Statista*. Available at: https://www.statista.com/outlook/cmo/food/confectionery-snacks/confectionery/ice-cream/romania#revenue (Accessed: 29 July 2023).

Ice Cream in Romania (2023) *www.marketresearch.com*. Available at: https://www.marketresearch.com/Euromonitor-International-v746/Ice-Cream-Romania-34544764/ (Accessed: 29 July 2023).

Ice Cream Market in Romania – Gen Consulting Company (2022). Available at: https://gen-cons.com/store/ice-cream-market-in-romania/ (Accessed: 29 July 2023).

Ice Cream Market Size, Share, Growth Analysis, By Product, Flavor, Distribution Channel – Industry Forecast 2022-2028 (2023) *www.skyquestt.com*. Available at: https://www.skyquestt.com/report/ice-cream-market (Accessed: 29 July 2023).

Johnson, G. *et al.* (2017) *Fundamentals of Strategy*. Pearson UK.

Kim, E.-A. (2019) 'An Analysis on the Core Competence Through the VRIO Model of CJ CGV', *Journal of the Korea Entertainment Industry Association*, 13(3), pp. 333–342. Available at: https://doi.org/10.21184/jkeia.2019.4.13.3.333.

Kotler, P. and Keller, K.L. (2016) *A framework for marketing management.* 6th edn. Boston: Pearson.

ltd, R. and M. (2019) *Romania Ice Cream Market Analysis (2013 – 2023) – Research and Markets, www.researchandmarkets.com.* Available at: https://www.researchandmarkets.com/reports/4773254/romania-ice-cream-market-analysis-2013-2023 (Accessed: 29 July 2023).

Osterwalder, A. *et al.* (2010) *Business model generation : a handbook for visionaries, game changers, and challengers.* Hoboken, New Jersey: Wiley.

Porter, M.E. (2008) *On competition.* Boston, Massachusetts: Harvard Business School Press.

Stobierski, T. (2020) *A Beginner's Guide to Value-Based Strategy, Business Insights – Blog.* Available at: https://online.hbs.edu/blog/post/value-based-strategy (Accessed: 4 August 2023).

Target group: Ice cream lovers in Romania (2022) *Statista.* Available at: https://www.statista.com/study/127152/ice-cream-lovers-in-romania/ (Accessed: 29 July 2023).

*Appendixes are available upon requested in order to better understand the financial analysis done by the author.

Radu–Ştefan Tărău

Analysing Operations Management and Balancing Design with Construction in the Iron Triangle – A Case Study of a Romanian Engineering Company Owned by a Larger Construction Company

EMBA Module: Operations and Supply Chain Management

Assignment task: Drawing upon either your own organisation (or previously worked for) or an organisation with which you are familiar, identify an area of activity and suggest how the current management of operations could be improved. It is important that you explain the area of activity and its purposes clearly by providing adequate information and contextual information of the chosen organisation. For the area of activity identified, define, and critically evaluate suitable operational objectives or performance outcomes, and suggest how the current management of the operations could be improved. It is important that you seek, where possible, to apply the various models, concepts, tools, and techniques considered during the course.

1. Introduction

The construction of high-voltage substations and high-voltage electrical lines is a critical component of the infrastructure needed to support modern electrical grids. A design company involved in such projects is crucial in ensuring the efficiency, safety, and sustainability of such infrastructures.

The *iron triangle* concept is more applicable to construction than to any other field. A construction project's greatest challenge is to balance quality, speed, and cost. Also, you can indeed have two, but not all of them. The *Iron Triangle*, also known as the *Triple Constraint*, is a fundamental concept in project management that highlights the interdependent constraints of **time, cost, and quality** (or **scope**). In the context of a design company working on the high-voltage substation part of construction projects, balancing these three elements is crucial for successful project completion. This balance is particularly challenging when integrating sustainable viability and Environmental, Social, and Governance (ESG) considerations.

High-quality construction requires the design company to have meticulous planning, highly experienced electrical and design engineers, and the highest compliance with standards. The above measures will ensure the safety, functionality, and durability of the energy infrastructure, as well as the use of superior-quality, premium materials and solid processes. Still, it can also lead to higher costs and longer execution times. However, speed is a priority when working in a competitive market, and clients and other stakeholders have strict deadlines and penalties. Improving construction timelines involves a design company having efficient project management, leaner processes, allocating more resources, and working much longer hours.

Budget constraints also drive the need to modify the design to reduce expenses. Nevertheless, optimising **cost** usually leads to a compromise of quality or time. This paper explores strategies for balancing design and construction within the Iron Triangle framework while ensuring sustainability and ESG compliance.

2. Organisational background

EBT is a competitive, solid, and trustworthy company in the Romanian energy sector. It is considered one of the major Electrical EPCs in the national market. The company has developed and offers a comprehensive range of services, including the production of electrical equipment (low and medium voltage), general contracting, construction, engineering, maintenance, and operational services. After almost three decades, EBT has remained an elite business partner highly appreciated by customers, suppliers, and the community. It has national coverage, three production units, and employs over 700 employees, of whom 200 are engineers.

ECS is an engineering company that is part of the EBT group, with its main activity being the design and consulting in the energy sector. ECS offers an extensive array of services, including the design of distribution and transmission grids (high-voltage substation and high-voltage electrical line design), energy installation design for industrial customers, renewable project design, various types of grid studies, and feasibility studies for large-scale energy infrastructure projects. It also introduced new services in the consultancy sector, including owners' engineering services and auditing services.

ECS is now a 70+ engineer Romanian electrical and design company based in Cluj-Napoca. It has experienced rapid growth and continuous improvement over the last four years, increasing its turnover tenfold and its workforce almost sixfold. By employing skilled and experienced engineers, developing new core competencies, and improving the quality of its services, ECS has extended its market share, and its services are in high demand. It was and is actively involved in the largest and most significant energy infrastructure project built in Romania. In terms of numbers, it has done studies for over 15 GW of wind, solar, and combined cycle projects; it covers the detailed design of several high voltage substations and high voltage electrical lines and is also responsible for approval of the most important feasibility studies that form the basis of changing the energy sector in Romania.

3. Organisational Aim and Objectives

ECS works with external clients (accounting for 70% of its turnover) and internal clients (EBT), tackling a complex array of projects that present several challenges. The three challenges related to the *Iron Triangle* (quality, speed, and cost) are most significant, especially when constructing a high-voltage substation, where effective communication between clients, the General Contractor, and the Designer is vital. The client is responsible for clearly communicating their priorities, budget limitations and the desired results. The EPC must also present alternative solutions or **value engineering options that balance quality and speed with budget.**

The **design and construction of high-voltage substations** are critical to the infrastructure needed to support modern electrical grids. A design company involved in such projects is crucial in ensuring the efficiency, safety, and sustainability of these infrastructures. There has been an increasing emphasis on sustainable viability and Environmental, Social, and Governance (ESG) considerations in recent years. This paper explores the intricacies of operations management and supply chain management (SCM) for a design company involved in constructing high-voltage substations, focusing on sustainable practices and ESG principles.

Working for the mother company (EBT) and working for external clients means encountering several challenges in managing resources and expectations. Aligning ECS's objectives with EBT's and the shareholders' intentions is not a straightforward task, and it can lead to potential conflicts if targets or expectations are not met. The Operations Management for ECS is critical. As is clearly defined, the OM "is the activity of managing the resources that create and deliver services and products" (Brandon-Jones, Slack and Johnston, 2016, p. 5).

Supply chain management involves coordinating and managing a network of interconnected businesses providing products and services required by end customers. SCM is "the management of the relationships and flows between the 'string' of operations and processes that produce value in the form of products and services to the ultimate consumer" (Brandon-Jones, Slack and Johnston, 2016, p. 399). For a successful EPC (EBT) and a design company (ECS) in the construction and energy sector, SCM includes sourcing raw materials, procurement of services, equipment and coordination with subcontractors, logistics, and delivering the final product. Effective SCM ensures that projects are completed on time, within budget, and to the required quality standards.

The design company aims to have lean and predictable operations management, balancing effectively the three key factors (time, cost, and quality) to ensure the overall performance of the organisation in supply chain management.

4. Operations Management for a Design Company in High-Voltage Substation Construction

1. The Role of a Design Company in High-Voltage Substation Construction

The design of substations plays a critical role in ensuring that high-voltage substations are efficient, safe, and sustainable.
Key design considerations include:

A. Conceptual Design: Developing the initial designs that meet the project requirements and adhere to regulatory standards.

B. Technical Specifications: Ensuring all components meet the required standards and performance criteria.

C. Detailed Engineering: Creating detailed plans and specifications for construction.

D. Compliance and Standards: Ensuring all design aspects meet local and international standards for safety and efficiency.

E. Sustainability: Integrating sustainable practices into the design to minimise environmental impact.

F. Innovation: Incorporating advanced technologies such as digitalisation of substations and smart grid capabilities.

Innovation, for an engineering company and for entrepreneurs, is a tool "the means by which they exploit change as an opportunity for a different business or a different service" (Drucker, 1985, p. 28). The operations within ECS create and deliver design services by changing the inputs they receive for a project or from customers into outputs. The service operations for ECS, with input and output, are shown in Figure 1.

2. The Role of Construction in High-Voltage Substation Projects

Construction involves translating design plans into physical infrastructure. The product operations for EBT, with input and output, are shown in Figure 2. Key construction considerations include:

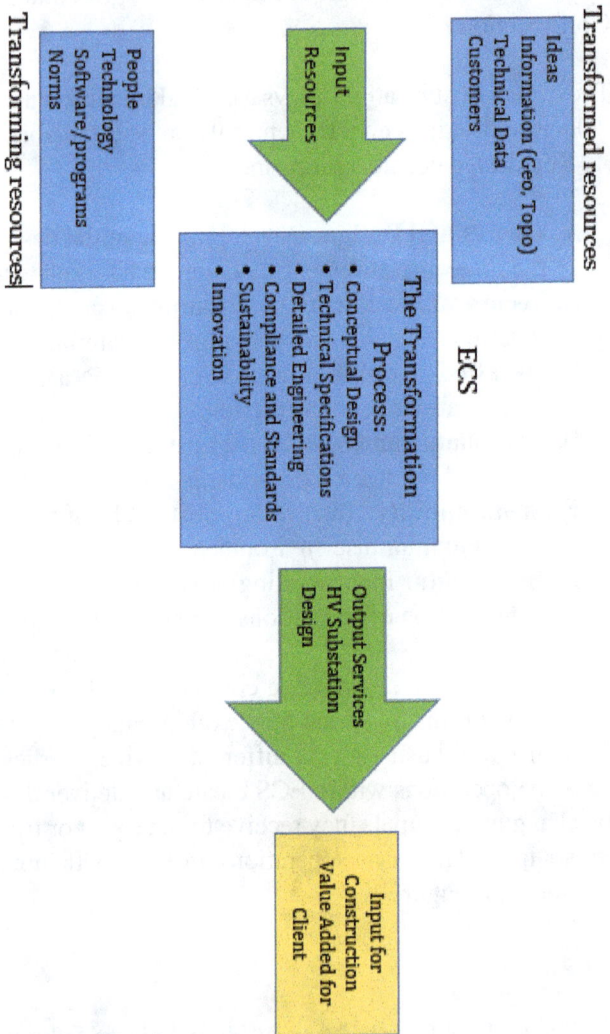

Figure 1. Input/output for ECS

A. Resource Management: Efficiently utilising materials, labour, and equipment.

B. Scheduling: Adhering to the project timeline and managing potential delays.

C. Quality Control: Ensuring that construction meets the design specifications and standards.

D. Safety: Maintaining a safe work environment and adhering to safety regulations.

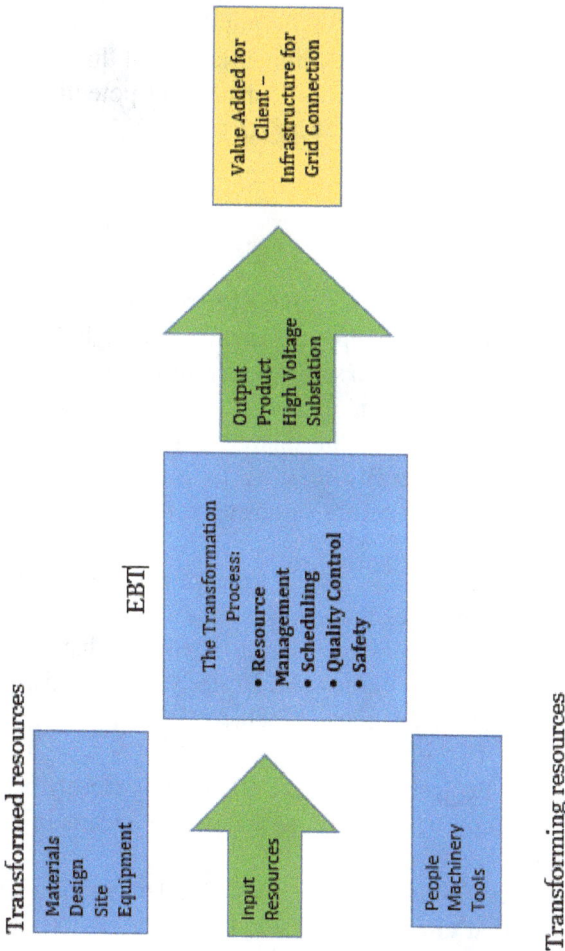

▲ Figure 2. Input/output for EBT

The 'input-transformation-output', from Figure 1 and Figure 2, follows the same principle: "All processes have inputs of transforming and transformed resources that they use to create products and services" (Slack and Brandon-Jones, 2021, p. 9).

3. Balancing Design and Construction within the Iron Triangle

The operation of ECS produces services, while the operation of EBT creates a product – the high-voltage substation. For both operations described above, the customer is the input, but they are also the reason for their existence. Therefore, "it is critical that operations managers are aware of customers' current and potential needs" (Brandon-Jones, Slack and Johnston, 2016, p. 18).

3.1 Time Management

Effective time management is crucial for balancing design and construction. The design company's operations are linked to the construction section, which can significantly influence the company.

Issue: Signing a design and execution contract has the disadvantage that delays in the design phase will impact the execution phase, potentially leading to missed deadlines or significant penalties; therefore, a strategy is needed from the design stage.

The Strategies for ECS operation management "is a sequential set of analyses and choices that can increase the likelihood that a firm will choose a good strategy; that is, a strategy that generates competitive advantages" (Barney and Hesterly, 2019, p. 5).

Strategies for time management include:

A. **Integrated Project Planning:** Collaborating closely between design and construction teams to develop a realistic project schedule.
B. **Phased Design and Construction**: Implementing a phased approach that allows design and construction activities to overlap enables adjustments based on real-time feedback.
C. **Agile Methodologies:** Using agile project management

techniques to adapt to changes and unforeseen challenges quickly.

ECS Strategy for OM	Proposed Actions	Advantage	Disadvantage
Integrated Project Planning	Each project has a PM from both design and construction to collaborate.	A more predictable timeline and a more proactive PM. If services or work fall behind schedule, actions can be taken quickly	More pressure from the construction side on design services is not always constructive.
Phased Design and Construction:	The design is split into objects, and for example, the civil design is finalised earlier.	Construction can start sooner.	The Client can request the entire design at once.
Agile Methodologies:	A software project for PM	A more realistic timeline	None

Table 1. ECS strategies for time management

3.2 Cost Management

Cost management involves controlling project expenses to stay within budget while achieving the desired quality.

Issues/Problems – Soil issues, supplier delays, weather, material shortages, contractual limitations, and liabilities.

Strategies for cost management include:

A. **Value Engineering:** Evaluating design options to identify cost-saving opportunities without compromising quality or sustainability.
B. **Budget Contingency:** Allocating a contingency budget to address unexpected expenses and risks.
C. **Sustainable Procurement:** Choosing cost-effective, sustainable materials and suppliers that offer long-term savings.

Selecting prefabricated components can reduce construction costs and time while ensuring consistent quality.

3.3 Quality (Scope) Management

Ensuring the project meets its specifications and standards is critical. Strategies include:

A. **Precise Specifications**: Developing detailed design specifications that clearly outline quality requirements.
B. **Quality Assurance (QA)**: Implementing robust QA processes during design and construction phases.
C. **Stakeholder Engagement**: Involving stakeholders early in the design process to ensure their requirements are met and to minimise scope changes later.

5. Supply Chain Management for Designing a Modular High-Voltage Substation

As stated before, high-voltage substations are critical components of the electrical grid, responsible for transforming voltage levels to ensure efficient power transmission and distribution. In an era where rapid deployment and scalability are essential, **modular high-voltage substations** offer a compelling solution. These substations can be prefabricated, transported, and assembled quickly, providing flexibility and efficiency. Effective supply chain management (SCM) is vital to successfully deploying and constructing modular substations.

The market demands the rapid deployment of high-voltage substations to energise the new renewables, solar and wind farms. The demand for high-voltage substations equipped with power transformers is at an all-time high and continues to increase. Completing the substation ensures the Client can energise and deliver energy to the grid, so the speed of construction and design is one of the investors' most sought-after aspects.

The shareholders of EBT and ECS have adopted this product as one of their key strategies for the near future, considering it a differentiator in the market. Therefore, ECS must adopt the fundamental SCM principles when designing a modular high-voltage substation for rapid deployment and construction. Table 2 represents the required principles.

Table 2. Supply chain management principles

Supply Chain Management Principles	Proposed Action	ECS current approach
Strategic sourcing involves identifying and developing supplier relationships to meet the project's needs.	Supplier Selection: Choosing suppliers with proven quality, reliability, and sustainability track records. Cost-Benefit Analysis: Evaluating suppliers based on cost, quality, and delivery capabilities. Long-Term Partnerships: Establishing long-term relationships with key suppliers to ensure consistency and reliability.	The company selects suppliers with expertise in modular components, focusing on those with strong sustainability practices. Long-term partnerships are established to ensure reliability and consistency in supply. Hitachi, Siemens, SEL, GE, ABB.
Lean manufacturing focuses on minimising waste and maximising efficiency in the production process.	Standardisation: Standardising components and processes to reduce variability and improve efficiency. Continuous Improvement: Implementing continuous improvement programs to enhance manufacturing processes and reduce lead times. Inventory Management: Optimising inventory levels to balance supply with demand and minimise holding costs.	Standardised designs for transformer and switchgear modules are developed for efficient mass production. EBT owns manufacturing facilities
Just-in-time delivery ensures that materials and components arrive precisely when needed, reducing inventory costs and improving cash flow.	Accurate Forecasting: Using precise demand forecasting to align supply with project schedules. Close Coordination: Maintaining close coordination with suppliers to ensure the timely delivery of materials. Flexible Logistics: Developing flexible logistics solutions to accommodate changes in project timelines.	Accurate demand forecasting and close coordination with suppliers ensure that modules are delivered on time for assembly. Flexible logistics solutions are developed to accommodate any changes in the project schedule.

Table 2. Supply chain management principles (continued)

Supply Chain Management Principles	Proposed Action	ECS current approach
Quality management ensures that all components and processes meet the required standards and specifications.	Quality Assurance (QA): Implementing QA processes throughout the supply chain, from raw materials to finished products. Supplier Audits: Conducting regular audits of suppliers to ensure compliance with quality standards. Testing and Certification: Ensuring that all components undergo rigorous testing and certification before deployment.	Comprehensive QA processes are implemented throughout the supply chain. All modules undergo factory acceptance testing before shipment to ensure they meet the required standards.
Sustainability and ESG Considerations Incorporating sustainability and ESG (Environmental, Social, and Governance) principles into SCM is crucial for modern projects.	Sustainable Sourcing: Procuring materials and components from suppliers that adhere to sustainable practices. Energy Efficiency: Designing modular substations to maximise energy efficiency and minimise environmental impact. Social Responsibility: Ensuring fair labour practices and engaging with local communities to support social initiatives.	Sustainable materials are used to construct the modules, and energy-efficient designs are incorporated to minimise environmental impact. Suppliers are selected based on their adherence to ESG principles.
Risk management involves identifying, assessing, and mitigating risks throughout the supply chain.	Risk Assessment: Conducting thorough risk assessments for all supply chain activities. Contingency Planning: Developing contingency plans to address potential disruptions, such as supply delays or quality issues. Supplier Diversification: Diversifying the supplier base to reduce dependence on a single source and mitigate risks.	Thorough risk assessments are conducted for all supply chain activities.

Modular high-voltage substations consist of pre-engineered, prefabricated units that can be transported and assembled on-site. These units include all necessary components, such as transformers, switchgear, control systems, and auxiliary equipment. The modular approach offers several advantages: speed, scalability, quality control, cost efficiency and flexibility.

Effective supply chain management is crucial for the successful deployment and construction of modular high-voltage substations. By implementing strategic sourcing, lean manufacturing, just-in-time delivery, quality management, sustainability, and risk management principles, design companies can ensure the timely and efficient delivery of high-quality modular substations.

Embracing future trends and overcoming challenges will be critical to the continued success of modular substation projects in a rapidly evolving global landscape. Figure 3 will show a SWOT analysis for designing and deploying a modular high-voltage substation.

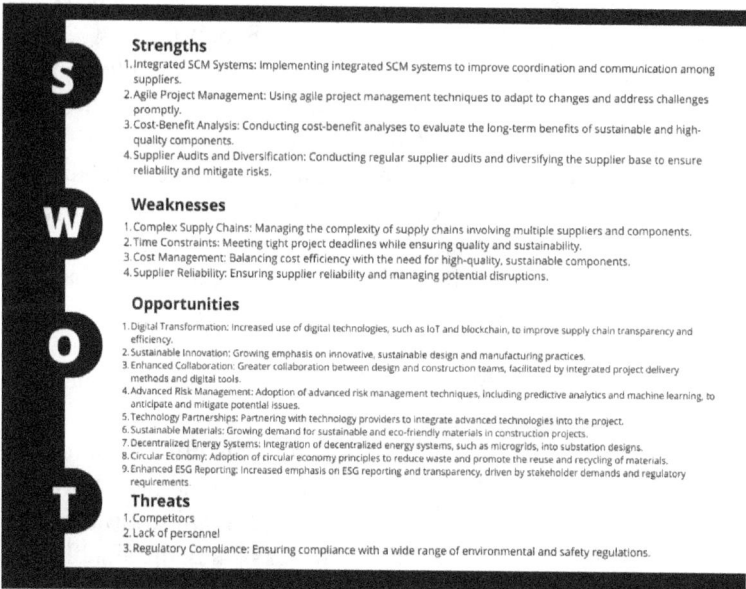

Strengths

1. Integrated SCM Systems: Implementing integrated SCM systems to improve coordination and communication among suppliers.
2. Agile Project Management: Using agile project management techniques to adapt to changes and address challenges promptly.
3. Cost-Benefit Analysis: Conducting cost-benefit analyses to evaluate the long-term benefits of sustainable and high-quality components.
4. Supplier Audits and Diversification: Conducting regular supplier audits and diversifying the supplier base to ensure reliability and mitigate risks.

Weaknesses

1. Complex Supply Chains: Managing the complexity of supply chains involving multiple suppliers and components.
2. Time Constraints: Meeting tight project deadlines while ensuring quality and sustainability.
3. Cost Management: Balancing cost efficiency with the need for high-quality, sustainable components.
4. Supplier Reliability: Ensuring supplier reliability and managing potential disruptions.

Opportunities

1. Digital Transformation: Increased use of digital technologies, such as IoT and blockchain, to improve supply chain transparency and efficiency.
2. Sustainable Innovation: Growing emphasis on innovative, sustainable design and manufacturing practices.
3. Enhanced Collaboration: Greater collaboration between design and construction teams, facilitated by integrated project delivery methods and digital tools.
4. Advanced Risk Management: Adoption of advanced risk management techniques, including predictive analytics and machine learning, to anticipate and mitigate potential issues.
5. Technology Partnerships: Partnering with technology providers to integrate advanced technologies into the project.
6. Sustainable Materials: Growing demand for sustainable and eco-friendly materials in construction projects.
7. Decentralized Energy Systems: Integration of decentralized energy systems, such as microgrids, into substation designs.
8. Circular Economy: Adoption of circular economy principles to reduce waste and promote the reuse and recycling of materials.
9. Enhanced ESG Reporting: Increased emphasis on ESG reporting and transparency, driven by stakeholder demands and regulatory requirements.

Threats

1. Competitors
2. Lack of personnel
3. Regulatory Compliance: Ensuring compliance with a wide range of environmental and safety regulations.

Figure 3. SWOT analysis for the design of the HV substation

6. Sustainable Viability in Supply Chain Management

As ECS grew as an engineering organisation, several questions and challenges emerged regarding the investment in people and time that the organisation is making. Additionally, what is the return on investment for maintaining an ever-increasing engineering team? The shareholders and the board must answer questions about why this is necessary and what is in the company's best interest. All parties involved must be educated.

All organisations and companies, whether small or large, must maintain their economic activity and performance (turnover and EBITDA) without negatively impacting the environment or society, meaning the organisation needs **to be sustainable**. An organisation must also be healthy and in good condition to perform and prosper. It needs **to be viable** in meeting the ever-changing and increasingly challenging market conditions and technological disruptions. Therefore, "sustainable viability is the state of an enterprise that enables it to benefit its stakeholders, the environment and society increasingly and indefinitely" (Gleadle 2018, p. iv).

A company's more valuable assets are its people. For an organisation to be viable and sustainable, it needs the right people. The task is for individuals who can combine their belief in sustainability and the environment with their understanding of economics to leverage these two areas. For a design company, the tasks to become a sustainable, viable organisation include using sustainable sourcing for its materials list, thinking and planning energy efficiency, examining waste management as a revenue stream, and incorporating lifecycle management into the design and specifications. Table 3 examines tasks and feasible methods for a design company to utilise.

Sustainable viability in SCM means managing resources to meet current needs without compromising the ability of future generations to meet their own needs. Any organisation needs to assess and understand its operational risks. In a sustainable and viable organisation, risk can be a chance to evolve. The shareholders should be able to understand and support "Sustainable Viability (SV) and its relationship to Enterprise Risk Management (ERM), think of it as a framework to quantify strategic, financial and operational risks better and, through this understanding, create opportunity for cost efficiencies and revenue enhancement" (Gleadle 2018, p. 44).

Tasks to obtain sustainable availability	Methods	ECS/EBT actions
1. Sustainable Sourcing: Procuring materials and services from suppliers that adhere to sustainable practices.	→ Use environmentally friendly materials. → Employ energy-efficient manufacturing processes. → Adhere to fair labour practices.	→ Transformers: Sourced from a manufacturer that uses eco-friendly insulation materials and has a low carbon footprint. → Cables: Made from recycled copper and manufactured using energy-efficient processes. → Concrete: Provided by a supplier that uses a high percentage of recycled aggregate and has implemented water recycling in their production process.
2. Energy Efficiency: Designing substations that maximise energy efficiency and minimise waste.	→ Optimising Equipment: Selecting transformers and other equipment that have high-efficiency ratings. → Smart Grid Integration: Designing substations that integrate with smart grid technologies to optimise energy distribution and reduce losses. → Renewable Energy: Incorporating renewable energy sources like solar panels to power auxiliary systems.	→ High-Efficiency Transformers: Using transformers with advanced cooling systems that reduce energy losses. → Renewable Energy Integration: Designing the substation to integrate with the solar farm seamlessly, maximising the use of renewable energy.
3. Waste Management: Implementing practices to reduce, reuse, and recycle materials to achieve the environmental footprint of substation construction.	→ Material Optimisation: Using design techniques that minimise material waste. → Recycling Programs: Establishing recycling programs for construction debris. → Hazardous Waste Handling: Properly managing hazardous waste to prevent environmental contamination.	→ Using building information modelling (BIM) to optimise material usage and reduce waste.
4. Lifecycle Management: Considering the entire lifecycle of the substation, from construction to decommissioning, to minimise environmental impact.	→ Durable Design: Designing substations to have a long operational life with minimal maintenance. → End-of-Life Planning: Developing plans for the safe and sustainable decommissioning of substations.	→ Using high-quality materials and advanced engineering techniques to ensure a long operational life. → Developing a maintenance plan that includes regular inspections and proactive replacements to extend the life of the substation.

Table 3. SV for design/construction

Investing in real sustainability issues also enhances shareholder value. A dynamic and flexible design company such as ECS should be sustainable and viable. It possesses all the necessary competencies and human resources to tackle this challenge and become a pioneer. The organisational culture that exists in the company serves as the basis for the changes needed to establish a solid SV enterprise and increase the benefits for all stakeholders.

7. ESG Criteria for Responsible Design

It is now a common fact that to stay relevant in tomorrow's market, Environmental, Social, and Governance (ESG) factors should be considered in any new investment plans. There are both risks and opportunities, and they should be front and centre for the development of ECS.

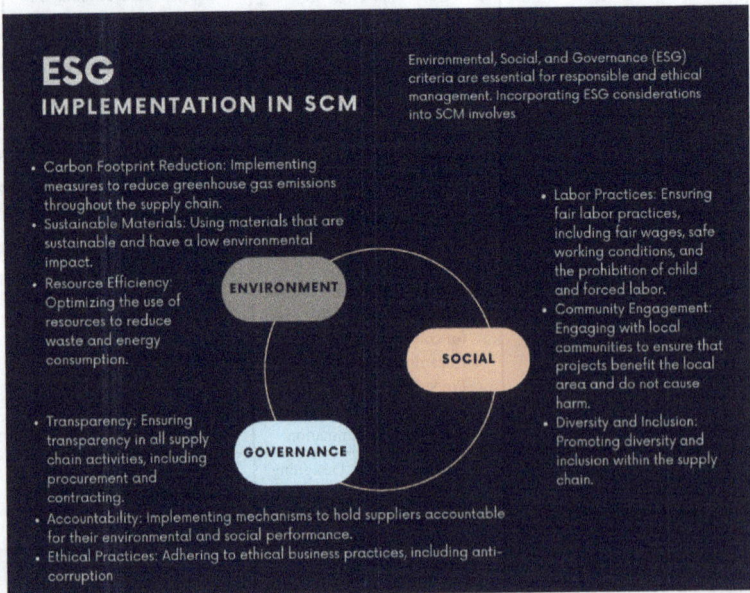

ESG
IMPLEMENTATION IN SCM

Environmental, Social, and Governance (ESG) criteria are essential for responsible and ethical management. Incorporating ESG considerations into SCM involves

- Carbon Footprint Reduction: Implementing measures to reduce greenhouse gas emissions throughout the supply chain.
- Sustainable Materials: Using materials that are sustainable and have a low environmental impact.
- Resource Efficiency: Optimizing the use of resources to reduce waste and energy consumption.

ENVIRONMENT

SOCIAL

GOVERNANCE

- Labor Practices: Ensuring fair labor practices, including fair wages, safe working conditions, and the prohibition of child and forced labor.
- Community Engagement: Engaging with local communities to ensure that projects benefit the local area and do not cause harm.
- Diversity and Inclusion: Promoting diversity and inclusion within the supply chain.

- Transparency: Ensuring transparency in all supply chain activities, including procurement and contracting.
- Accountability: Implementing mechanisms to hold suppliers accountable for their environmental and social performance.
- Ethical Practices: Adhering to ethical business practices, including anti-corruption

Figure 4. ESG Criteria

To implement and quantify ESG elements within the organisation, clear ESG goals should be set that are specific, measurable, achievable, relevant, and time bound. The ESG factors should be considered a core part of the company's strategic planning and decision-making processes. For the process to be smooth, the stakeholders should be engaged. It should include the customers, employees, investors, and the community, who must understand their expectations and incorporate feedback. The company should be committed to continuous improvement and regularly review and update its ESG policies and practices. By integrating these ESG principles, an energy design company can enhance its sustainability and ethical standards, improving its market competitiveness and attractiveness to clients who prioritise sustainability.

8. Conclusions and learnings

Effective operation and supply chain management for ECS is essential for successfully deploying and constructing modular high-voltage substations. By implementing strategic sourcing, lean manufacturing, just-in-time delivery, quality management, sustainability, and risk management principles, **design companies** can ensure the timely and efficient delivery of high-quality modular substations. Embracing future trends and overcoming challenges will be critical to the success of modular substation projects in a rapidly evolving global landscape.

The approach for designing high-voltage substations can be replicated in other areas of expertise to create a better practice system within the organisation. By integrating sustainable viability and ESG considerations into SCM practices, such companies can meet regulatory and stakeholder demands and contribute to the long-term sustainability of the infrastructure they help create.

Through sustainable sourcing, energy-efficient design, effective waste management, and comprehensive lifecycle management, design companies can ensure that their projects are environmentally responsible, socially beneficial, and governed by strong ethical principles. Embracing these practices and overcoming the associated challenges will be critical to the future success of ECS in a rapidly evolving global landscape.

References

Slack, N., Brandon-Jones, A. and Johnston, R. (2016) *Operations Management,* Pearson Education Limited: Edinburgh Gate, United Kingdom.

Slack, N. and Brandon-Jones, A. and Johnston, R. (2021) *Operations and Process Management,* Pearson Education Limited: Harlow, United Kingdom.

Gleadle, C. (2018) *The Five Essential Steps To Sustainable Viability,* ResearchGate.

Barney, J. B. and Hesterley, W.S. (2019) *Strategic Management & Competitive Advantage,* Pearson: New York, NY.

Drucker, P. F. (1985) *Innovation and Entrepreneurship,* Harper & Row, Publishers, Inc.